P9-CCO-209

Praise for *The Decision to Trust*

"This book provides an invaluable perspective on what organizational trust really is all about and how it can be influenced by individuals, teams, and leadership systems. Dr. Hurley's research is both comprehensive and compelling. More important, it offers the reader practical guidelines and tools."
—**Jon R. Katzenbach,** coauthor, *Leading Outside the Lines,* and senior vice president, Booz & Company

"For executives and managers who aspire to create high-trust organizations, Robert Hurley's *The Decision to Trust* is the book to read. The framework he proposes is eminently sensible and powerful. *The Decision to Trust* will help leaders reap the myriad benefits of trust within their own organizations."
—**Roderick M. Kramer,** William R. Kimball Professor of Organizational Behavior, Graduate School of Business, Stanford University

"Nothing much happens within an organization unless there is a foundation of trust between its members. Robert Hurley makes building that fundamental trust very actionable. For a leader who is attempting to build a team, this model is invaluable. We've seen a lot of books on trust, but none come close to examining the issue of trust in working relationships with the rigor that Dr. Hurley has provided."
—**Doug Lennick** and **Fred Kiel,** coauthors, *Moral Intelligence*

"This well-researched book provides valuable information for individuals, as well as for leaders of organizations, on how they can increase the trust that others have of them."
—**Morton Deutsch,** E. L. Thorndike Professor Emeritus of Psychology and Director Emeritus of the International Center for Cooperation and Conflict Resolution, Teachers College, Columbia University

"Dr. Hurley's deep experience in research and in the trenches of organizational practice allows him to offer some powerful ideas on how to manage trust. *The Decision to Trust* is full of useful insights and should be required reading for leaders and anyone seeking to earn and keep others' trust."

—**Chester Cadieux,** chairman and CEO retired, Quiktrip Corporation

"In these times, when working with organizational executives, the issue that constantly tops the list is trust—that is, the lack thereof. Mistrust is pervasive, cutting across all kinds of organizations, and is highly stable, whereas trust is delicate and can be destroyed in a nanosecond. Trust, therefore, can never be taken for granted, as Hurley makes abundantly clear in this excellent book. His invaluable contribution has been to provide a model for (a) how to understand the nature of trust and (b) what the key criteria are in deciding whether to trust in the first place. Hurley has addressed one of the most important issues in human relationships today."

—**W. Warner Burke,** Edward Lee Thorndike Professor of Psychology and Education, Teachers College, Columbia University

The Decision *to* Trust

How Leaders Create High-Trust Organizations

Robert F. Hurley

JOSSEY-BASS
A Wiley Imprint
www.josseybass.com

Published by Jossey-Bass
A Wiley Imprint
989 Market Street, San Francisco, CA 94103-1741—www.josseybass.com

Jossey-Bass books and products are available through most bookstores. To contact Jossey-Bass directly call our Customer Care Department within the U.S. at 800-956-7739, outside the U.S. at 317-572-3986, or fax 317-572-4002.

Wiley also publishes its books in a variety of electronic formats and by print-on-demand. Not all content that is available in standard print versions of this book may appear or be packaged in all book formats. If you have purchased a version of this book that did not include media that is referenced by or accompanies a standard print version, you may request this media by visiting http://booksupport.wiley.com. For more information about Wiley products, visit us at www.wiley.com.

Library of Congress Cataloging-in-Publication Data

Hurley, Robert F.
The decision to trust : how leaders create high-trust organizations / Robert F. Hurley.—1st ed.
p. cm.
Includes bibliographical references and index.
ISBN 978-1-118-07264-6 (cloth); ISBN 978-1-118-13186-2 (ebk); ISBN 978-1-118-13187-9 (ebk); ISBN 978-1-118-13188-6 (ebk)
1. Trust-Psychology. 2. Leadership. 3. Trust-Case studies. I. Title.
BF575.T7H87 2012
658.4′092-dc23

2011030029

Printed in the United States of America

FIRST EDITION
HB Printing 10 9 8 7 6 5 4 3 2 1

This book is dedicated to the two people who have affected my life in the most profound ways.

To my wife, Kathleen Conway Hurley, whom I have been blessed to call my wife and trusted partner for over thirty years. No one lives the ideas concerning trustworthiness found in these pages better than you.

To my father, Francis Joseph Hurley, who in life's brief moments, between baseball games and at the dinner table, somehow instilled in me self-trust and an interest in the world of ideas.

CONTENTS

The Decision *to* Trust

INTRODUCTION

Having helped business leaders solve problems for more than thirty years, I have seen as both a researcher and a practitioner that organizational life has changed in fundamental ways. One of the most profound changes has been the loss of loyalty and trust, both of which have declined globally in nearly all industrialized democracies over the past three decades. If we define loyalty as a sense of duty and support among parties in a relationship, we are safe in saying that in most organizations today, loyalty is largely contingent on favorable economics and that this foundation is increasingly unstable and uncertain. The decline of loyalty in organizations may be the irreversible consequence of globalization, the growth of market-based economies, and the dynamics of creative destruction and innovation.[1] In fact, many would argue that organizations that must be agile to respond to rapidly changing markets can operate more effectively with less loyalty. But what happens when trust is lost? To what degree can an organization continue to be agile and effective when feelings of trust among employees, customers, investors, or other stakeholders have been replaced by distrust or suspicion?

Trust is the degree of confidence you have that another party can be relied on to fulfill commitments, be fair, be transparent, and not take advantage of your vulnerability. A simple thought experiment shows the consequences when trust is lost. Ask yourself, in the absence of force or coercion, how sustainable and vigilant would your commitment be to a partner who you thought would take advantage of you if given the opportunity? What about your commitment to a company where you believed that the CEO was exclusively concerned with his own income? Would you be willing to give up some resource (money, energy, water) to another party (person, organization, nation) if you felt that others would take advantage, squander your donation, and never reciprocate? Of course, the answer is that distrust reduces your willingness to cooperate, and therein lies the danger of a loss of trust. When we lose trust, we lose cooperation. Without trust, organizations and societies begin to break down. The loss of trust is much more dangerous than the loss of loyalty because it is an essential element to all effective relationships.

This book is the result of decades of working to apply research on trust with individuals, teams, and organizations. It is the product of a commitment to understand what trust really is and how it can be influenced in the variety of environments that we vulnerable humans must navigate. Most important, this book explains why some people, groups, organizations, and institutions have been able to defy the overall trend of declining trust—how they have created trust even in environments where change, uncertainty, and risk exist.

The essence of this book is the Decision to Trust Model (DTM), which can be used to make better trust decisions and to help diagnose and build trust. The development of the DTM involved going back and forth from research to practice to create a model that was grounded in the science of trust but also useable with leaders, teams, and organizations. I examined much of the vast theoretical and empirical research on trust, then tested the model in practice with many individuals, teams, and organizations over a twenty-year period. Beginning in 1990, I used the model in sessions on trust in an ongoing Columbia Business School executive program called High Impact Leadership and in Executive MBA classes at the Fordham Graduate School of Business. In these sessions, executives were asked to talk about how they made decisions to trust or distrust, and we covered trust at multiple levels: trust in a person, group, and organization. Each time, we used the latest iteration of the trust model to help them diagnose a trust relationship. Each year,

I refined the model, balancing the goals of making it both thorough and practicable.

In 2006, a version of the model was published in the *Harvard Business Review*.[2] Many people and companies found the model useful; this led to more experience applying the model with executives, teams, and in some cases entire organizations, helping train leaders about what trust is and how it can be managed. The DTM has been used by over a thousand executives in Asia, Europe, and North America to understand, diagnose, and build trust relations. These experiences led to further refinement of the model and to the development of a variety of tools and techniques to diagnose and build trust. All of these tools and techniques for diagnosing and building trust are presented in this book.

The model uses ten specific factors that have a bearing on whether people will be comfortable trusting. The ten factors are risk tolerance, adjustment, power, situational security, similarities, interests, benevolent concern, capability, predictability and integrity, and communication. Each of these factors will be reviewed in detail in this book, but for now what is important to know is that this list of ten items is both comprehensive and useful for addressing a variety of trust issues at the individual, group, and organizational levels. The DTM enables a clear diagnosis of why trust is high or low and, perhaps more important, aids in pinpointing areas for interventions and designing concrete actions to improve trust.

Using the DTM to make trust more understandable and manageable enables us to

- Make better decisions concerning whom to trust, so as to avoid harm and to increase pressure on untrustworthy agents to reform themselves
- Allocate our trust-building energy better by appreciating how different people approach the trust decision
- Identify the root cause of trust issues

- Offer concrete interventions and reforms that can enhance trust
- Distinguish situations in which building and repairing trust can work from those where it may not work
- Enhance trust at different levels: with a person, within teams, across teams, across national cultures, within organizations, and in leadership

This book is organized as follows. Chapter One, The Decision to Trust, explores trust as a decision-making process, reviews the trends of declining trust, and offers some explanation for the loss of trust. Chapter Two, The Decision to Trust Model, reviews the inputs to the trust decision and outlines the DTM, which can be used to understand and diagnose situations requiring a decision to trust. Through real examples and common trust scenarios, the model shows how to determine which of the ten factors are most trust deficient and what steps can be taken to improve the prospects for a successful trusting exchange.

Chapter Three, How We Differ in Trusting, focuses on the three DTM factors that measure one's personal proclivity to trust: risk tolerance, adjustment, and power. We will witness the toll that compulsive mistrust—commonly called micromanagement—can take on a company's or division's bottom line.

Chapter Four, Situational Factors in the Building of Trust, examines situational and relationship issues between parties that build or destroy trust. Special attention is paid to the seven DTM factors that affect relationships, such as the alignment of interests, predictability, integrity, and benevolence. Chapter Five, Tools for Diagnosing, Building, and Repairing Trust, explains how to use DTM analysis to remedy and repair areas of trust where needed, drawing on the trust workshops I have held across Asia, Europe, and North America in recent years.

Chapter Six, Trust in Leadership and Management, offers some concrete ideas on how to lead with trust, and discusses how leaders at any level can take active steps toward making their companies high-trust organizations. Chapter Seven, Trust in Organizations, examines the process of embedding a high-trust culture; it profiles examples of companies that have defied the trend of declining trust. Chapter Eight, Building Trust Within Teams, covers how trust can be developed within groups and teams. How to create a unifying identity and common goals is a key focus. Chapter Nine, Building Trust Across Groups and National Cultures, addresses how trust and trust building operate across functional, geographic, company, and national cultural partitions. The book concludes with Chapter Ten, Hope for the Future of Trust, which offers three major paradigm shifts that will be necessary to restore trust in our more cynical age.

My hope is that after reading this book, you will never think about trust and trustworthiness the same way. You will know why you trust or distrust, you will be better able to repair trust, and, most important, you will understand how to build trustworthiness in yourself, your teams, and your organization. In doing so, you will ensure more sustainable progress and eliminate a great deal of angst in your life and in the lives of those around you.

ONE

The Decision to Trust

Trust is central to human existence. Like all social animals, human beings have an instinctive need to cooperate and rely on each other in order to satisfy their most basic emotional, psychological, and material needs. Without trust, we are not only less happy as individuals but also less productive in groups. Research has linked the virtues and benefits of trust to economic prosperity, societal stability, and even human survival.[1] The powerful effect of trust is that it enables cooperative behavior without costly and cumbersome monitoring and contracting. In short, trust is a form of social capital that enhances performance between individuals, within and among groups, and in larger collectives (for example, organizations, institutions, and nations).

Yet even though the decision to trust is so important, most of us can provide only rudimentary explanations of why we choose to trust certain people, groups, and institutions and not others. Trust, like love and happiness, is difficult for people to explain in clear, rational terms. This often makes us very bad trustors (a person deciding to trust or distrust). It also can create problems for us in life. We extend trust with only a vague sense of our reasons for trusting, and we unknowingly create an incentive and a market for untrustworthy opportunists who rely on a steady supply of naïve trustors. In not understanding trust, we may also fail to grasp why someone might be wary of giving us his or her trust. Worst of all, we may sometimes act unintentionally in ways that erode others' trust in us.

We make different kinds of trust errors. Sometimes we choose to trust people, groups, and organizations that do not warrant that trust. Other times, we choose not to trust even though trust is warranted, and we miss out on opportunities as a result. For example, studies have shown that many people underestimate the trustworthiness of others and that this induces these others not only to be less trusting but also less generous.[2] Emotions and gut feelings can often outweigh data. There are even people who err by adopting a default decision of distrust in order to protect themselves from the pain of betrayal and disappointment. They might be happier on the whole if they chose to trust more often and to endure some betrayal as a necessary price in the pursuit of happiness.[3]

By trusting, you make yourself vulnerable to loss. Questions of whom to trust, how far to extend that trust, and how to avoid betrayal of trust extend into all our important relationships, including those with our employers, the government, and other large institutions. The choices we make in answering these questions can have profound effects on the course of our lives, which is why so many classics of world literature are suffused with themes of trust and betrayal. From *The Odyssey* to *Hamlet,* all the way through to such modern classics as *The Brothers Karamazov* and *Catcher in the Rye,* the question of how much one can trust—whether it be a loved one, authority figure, or government—has plagued literature's heroes.

Distrust can be healthy and advisable, but when present in the extreme and in the wrong situations, it corrodes the cooperative instinct. It turns collaborative exchange into a slow and anxious mess of protective maneuvers.[4] We know from research that our beliefs and judgments about trustworthiness affect our intentions and behaviors toward others in fundamental ways. Consider the consequences that research shows are related to high or low trust (illustrated in Figure 1.1).[5]

Without trust, people are more anxious and less happy; leaders without trust have slower and more cautious followers; organizations without trust struggle to be productive; governments without trust lose essential civic cooperation; and societies without trust deteriorate. In short, if

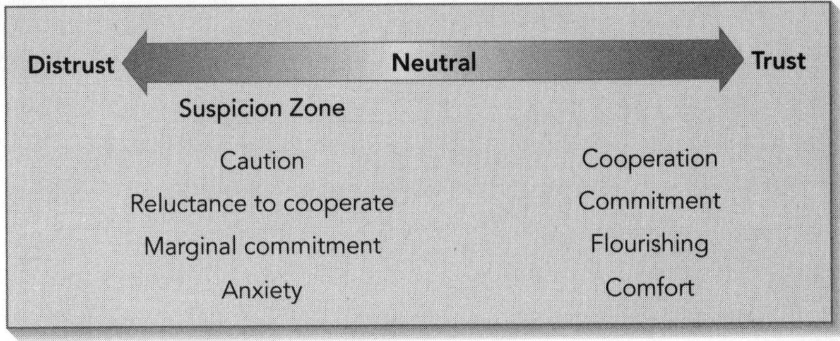

Figure 1.1 The Distrust-Trust Continuum

we cannot generate adequate and reasonable perceptions of trust, through agents acting in a trustworthy manner, our lives will be more problematic and less prosperous.

A DEEPER LOOK INTO THE DECISION TO TRUST

Researchers have studied trust as a decision process and identified the inputs we typically consider in making this decision.[6] We will consider the inputs to the trust decision in the next chapter, but for now we will concentrate on the trust decision process. As Figure 1.2 shows, every decision to trust is made within a situational context. You decide to trust person B in matter X, and this will be influenced by the situational factors represented by C. For example, you may trust your spouse with home repair (matter X), but not with your home finances. You would never trust a total stranger with your expensive digital camera—unless the stranger is standing a few feet away and you've asked him to snap a vacation picture of you and your companion at the Grand Canyon (situation C).

The decision to trust presents itself when both uncertainty and vulnerability are at hand. When things are totally predictable, the question of trust does not arise. But when you hand that stranger your camera at the Grand Canyon, you can't be absolutely certain that he

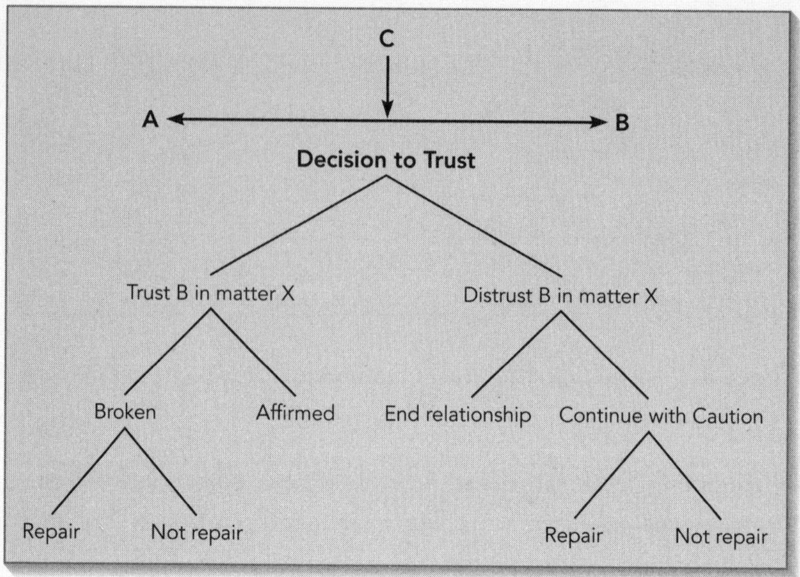

Figure 1.2 The Decision to Trust

won't either drop it or run off with it. Your decision to trust—your confident reliance that he will return the camera to you unharmed—is partly based on your choice to accept some uncertainty in the situation. But even in an uncertain situation, if you don't feel any true vulnerability, then trust is really not an issue. If you were to lend a cheap pen to that same stranger at the Grand Canyon and you have three others in your pocket, you haven't made a substantive decision to trust because whether or not you get your pen back is not of any real concern to you. Trust is most helpful when we are faced with risk and uncertainty and the possibility of injury. In important matters, when we decide to distrust, a relationship usually ends or continues under duress unless it can be repaired.

Consider the following scenarios that involve the decision to trust:

- You and your spouse are about to purchase a house. You are torn about how much to rely on your real estate agent, who has told you that the price is fair, the schools are great, and the neighbors are wonderful. It is the biggest decision you and your spouse have made since marrying.

- Your company has just announced that it is merging with another firm. Your boss tells you that your position is safe. How much of your energy do you put into making the merger work versus actively seeking other job opportunities?
- You have just taken over as CEO of a firm, and you realize that your direct reports and the functions they lead do not trust each other or share information, and your customers and profits are suffering. You are leading a collection of groups that are not integrated and not performing, and you know that you will lose your job if you cannot repair this sinking ship.

You may ruminate more in some scenarios, and you may have more options in certain cases, but in each situation you will come to some judgment about how comfortable you are relying on a trustee (a person, group, organization, or institution to whom something is entrusted). Research shows that this trust judgment is related to your disposition to trust and your perceptions of the trustworthiness of the trustee.[7] You assess attributes of trustworthiness and the situation in making a trust judgment. The judgment you make influences your behavior toward the trustee—for example, whether you share information or the degree to which you take protective measures with this trustee in this situation.

Interdependence is an inescapable fact of life, and we cannot predict the future with certainty, but we can understand the set of factors that go into making a good trust decision. Trust errors often occur when we fail to consider one or more of these key trust factors. If you familiarize yourself with the mental calculations involved in the decision to trust, if you understand the underlying causes of trust, it stands to reason that you will make wiser, better-informed decisions. Furthermore, if you are able to predict the conditions under which people will trust, then you should be able to manage trust and earn the trust of others.

THE STATE OF TRUST OVER TIME

One way to understand the trust decision is to examine it over time. Fortunately, social scientists have been measuring the degree to which we trust or distrust for a long time. The findings show a disturbing trend of declining trust in major social institutions, including government, in nearly all advanced industrialized democracies.[8] In the United States, trust has been in gradual decline since the early 1970s, following a dramatic drop in the 1960s. In the 1960s, surveys indicated that about 59 percent of people agreed with the statement "Most people can be trusted." Figure 1.3 presents this generalized trust data from the General Social Survey beginning in 1987, when they began to be collected regularly. The data represent face-to-face in-person interviews in the United States with a randomly selected sample of adults.[9] The survey results indicate a steady decline, with the most recent scores showing that only about one-third of respondents agree that most people can be trusted.

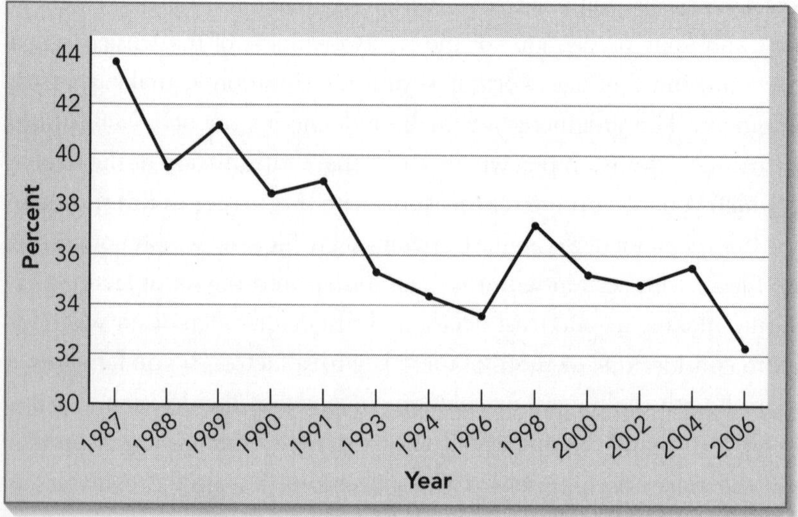

Figure 1.3 Percentage of People Who Say That "Most People Can Be Trusted"

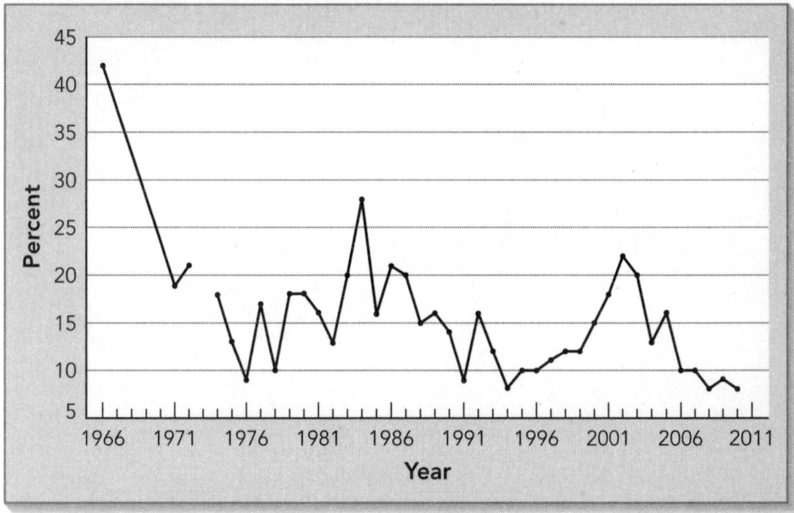

Figure 1.4 Percentage of People Who Have a Great Deal of Confidence in Congress

Because trust is often defined as "confident reliance," many surveys measure confidence rather than asking directly about trust. As illustrated in Figure 1.4, Harris Poll data on confidence in the U.S. Congress shows the bleakest trend. Except for 1985, when the Congress protected Social Security from cuts under Reagan, and the extended period of economic growth leading up to the dot-com crash in 2000, the public's confidence in Congress has been in steady decline. In the most recent data, less than 10 percent of people said they had a great deal of confidence in Congress.

Given the low generalized trust scores and low scores on trust in Congress, we would hope that people can at least trust where they get their information, the press. Unfortunately, according to the Harris Poll, the long-term U.S. trend for confidence in the press also shows declines (see Figure 1.5).[10] Trust has declined since 1966, with the exception of two periods when there was a positive bounce: coverage of Watergate in the mid-1970s and of the Iran hostage crisis in the late 1970s into 1980. In 2009, a Pew Research Center survey that asked directly about bias and accuracy showed rising perceptions that the media is biased in its reporting.[11]

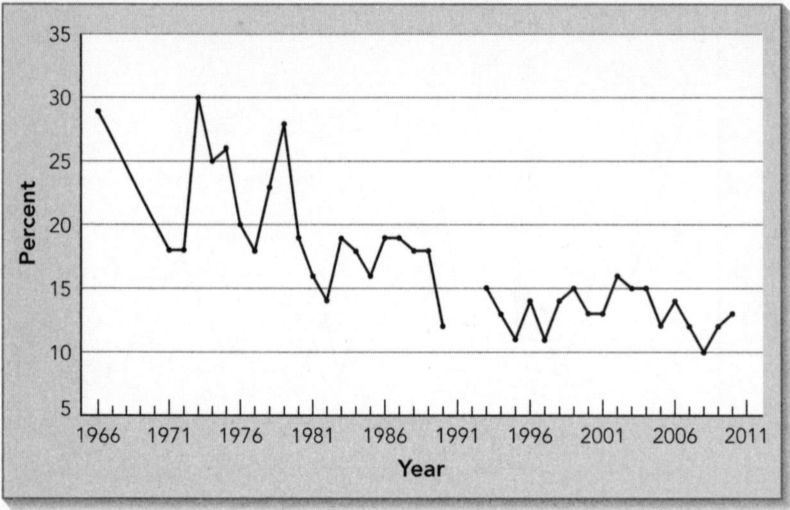

Figure 1.5 Percentage of People Who Have a Great Deal of Confidence in the Press

Data on trust in business are even bleaker. The Harris Poll data on confidence in business in the United States is shown in Figure 1.6. Starting at a high of 55 percent in 1966, scores since 2008 are trending at or below 15 percent of people who have a great deal of confidence in business. The only periods when scores increased were from 1992 to 2000, when there were eight years of above-average GDP growth, and during the mania leading up to the dot-com bust, 2000 to 2002. The 2009 Edelman Trust Barometer, which is a global measure, showed that trust in business declined across the globe after the financial crisis. Across twenty countries, 62 percent of respondents trusted business less than the year before.[12] In another Edelman survey of more than four thousand people, only 30 to 40 percent of respondents in the United States, the United Kingdom, France, and Germany felt that business could be "trusted to do what is right."[13]

A deeper look at the loss of trust in business during the global financial crisis reveals poor decision making and a failure of trustworthiness across the individual, organizational, and governmental levels, with

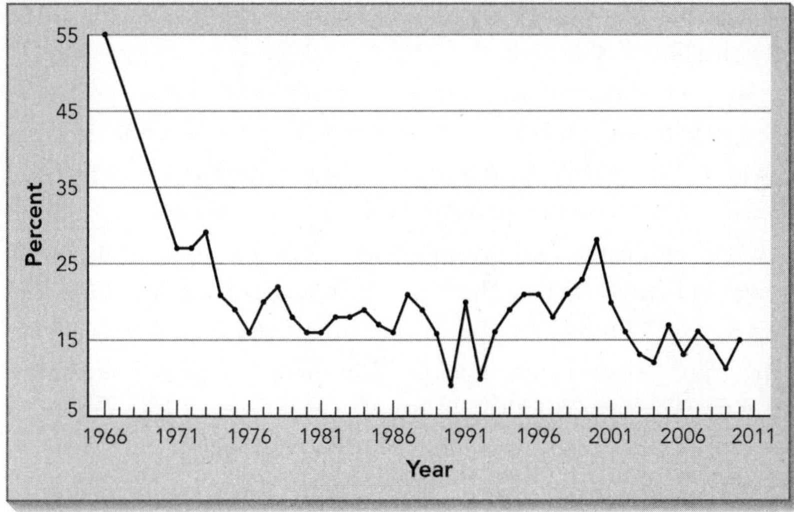

Figure 1.6 Percentage of People Who Have a Great Deal of Confidence in Business

disastrous effects. The Financial Trust Index showed that between September and December of 2008, 52 percent of Americans lost trust in the banks. Similarly, 65 percent lost trust in the stock market.[14] Although many articles and books have been written about the global financial crisis, none have properly analyzed this betrayal from a trust perspective. Preceding this massive loss of trust was a systematic erosion of the foundational elements of trustworthiness.

Financial institutions were changing their business models to grow, but they were not increasing their capability to systematically understand and manage these new products (derivatives, credit default swaps, mortgage-backed securities).[15] There was also a fundamental misalignment of interests and incentives in the system. Politicians leading financial regulation in Congress (for example, Barney Frank and Chris Dodd) were receiving millions of dollars from the industry they were regulating. The government was not only reducing regulation and enforcement but also contributing to inflation in home prices by keeping interest rates artificially low and forcing Fannie Mae and Freddie Mac to buy mortgages and take the default risk from banks whose mortgage brokers received bigger commissions to sell mortgages with a higher likelihood of default.

Adding to this list of perverse incentives, the investment bank CEOs were receiving large bonuses that were based on questionable earnings growth and at odds with risk-adjusted long-term shareholder value. These incentives also turned out to be at odds with Main Street's desire for a healthy financial system to achieve some stability in retirement savings and employment. There were also major lapses in ethics and integrity as CEOs assured the markets that their firms were in great shape—just prior to their failures. The failure of proper disclosure and transparent communication between investment banks and their own clients was noted in a number of fines levied by the Securities Exchange Commission (SEC). Finally, there was a major failure of boards of directors to hold management accountable; and in firm after firm, co-optation replaced rigorous stewardship of shareholders' and citizens' best interests. The story of the global financial crisis that is just beginning to be written is a story of trust and eventual betrayal in a system that was inherently untrustworthy. It is a story of poor trust decision making that led to trillions of dollars of wealth destruction and immensely painful job losses on a global scale.

MAKING SENSE OF THE DECLINE IN TRUST

How did we reach this poor state of affairs concerning trust in business, government, and the media? Why is trust such an issue today? Was it a problem for previous generations? Although different types of trust (of government, leaders, Congress, and people in general) may have some specific reasons for decline, larger themes and some answers for the decline of trust emerge from research.

Change, Complexity, and Inflated Expectations of Trustees

Some of the failures noted earlier on the part of business and government leaders were due to misguided decisions made in the face of great change and complexity. When matters grow beyond the capability of the trustee, distrust is a logical posture. In his book *Trust,* Russell Hardin makes the point that trust in government began to decline with the advent of Lyndon Johnson's Great Society program and the expanding scope of government, which tried to solve issues concerning poverty and crime, with generally poor results.[16] Surveys of trust in government often cite waste and inefficiency (incompetence) as one of the major reasons that citizens lack confidence and trust in government.[17] There is also evidence that trust in business leaders has declined because employees do not feel confidence that their leaders know how to handle the challenges confronting them. A survey by the European Leadership Program of one thousand midlevel executives in U.K. companies showed that just 53 percent felt confident that their leaders could manage their companies through challenges.[18] In this sense, the decline in trust is simply good judgment in the face of more challenging times and less dependable trustees.

Compounding the limited ability to deal with change and complexity is the problem of inflated expectations. Expectations have increased along with a sense of entitlement, so trustors are more frequently disappointed. Often our reaction to disappointment is to decry the trustee without asking ourselves whether our expectations were fair or reasonable. It is more comforting to blame loss or failure on a flawed trustee (scapegoat) because it offers us the hope that success is achievable, even in dealing with the most challenging problems, if only we have the right president or CEO. It is more troubling to admit that sometimes situations are beyond our control and that there is no all-knowing authority figure who can change this. There is evidence that these inflated expectations explain some of the loss of trust in government.[19]

An excessive entitlement mentality can lead to a feeling of betrayal even when the trustee has been trustworthy by all objective assessments. This is not meant to take leaders off the hook for acting in good faith, but merely to recognize that it is hard to maintain high trust when we project unreasonable expectations onto trustees.

Radical Change in Interdependence and Social Networks

Simply put, the world used to be a much smaller place for most of us. In a small village, people depended on direct face-to-face exchanges with people they knew. Violating norms of trust and of reciprocity would result in sure and quick punishment by the community. Today in our larger, more fragmented social networks, we are forced to depend on many more people and groups that we do not know well. This increases the chances that we will be betrayed and lose trust.[20] It also is harder to locate and penalize violations of trust. Many social networks comprise fragmented, shallow connections based on online interaction rather than personal relationships. This changed dynamic makes it harder to regulate distrust and presents more opportunities for betrayal.

Widening of Income Disparity, Prevalence of a Sense of Unfairness, and Decrease of Optimism

Studies have shown that lower levels of trust are found in nations with greater income disparities.[21] The explanation given for why low trust tends to be associated with more income disparity is that trust is connected with people's sense of optimism and hope for a better life, both of which suffer when there is great variance in wealth. When we feel hopeful that we can have a better life, we tend to be more trusting. In contrast, if we feel despair and that others have advantages that are not available to us (lack of fairness), we tend to be suspicious. Low trust tends to be the result when there are many "have nots" looking at the "haves." Some argue that redistributing wealth robs people of the chance to build self-esteem through hard work, and creates incentives for sloth and disincentives for entrepreneurship. Although this may be true in certain circumstances, these arguments do not change the empirical fact that trust goes hand in hand with higher levels of income equality. If a nation values a high level of societal trust as a goal, it is clear that fairness in the ability to earn income and some mechanism for avoiding excessive extremes in income distribution must exist.

The ability to increase one's standard of living is connected with a more general issue of generational optimism and pessimism. Each generation views its environment and adopts a mind-set that falls somewhere along a continuum of optimism and pessimism; this mind-set colors how trusting the people in that generation are likely to be. In an analysis of trust data, Uslaner found that optimistic people were 36 percent more likely to trust others than the most pessimistic people.[22] Increasing life spans, affluence, and technological progress have not made younger generations more optimistic. A world leadership survey by the Center for Creative Leadership indicates that only 30 percent of employees ages twenty-five to thirty-five trust the people they work with "a lot," versus 45 percent for employees ages thirty-six to sixty-five. The survey was conducted in January 2009 and surveyed 1,750 people, covering the Americas, Asia Pacific, Europe, Middle East, and Africa. The data suggest that across the world, younger generations are increasingly less trusting; this has major implications for retaining talent and building effective organizations.[23]

Decline in Civic Mindedness and Increase in Isolation

When we come together and prevail in a crisis, we feel better about human nature and our ability to count on those around us. Putnam and Uslaner makes a convincing arguments that the generation that came together to overcome the challenges of the Great Depression and World War II—food and material shortages, deaths of loved ones in combat, and the threat of an expansionist aggressor—embedded a belief in the power of a civic-minded community to prevail by looking out for each other. They refer to the people born from 1910 to 1940 as the "long civic generation." Generations since have all shown some decline in civic mindedness, the willingness to sacrifice for the common good and trust in others.[24] Other research suggests that the advent of television increased isolation and reduced community building, which led to a decline in trust.[25] The math is very simple. As of the twenty-first century, no one under the age of fifty can remember a time when a majority of the public trusted government, social institutions, and major corporations. Everyone ages sixty or younger has spent his or her entire working life in a world characterized by eroding trust and growing suspicion.

Extreme Capitalism and an Age of Opportunism

It is clear that the global financial crisis and the opportunistic behavior of banks, ratings agencies, and mortgage brokers, as well as some boards of directors and senior managers, contributed to a near depression and an erosion of trust. In the United States, data from the Edelman Trust Barometer showed major declines in trust in business among the public during the 2008 to 2009 time period of the financial crisis.[26] But this trend is not a recent or isolated one. Increased competition and globalization have contributed to the evolution of a more economically driven and less social and humanistic model of capitalism.[27] Consider the difference between IBM as a blue-chip company in the 1960s, where employees could largely assume lifetime employment, versus the leaner and arguably more agile and meaner 2010 version, where jobs move to countries based on economics, and workforce reductions are made more regularly.[28] More competition, more stress, and less slack in the system increase risk and make trust more difficult.

Deutsch's research established that a competitive, winner-take-all orientation promotes suspicion, not trust.[29] Creating types of competition in specific areas of business and society can be associated with progress through innovation and creative destruction of poorly performing firms and non-value-adding industries.[30] The problem comes when capitalism becomes an unbridled race to profit without concern for ethics, morality, and the interests of all stakeholders in the social and economic system. Organization theories have contributed to this problem. For example, the transaction cost theory of organization starts with the assumption that people will act opportunistically with guile, which some have argued has induced this very behavior.[31] Shareholder maximization theories have elevated shareholders over other stakeholders and led to conflicts rather than to integration of interests.[32]

The general lack of integration of ethical, moral, and stakeholder theories into business models and organizations has contributed to what I refer to as extreme capitalism.[33] For example, we sometimes hear the expression "This is a business" or "I am running a business" to justify, on economic grounds, what we feel may be questionable from a moral or ethical perspective. Edward Freeman, one of the leading stakeholder theorists, referred to this as the "separatist principle," whereby we separate business from ethics, morality, and humanism. For this reason, as a means of restoring trust, Freeman and other scholars advocate new forms of governance and incentives to correct some dysfunctions of our current form of capitalism.[34] Capitalism has proven to be an incredible vehicle for the allocation of human and financial capital to increase prosperity, but, like all systems, it needs to be occasionally changed and reformed.[35]

Increased Negative Content and Tales of Betrayal in the Media

Survey data indicate that 72 percent of Americans get their impression of government from the media rather than from personal experience (18 percent) or friends and family (8 percent).[36] There is also evidence that after the 1950s, which is when trust scores began their long decline, the media transitioned from being a simple carrier of the politician's message to active critic of the politician.[37] Estimates suggest that negative accounts in TV, newspapers, and magazines increased from about 25 percent of stories to 60 percent during the 1970s and 1980s.[38] In modern elections in the United States, some of the most frequent government bashing in the media comes from politicians themselves using pejorative terms like "government is broken," "beltway bandit," and "Washington elite."

The vast increase in the volume of media also hurts trust in some ways. Contrast the Kennedy White House years with the Clinton era. For weeks if not months, the American public heard about President Clinton's betrayal with Monica Lewinski. Similarly with Richard Nixon and Watergate. Unfortunately, tales of the noble politician seem rare and are drowned out by the stories of investigations and indictments. Senator Bill Bradley once said of media coverage, "If it bleeds it leads; if it thinks it stinks."[39] Beyond the news, nearly all of the reality TV shows and many of the talk shows supply a steady diet of stories of betrayal, with what seems like a preference for the most uncivil and outrageous.

THE IMPLICATIONS OF THE DECLINE IN TRUST

But what do a decline of trust and perceptions of trustworthiness mean at a more granular level? At the individual level, it means that people feel that they must protect their interests because they believe others will not. At the organizational level, it means that one department is reluctant to cooperate or share with another, or is resistant to doing so. At the system level, an atmosphere of distrust ensures that more and more energy and attention are devoted to cautious self-protection rather than to productive exchange, whether that be in an economic or a political system. The result can be disorder, chaos, and, in the case of the 2008 financial crisis, $4.1 trillion of wealth destruction on a global scale.[40]

The defining characteristics of successful institutions, societies, and organizations are interdependence, cooperation, and coordination, all of which are enabled by trust. Followers depend on leaders, leaders depend on followers, the marketing group depends on manufacturing, and so on. Group life requires the development of "dependable" working relationships with others who affect outcomes and our futures. Without trust, we move from dependable working relationship to stressful adventure as we try to make things work with those on whom we must rely.

If there is any good news at all to be found here, it's that a worldwide scarcity of trust means that trust has never been so precious and so valuable. In an atmosphere of general distrust, those leaders with a good grasp of trust—who know how to judge it, build it, and rely on it—have an enormous edge over their competitors. Those who can succeed in the task of building high-trust relationships and high-trust organizations are more likely to be rewarded, because research shows that people instinctively gravitate toward individuals and organizations who are trustworthy and who manage trust well.[41]

Research in economics suggests that on a global scale, investment as a share of GDP increases 1 percent for every 7 percent increase in trust, and the average economic growth rate increases 1 percent for every 15 percent increase in a country's level of trust.[42] Research in organizations shows that trust improves the internal effectiveness of groups and organizations; there is lower turnover, higher commitment, and better mutual adjustment. There is also evidence that trust improves external performance through increased goal attainment, better completion time, more positive impact on stakeholders, and higher return on investment.[43] In high-trust collectives, people and groups are invited to move beyond their narrow self-interests and commit to common goals. They aren't excessively distracted by the need to protect themselves from others' self-promoting agendas. It is for this reason that trust is the primary measure that *Fortune* magazine uses to select its annual list Fortune 100 Best Companies to Work For. In these companies, employees acknowledge that change brings inevitable uncertainties, but that they nonetheless have a sense of comfort that they are acting in concert with their coworkers, pulling together toward a common goal.

Too few environments match this description of high-trust organizations today. To move from a low-trust to a high-trust environment requires effort, but above all, as we'll see in the next chapter, it takes a more thorough understanding of what we really mean when we use the word "trust."

TWO

The Decision to Trust Model

What is trust? In the most general terms, trusting means feeling comfortable with how a party will act in a situation in which you could be hurt. In terms of one-on-one relationships, it's been described as a willingness to make yourself vulnerable to someone else, based on positive expectations that the other person will either serve your interests or at least not hinder them.[1]

Drawing on prior research, I define trust as having "confident reliance" in another party whenever an uncertain situation entails some vulnerability or risk.[2] This notion of confident reliance allows room for discussing both "relational trust" from an interpersonal perspective as well as "organizational trust" and "system trust" from a more impersonal perspective. Your decision to trust involves your degree of confident reliance in a wide spectrum of possible trustees in your life—a person (your spouse, your colleague), group (your department, your tennis team), organization (your company), institution (the federal government, the Catholic Church), system (air traffic control, the financial system).

This wide spectrum of trustees presented the first challenge to developing the Decision to Trust Model (DTM)—how to make the model robust enough that it could be used with individuals, teams, and organizations without making it unwieldy. I decided to focus on the factors that could explain the major proportion of trustworthiness across multiple levels of trustees. The model is thus very effective in assessing basic trust in people, teams, and organizations, but it ignores some nuances in trust at each level that a more complicated model would cover.

Another challenge was making the vast research and diverse perspectives on trust practicable. I chose to follow Deutsch's and other scholars' lead in framing trust as a judgment that the trustor (the one deciding to trust or distrust) makes concerning the trustworthiness of another (the trustee).[3] The trust decision is an "all things considered" overall belief about the degree of confidence we have in relying on the trustee where there is uncertainty and possible injury. In making this judgment, we may uncover reasons to both trust and distrust, and we weigh and balance them to take an overall trust stance regarding the trustee.[4] This stance, or orientation, affects our intentions and behavior toward the trustee. When we trust, our stance is characterized by sharing and cooperation; when we distrust, we tend to be more cautious or reluctant to share or cooperate.

Having framed trust as a decision that derives from our assessment of the trustworthiness of another, my next key question became: What are the inputs to the trust decision? Fortunately, there are thousands of studies in economics, psychology, and sociology that answer this question quite well. The challenge was to integrate related concepts into a limited but useful model for managing trust. This research proved invaluable, and the findings and integration are summarized in Appendix A, Research on the Antecedents to Trust. The ten factors in the model cover those that research has shown are the antecedents to trust. In some cases, I chose broader labels to connect related constructs and limit the number of factors to one that would be both powerful and practical in managing trust. For example, the term *similarity* was used to cover value congruence and social identity, and *benevolence* includes elements of caring, altruism, and goodwill. These labels were tested for understanding and usability among executives as the model was being developed.

Because researchers had suggested that in any relationship there may be reasons both to trust and to distrust someone, the model was framed as a balancing or "compensatory" process whereby the decision maker weighs the various factors in coming up with an overall judgment.[5] I deliberately chose not to weigh the relative importance of factors; this would have made the model unreliable for use across different situations and cultures, which research shows affect the relative importance of various factors of trust.[6] In fact, how the parties in the trust relationship weigh the factors can be uncovered as part of the process of using the model as a diagnostic tool to assess and build trust.

Finally, researchers have suggested that the trust judgment involves both emotions and cognition, and that they interact.[7] I trust you because I have a good feeling (emotion) about you; or, perhaps, I trust you because I believe (cognition) that you manifest trustworthy characteristics. The model takes the perspective that the trustor's thoughts and beliefs (cognitions) about himself or herself and about the trustworthiness of the trustee are generally the most powerful factors influencing trust. Because the goal of this book is to help manage trust, this focus on cognitions rather than emotions is also practical, because there is much research supporting the notion that changing beliefs can, over time, lead to changes in emotion.[8]

TEN ESSENTIAL ELEMENTS OF TRUST

The ten factors included in the DTM are divided into two categories, as illustrated in Figure 2.1. In the first category are the three *trustor* factors, which assess the general disposition of the decision maker to choose to trust or distrust. The second category comprises seven *situational* factors that define the antecedents to trust as they relate to the situation and the relationship with the trustee. The research that underpins the DTM was discussed in Chapter One and will be touched on again in Chapters Three and Four. The focus in this chapter is to offer a straightforward review of the model and describe how it is used in practice.

The Three Trustor Factors

Most of us know some people who trust nearly everyone and other people who seem to trust no one. Three factors help explain differences in people's disposition to trust: risk tolerance, adjustment, and power.

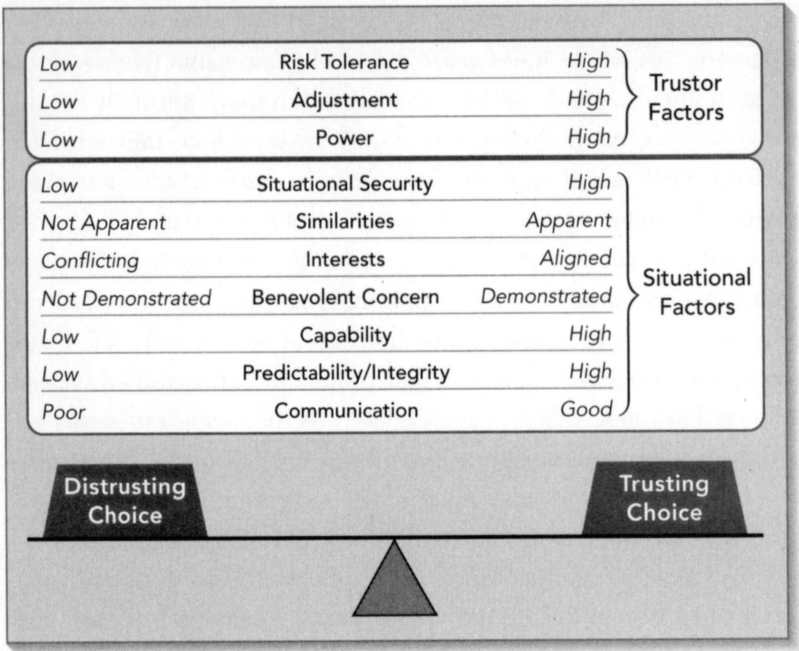

Figure 2.1 The Decision to Trust Model

These intrapersonal aspects of trust describe an individual trustor's generalized tendency to trust—regardless of the other party (the trustee). They are the result of a complex mix of personality, culture, and experience and account for the fact that building trust takes more time and effort for some people than it does for others. More important, we can use these three factors to predict which people will tend to be more or less trusting.

Risk Tolerance

Some people are natural risk takers; others are innately cautious. How tolerant people are of risk has a big impact on their willingness to trust—regardless of who the trustee is. Psychologists have measures of "mischievousness" to assess risk seeking and "cautiousness" for those for whom risk is more uncomfortable. Risk seekers don't spend much time calculating what might go wrong in a given situation. In the absence of any glaring problems, they tend to have faith that things will work out. Risk avoiders, however, often need to feel in control before they place their trust in someone. They tend to want more assurances before they will trust, regardless of the situation. They can be reluctant to act without approval, because some risk avoiders don't even trust themselves.

Psychological Adjustment

Psychologists have shown that individuals vary widely in how well adjusted they are. Like risk tolerance, this aspect of personality affects the amount of time people need to build trust. Well-adjusted people are comfortable with themselves and see the world as a generally benign place. Their high level of confidence often makes them quick to trust, because they believe nothing bad will happen to them. People who are poorly adjusted, which is commonly called neuroticism, tend to see many threats in the world, so they carry more anxiety into every situation. These people take longer to get to a position of comfort and trust, regardless of who the trustee is.

Relative Power

Trustors in positions of authority are more likely to have confident reliance in the actions of people subordinate to them because they have the power to punish betrayal. In contrast, subordinates with little authority, and thus no recourse, feel more vulnerable to those with power. They are less comfortable trusting. A corporate culture that is characterized by powerlessness, and therefore nurtures distrust, is one of the central impediments to building a high-performance, high-trust organization.

The Seven Situational Factors

The remaining seven factors in the DTM concern aspects of the situation and of the relationship between the parties. These are the seven factors that trustees can most effectively address and influence in order to gain the trust—the confident reliance—of trustors.

Security

In looking at the three trustor factors, we examined risk tolerance as an internal dispositional factor of the trustor. Here we look at the opposite of risk—security—as it relates to a given situation. A general rule to remember: the higher the stakes, the less likely people are to trust. Distrust follows naturally from risk. An employee of mine might not need much assurance to trust me to gain approval to fund his attendance at an expensive training program, but he might need a lot if I am deciding who the survivors will be in a reduction in force. With global competition and rapidly changing markets and competitive dynamics, there is greater situational risk and uncertainty for most people and organizations today.

Similarities

Social identity theory suggests that we are at heart still quite tribal, which is why people tend to more easily trust those who appear similar to them. For some cultures, "in-group" status is key to trust. Similarities that can prime trust may include common values (such as a strong work ethic), membership in a defined group (such as the manufacturing, editorial department, a local church, or gender), and shared personality traits (extroversion, for instance, or ambition). In deciding how much to trust someone, people often begin by tallying up their similarities and differences. Often this leads them to make foolish choices based on trivial similarities. Most Ponzi schemes, for instance, begin by relying on existing networks of people who trust each other on the sometimes weak basis of social, ethnic, or religious affiliations.

Alignment of Interests

Before we place our trust in someone else, we weigh the question *How likely is this person to serve my interests?* When the trustor's and trustee's interests are well aligned, it's much easier for both parties to trust. When we board a plane, we trust the airline pilot in part because we assume that he has as much interest in getting to our destination safely as we do. Used car dealers, in contrast, are typically considered untrustworthy because buyers assume that the dealer's self-interested goal—getting a higher price by concealing a car's faults and defects—is directly at odds with the buyer's goal of obtaining a safe and inexpensive car.

Benevolent Concern

We tend to trust and feel positive affection for those who are willing to put our interests above their own—to demonstrate benevolent concern for us. By contrast, a trustee who appears self-centered inspires distrust. We have all known managers, for instance, who aren't trusted by their employees because those employees don't believe that the manager will stick up for them or fight for them. The result is that those employees probably wouldn't advocate for the manager's goals on their own—that is, when performance is not subject to coercive control. Therein lies the tremendous cost that burdens low-trust organizations. When trust is absent, so is real effort and concern for the enterprise.

Capability

Because trust involves an assessment of how comfortable we are in relying on someone, judgments of simple competence can be paramount. We are only trustworthy to the extent that we can capably fulfill a given responsibility. Some trustors make the mistake of relying on other factors, such as similarities and benevolent concern, to make up for a lack of evident capability. They hire friends and family under the assumption that caring is a substitute for capability, and soon find out otherwise. Michael Brown, the head of the Federal Emergency Management Agency (FEMA), which did such a disastrous job in emergency relief after Hurricane Katrina in 2005, was a friend of then President Bush. FEMA, under Brown, was described as a glaring example of incompetence due to cronyism.[9]

Predictability and Integrity

At some point in the trust decision, the trustor asks, "How certain am I about my prediction as to how the trustee will act?" For example, managers who are excessively passionate and not detail or process oriented often overpromise and underdeliver. Their enthusiasm leads them to commit to deliverables that they have not yet figured out how to produce. Inevitably, promises cannot be fulfilled once the details and methods are understood. These managers may be hardworking and have good intentions, but they are not trusted because their track records of delivery are poor.

Communication

Because trust is largely a relational concept, communication is critical to each of the other six relational factors in the DTM. On the one hand, frequent and open communication can lead to trusting relationships even when other relational factors are low in trust. On the other hand, poor communication almost always leads to a tendency not to trust. Spirals of distrust often begin with miscommunication, leading to perceived betrayal that causes further impoverishment of communication and eventually ending in a state of chronic distrust (see Figure 2.2). By the same token, trustees who excel at communication and are able to create emotional bonds with trustors can set off a virtuous cycle of trust, in which their openness induces others to open up and reciprocate with feelings of confident reliance.

The DTM is broad enough to be used with different types of trustees and in different situations. When we are trustors at the organizational or system level, the signals we use to judge trust are more impersonal

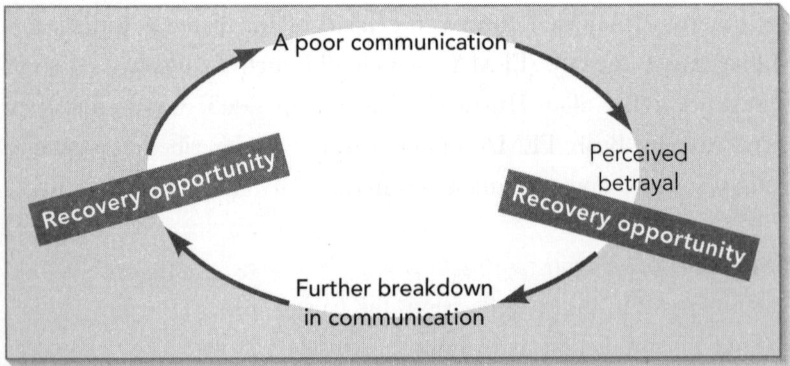

Figure 2.2 Miscommunication and Distrust

than when we are looking at an individual or group. This alters the trust judgment because some trust factors become more important (capability and predictability) and others less important (for example, similarities and benevolence). The judgment also changes to some degree depending on the type of trust situation. Situations can vary in terms of the amount of uncertainty and risk, the length of the relationship, the number of alternative options we have, and the amount of experience and information available in assessing the trustee. These situational variables affect the amount of time we invest in assessing trust and how deeply we might get into assessing some of the dimensions of trust. For example, I am likely to invest more time and probe deeper to assess the competence of a direct report than I would to assess the trustworthiness of the global conglomerate that owns my company. Why? I might conclude that the larger organization will not affect me directly in a major way, that I do not have any other options but to trust, or that I simply cannot know enough to make an accurate assessment.

TESTING THE DTM

The DTM is a deliberately broad diagnostic tool that can be used to capture the nuances of many different types of trustor-trustee situations. Used properly to think through the trust decision, the DTM helps us match the degree of trust with the actual trustworthiness of the trustee. As shown in Figure 2.3, the model helps us avoid the errors in the upper left and lower right quadrants while locating caution and appropriate reliance where they belong. The DTM also enables us to diagnose which variables are most critical to trust in a given situation and then focus on enhancing those factors to maintain, build, or repair trust.

Let's return to the three trust scenarios posed in Chapter One to see how the DTM can be used to confront a potentially negative, distrustful situation and create a result that benefits both parties.

1. In the case of the real estate agent who is influencing your decision to buy a house, the DTM helps us focus on some key questions. Is the agent more apt to say and do things that protect her interests

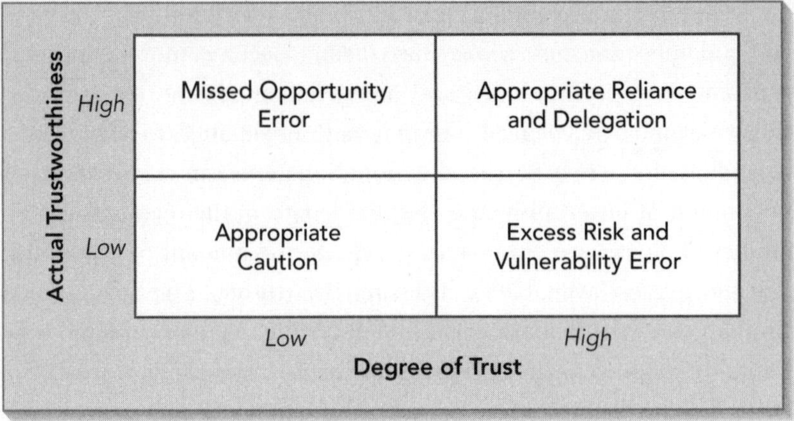

Figure 2.3 Aligning Trust and Trustworthiness

(commission) or that protect your family? How does she balance benevolence (concern for you) with her self-interest? Is she candid about key issues (integrity and open communication)? Also, how risk tolerant are you? Do you have any recourse if she lies to you? How competent is she? Does she really know schools, pricing, and the neighbors? Is she able to discern "good" and "bad" in these areas? Considering these factors of the DTM can prevent you from blindly trusting or blindly distrusting and making a mistake. It may also cause you to get another agent because you really need someone whom you trust to help you make the best, most informed decision. You need to trust an expert.

2. What about our fellow whose company has merged and whose boss says he is safe? The DTM helps him make a better trust decision by encouraging him to ask, How much situational risk is there? Are my skills in great demand? If so, no problem; if he betrays me, I will move on. If not, maybe I would like to reduce my situational risk with a contract or at least an agreement for extended severance. If this is not an option, I really do need to assess my boss's benevolence toward me and his competence (Is he really in the know?), and I need to assess the interests not only of my boss but of the company we are merging with, especially because there are really very few "mergers of equals," despite the frequent use of this term.

3. What about our CEO who has inherited a distrustful top team and is now captain of a sinking ship? He needs to figure out how to eradicate the poisonous, distrustful culture. How much trust is needed for the company to succeed? Are the staff members team players who can go beyond self-interest to be benevolent with their peers? Has trust eroded because of lack of competence among a few players? What values and goals need to be embedded in the organization to foster trust and cooperation? What forms of communication can keep people on the same page and transmit the new values?

The model helps you think through the factors that come into play in making good trust decisions and in figuring out how to build trust and trustworthiness. Now let's try a more strenuous test of the DTM by considering a new, more complicated scenario. A young manager, Sue, had been selected by her boss, Steve, to take over a department at their Fortune 500 company. She accepted the position knowing that Steve would be exerting significant pressure on her to improve the unit's financial performance. From Sue's perspective, the challenge was to make some aggressive personnel moves without destroying the trust among members of the department as a whole. First on her list of challenges was Joe, an employee who was three years short of his retirement date. He was a chronic underperformer, and previous department heads had identified him as someone who needed to be moved out.

Joe was unsure of how much he could trust Sue when she took over the department. Using the DTM in Figure 2.4, we can analyze this trust situation. Joe's self-confident personality (high adjustment) helped him see clearly that he was poorly suited for his current job. But his overall trustor factors entering the situation were low. He felt that he had little or no power, and, with just three years left before retirement, his tolerance for risk was extremely low. So although he would have liked to request a transfer to another job, Joe was too afraid of being terminated to share this desire openly with Sue.

Because Joe didn't know Sue very well, the DTM's seven relationship factors in Joe's decision to trust also trended low. He had little to

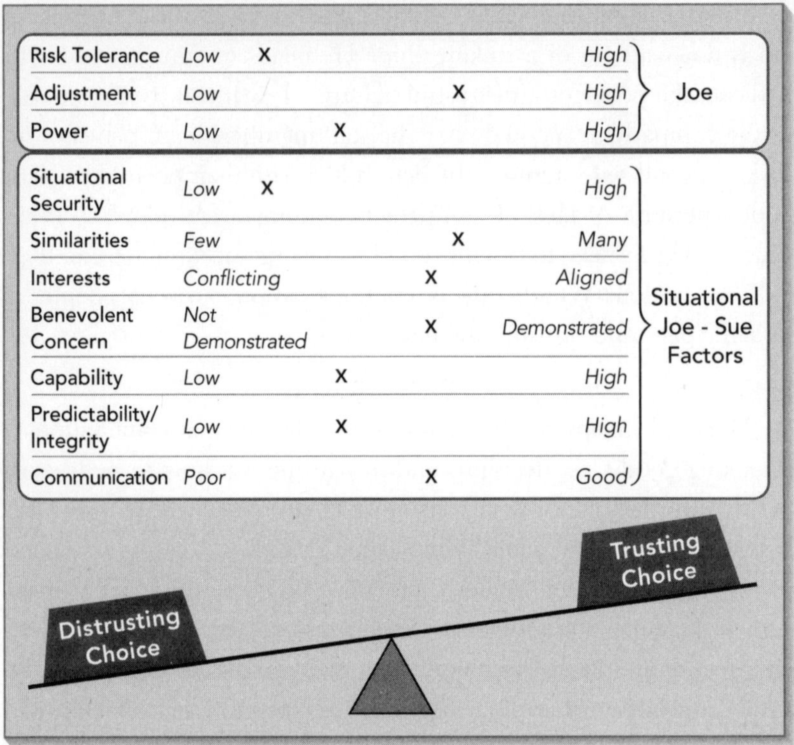

Figure 2.4 Trust Analysis: Joe and Sue

no situational security. Sue was a woman several years younger than he, which reduced their similarities. It was not self-evident to Joe that their interests were aligned; Sue might prefer to fire him rather than transfer him. Joe was unaware also of whether Sue was capable of showing him benevolent concern, and although he was aware that she had a reputation for integrity and capability, he could not be sure that she was the actual decision maker in his fate, so those two factors were low as well. The communication between the two was extremely low up to this point.

Sue's overwhelming power in this situation made it incumbent upon her to take the lead in building trust. Her goal was to remove Joe from this position, but not in a way that would damage his self-respect or her reputation for integrity and capability. Figure 2.5 maps the situation

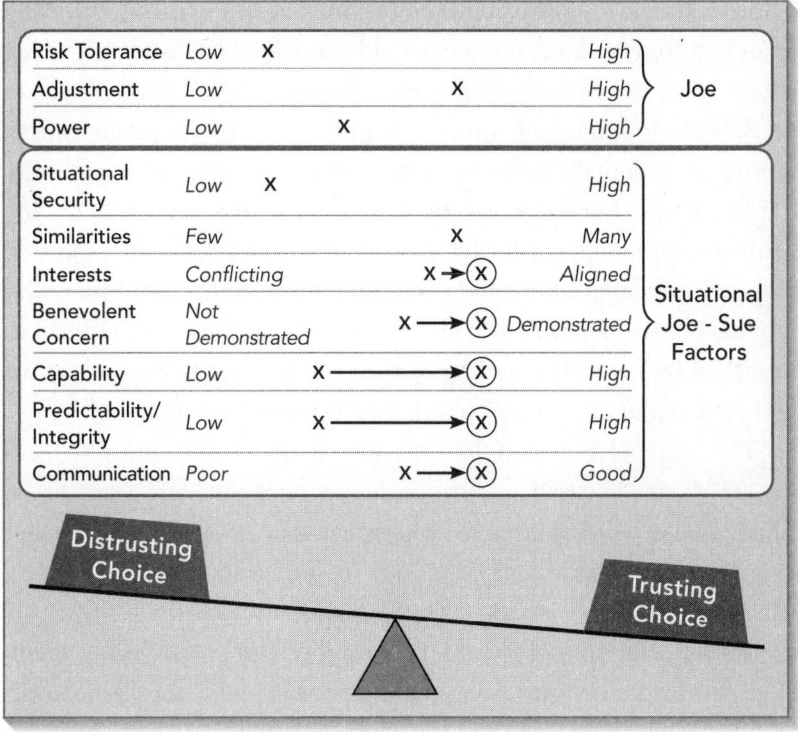

Figure 2.5 Trust Interventions: Joe and Sue

across the DTM. The first step was for Sue to acknowledge the reality that there was little that could be done to lower the risk to Joe. So Sue began by having a very candid but supportive conversation with Joe in which she introduced the idea of Joe's going through a self-evaluation self-discovery process with an outside consultant.

By having Joe meet with the consultant, Sue was able to demonstrate her benevolent concern for Joe, while also assuring him that it was possible that their interests were aligned. This step led Joe to come back to Sue requesting a transfer to a position for which he was better suited. Sue also decided that she should adopt a clear influence strategy with her boss, Steve, to ensure that she would gain approval for some alternative options for Joe (increase capability and predictability). Sue communicated frequently and openly with Joe about his options in the organization (increase communication) and expressed her empathy about how his career uncertainty would affect Joe and his family, which increased her demonstrated benevolent concern for Joe as he arrived at this difficult choice. It took some work and a lot of open communication, but Joe was eventually moved into another job—one with less authority and lower pay, but for which he was better suited. This was by any measure a demotion, but Joe felt very positive about it, and he expressed his positive feelings about the process to those of his colleagues who remained in the department. The result was that Sue's reputation was burnished by her deft handling of the relationship. Her level of trust increased among her employees, despite this risky situation.

The story of Sue and Joe provides a direct case study of how the DTM can be used to turn a thorny personnel problem into a valuable trust-building exercise with a win-win resolution. This is not how situations of this kind often end. In some organizations, poorly performing veteran managers are allowed to run out their years, for fear of engendering bad feelings in the process of getting rid of them. That can lead to a pervasive malaise of distrust: if the department head is willing to accommodate obvious incompetence, why should I knock myself out? But if Sue had demoted Joe without engaging him in a manner that built trust, even those colleagues who knew that Joe deserved to be demoted would have had cause to fear and distrust Sue. Employees will generally get behind even a negative decision if they perceive the process for arriving at the decision as fair.[10] Conversely, they will distrust a manager who makes good decisions in a way that seems heedless and unnecessarily painful.

As was the case with Joe's decision to trust Sue, simple and direct interpersonal interventions can be very effective in building trust in a speedy and fairly reliable way. When we approach such matters as developing group trust, however, there are more people involved, so trust decisions must be made in ways that go beyond one-on-one conversations (while still including them). At the organizational and system levels, the building of trust becomes far more complex and challenging, because the signals we rely on to judge trust are "noisier" and filled with ambiguities and inconsistencies. Most large corporations, for instance, are made up of so many divisions and departments that it is impossible to assess trust with the same level of certainty you have in determining whether to trust your boss.

TRUST AND ETHICS

Now that we have covered the DTM and how it is applied, we can focus on an important question that should be addressed early in this book: What is the relationship between trust and ethics? Organizations often spend a good deal of time on ethics policies and programs but often fail to properly relate them to trust. As we shall see, ethical people and companies are not always trustworthy.

To address this question, let's consider an example. Imagine that there is a natural disaster on an island, and the water supply is contaminated. You are the CEO of the only bottled water company within a thousand miles. Rational principles of economics suggest that you raise the price to the point where demand will be lowered to meet the supply, and you will earn handsome profits. One group of observers might call this good economics. Another group might call it price gouging. But does raising the price to an extremely high level feel right? Research on social reciprocity and ethics indicates that most people would think it is not "right" because it seems to be an extreme case of taking advantage of misfortune and maximizing self-interest in a socially inappropriate way. That is, most human beings will expect you not to act based solely on the laws of economics in this situation. There is a definition of trustworthiness that relates to ethics and explains why it feels wrong: "A trustworthy party is one that will not unfairly exploit the vulnerabilities of the other party in the relationship."[11]

In most codes of morality, ethics, and virtue there is a concept of fairness. We expect members of a society to treat one another fairly just as they themselves would want to be treated. With regard to trust, fairness expectations are situation dependent and must be defined among the parties within a specific context. For example, if the context is a price negotiation at a used car dealership or a job interview, we would not consider it a betrayal of trust if the other party was not completely transparent. What parent would suggest to one of their children going to a job interview that he should be sure to offer that company all relevant negative information about himself? In contrast, we would have less tolerance for material deception by a businessperson of an elderly counterparty whose lack of awareness or knowledge may put her life savings at risk. This is where communication and establishing mutual expectations among parties become central to manifesting both ethics and trust.

Certain factors in the DTM could be said to demonstrate aspects of a moral, ethical, or virtuous character. Research indicates that we can relate ethics to the DTM as follows:

- Alignment of interests—ethical principles of fairness, respecting others, and self-interest constrained by not infringing on others' rights[12]
- Benevolence—virtue and ethical principles of courtesy, reciprocity, and justice, especially for the disadvantaged[13]
- Integrity—moral and ethical principles of living up to your word and of truthfulness[14]

People of good moral and ethical character will tend to be more trustworthy, but it does *not* follow that they should always be trusted. Why? Because there are some elements to the trust decision that have nothing to do with ethics (situational risk, competence, trustor disposition). For example, an ethical trustee may be untrustworthy because he lacks competence or the ability to control events. This makes his betrayal of trust excusable on moral grounds (if he has not misled) but not on practical grounds (you are still hurt). The ethical behavior of the trustee is only a component in gauging trustworthiness. Although the selection and training of ethical people increases trustworthiness and trust, we still need the DTM to make more robust assessments of trustworthiness when there is risk and vulnerability. To further expand our understanding of trust and its elements, we will explore the ten DTM factors more deeply, beginning with a closer look at the three decision maker or trustor factors in the next chapter.

THREE

How We Differ in Trusting

John, a senior executive at a technology company, ran a business unit with about ten thousand employees. He was well regarded within the company as a man of high integrity and ethics, someone who had worked for the company for about twenty years. After a series of promotions, he reached this senior role as the pinnacle of his career. It also marked his downfall. Within a few years, John had failed in the job and was forced to take a demotion, largely because he could not learn how to trust.

John had a good handle on his operation. He knew the business well; he was smart, very well organized, and extremely detail oriented. It didn't take long, however, before some problems with his leadership style emerged. He often took his attention to detail to extremes. He had a hard time trusting even his most competent employees with the simplest decisions. As a result, he had to involve himself in tiny details of projects before he could feel comfortable with the end product. Simply put, John was a micromanager.

John's subordinates, in confidence, described John as too focused on "minutia." They complained that John didn't give them much running room, and as a result they didn't feel challenged in their jobs. They were frustrated at John's insistence on having each thing done in a particular way, closing off their creative contributions to the work.

One of the managers who reported to John wrote in an evaluation, "I don't think he saw himself this way, but his style of leadership devalued the people around him. We never really felt like he trusted us. The end result was that the whole management structure worked just to give him what he wanted. Nobody really owned anything because he had his fingers in everything. All authority flowed through him. As a result, there was little or no creativity, and no one felt empowered or fulfilled."

When we think about trust, we typically consider the trustworthiness of a person, group, or institution on whom we depend. In this sense, trust has a great deal to do with what we think of the other party. Because this tends to be our focus, we often fail to realize that the decision to trust sometimes has nothing to do with the other party (the trustee) and everything to do with the person making the decision to trust (the trustor).

In John's case, for instance, it didn't matter how trustworthy some of his employees were. He simply could not bring himself to trust them, to have confident reliance in their abilities. A contagion of distrust and anxiety thus spread through the business unit, and John was labeled a "control freak" or micromanager. Productivity suffered because people were not empowered to use their talents and solve problems that emerged, without constantly checking in with John.

But even in companies with high-functioning, high-trust cultures, where general conditions are conducive to trust, you will always find some people like John. It's important to recognize that in every workplace, there are people who will always require more tangible proof—of aligned interests, benevolent concern, predictability, and capability—before they feel comfortable to trust. If we understand this, we can draw on the DTM to identify situational and relationship factors that can offset a low disposition to trust and tilt the scale toward confident reliance.

This chapter will explore the three decision maker or trustor factors in the DTM: risk tolerance, psychological adjustment, and power, highlighted in Figure 3.1. Before we are able to examine the challenges of building trust using the seven situational factors of the DTM, we

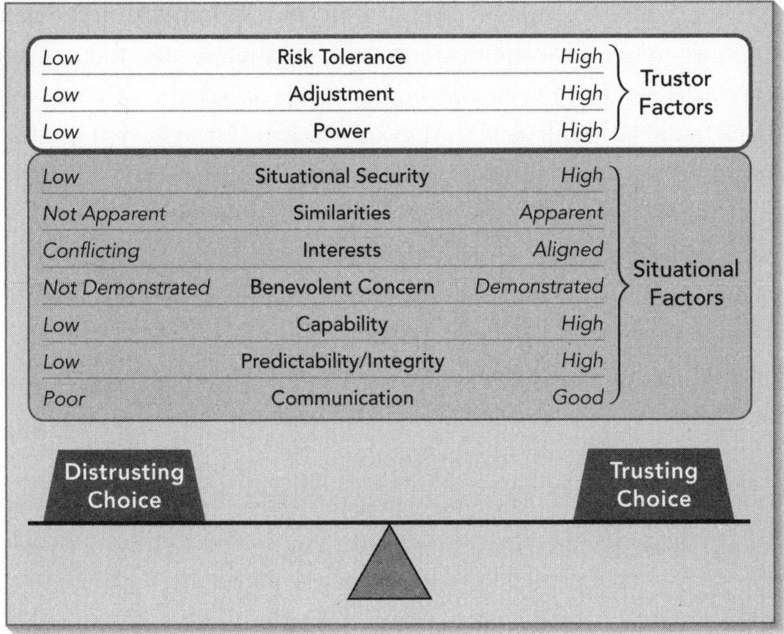

Figure 3.1 The Decision to Trust Model—Trustor Factors

must first explore how and why trust building will always require more effort and patience with some people than it will for others.

RISK TOLERANCE AND TRUST

Trust bears a close, inverse relationship with risk. When risk is high in a situation, trust levels tend to be low, and vice versa. The most common source of perceived risk is simple ignorance. A situation appears risky to us because we don't understand it, or perhaps because it involves something we've never done before. Anxiety caused by the presence of risk and uncertainty can leave us reluctant to trust others, or even ourselves. Psychologists find, for example, that one effective way to treat patients with a fear of flying is to expose them, carefully and step-by-step, to air travel. In fact, it is not uncommon for aviophobic people to learn to become pilots as a way to overcome their fear.

Economists and psychologists also accept a related trait in human nature: when a favorable outcome in any situation seems all but guaranteed, trust tends to fall away as an important concern. Our minds can turn off our need to calculate trust in an extremely low risk circumstance because we assume that trust isn't necessary. When we turn on a light switch, for instance, we don't think of the spark inside the wall as presenting a serious risk of fire, so we trust the switch without a second thought. To some extent, this thought pattern may help explain the 1990s Internet stock bubble, the 2000s housing bubble, and other cases of market euphoria, when investment success in the short term seemed as sure and simple as switching on a light, and many investors dropped their habit of calculating trustworthiness.

There were plenty of investors, of course, who did not trust either of these market bubbles and escaped harm when the bubbles burst. People vary widely in their perceptions of risk and accompanying inclinations to trust. More than a million people cancelled airline tickets after the 9/11 terror attacks, despite increased air security measures. Airline revenues remained in a slump for much of the following year, even though there was not a single commercial airline fatality during all of 2002. Air travel had statistically never been safer, but terrorist attacks had caused more than a million people to fear to trust the system.

In a less emotional and more calculated example of risk aversion and prudent distrust, there were a handful of money managers who resisted Bernie Madoff's invitation to invest with him because they were by nature very cautious. After Madoff's Ponzi scheme was exposed in 2008, some of these money managers told the media that Madoff had never been able to explain satisfactorily just how he was achieving the market-defying results that induced so many to invest with him. Despite years of steady returns enjoyed by Madoff's investors, these money managers simply refused to put their trust in an investment strategy that did not make sense to them.

The perception of risk, the willingness to tolerate risk, and the inclination to trust vary from person to person. To win someone's trust, it's not enough to make ourselves trustworthy in our own eyes. We must understand whom we are dealing with. No matter how trustworthy we feel we are, no matter how glowingly we view our own track record, a certain percentage of the people we want to exchange with will need us to pay special attention to their risk-averse perceptions if we wish to gain their trust.

PSYCHOLOGICAL ADJUSTMENT AND TRUST

It took several years to get to the bottom of what was going on with John the micromanager. Over that period of time, various meetings and team-building sessions exposed John's counterproductive and controlling behaviors. One day he finally snapped at the suggestion that there was anything wrong with him. His employees came away with the impression that retribution might await anyone who even suggested that John's management style needed some change.

After a while you could see the writing on the wall. John's unit was failing to meet its growth goals, quarter after quarter, and one day a close confidant told John that he thought his job might be in danger if he did not change. He was running out of rope, and this friend suggested that it might be a good time to figure out why. That got John's attention. He went through a rigorous process to understand his personality, his mental model of management, and his background thinking as he navigated working with others.

What the process revealed was that underneath his successful executive exterior, John was a tremendously insecure individual. He had a deep-seated fear of failure and embarrassment that was triggered by the slightest possibility of a mistake. This had been drummed into John from early childhood. His parents had had a hard life, and they had conditioned John to see the world as a place where bad things happen. John grew up believing that the only safe haven in a world of threats was to be constantly vigilant in preventing even small errors. He needed to be perfect.

Psychologists use the term "low adjustment" to describe people who tend to have low self-esteem and negative emotions, who experience the world as a threatening place. Low-adjustment people are also hard on themselves and sometimes moody and tense. By contrast, high-adjustment people are generally comfortable with themselves and see the world in a benign or positive manner, with less negative emotion or angst. They are also more likely to trust.

Tests with twins who were separated at birth indicate that some of these personality traits are inherited.[1] But harsh childhood circumstances can also leave indelible and recognizable patterns of distrustful inclinations. Developmental psychologists have viewed the capacity to trust as a foundational element that sets the stage for the giving and receiving behavior (reciprocity) that is crucial for social relations in later life.[2]

An example of how nature (personality) and nurture (environment) can combine to affect trust came from a high-ranking airline executive. This manager's personality tests showed very high scores on "diligence," which measures the tendency for perfectionism, and "cautiousness," which measures a person's fear of failure or embarrassment. Further work revealed that he grew up in an unstable household, and his perfectionism and caution were psychological reactions to his lingering fear of instability. Growing up in such an unstable environment can condition a child to see life in terms of threats and insecurity. The child grows into an adult believing that safety can be achieved only by being in control rather than by relying on or trusting others.

The legacy of ethnic and race discrimination often creates skepticism or even distrust among members of minority groups.[3] This should not be surprising, considering that many minority groups have been unfairly deprived of opportunities and even threatened with violence. When people's personal experience and upbringing have conditioned them to be skeptical or suspicious, it is reasonable to expect that it will require more effort to build trust.

High adjustment, incidentally, does not necessarily mean high achievement, high intelligence, or high integrity. Some highly adjusted people lack drive and ignore corrective feedback, which will hurt their chances to grow and succeed. Many low-adjustment people channel their angst and end up being more accomplished and even happier—if they can figure out how to de-stress their lives. There are strengths and weaknesses to both personality profiles; however, when evaluating them in terms of trust, low-adjustment individuals will tend to need more assurance to trust.

Every workplace requires a healthy mix of high- and low-adjustment people. Some of us who have been trained from an early age to be skeptics or to distrust nonetheless provide significant benefits to society. Certified public accountants, certain types of lawyers, and security and intelligence personnel are often trained and socialized in their organizational cultures not to assume that people are honest and to look for fraud or deception. The larger public accounting firms tend to hire high-prudence and fairly cautious people and provide them with a workplace culture that reinforces the importance of avoiding errors and omissions in their audit work.

We might call these people "professional distrusters." When they perform this role, many of us can invest more freely, sign contracts, and fly airplanes knowing that they are on the case. Just remember that when dealing with people who are trained and operating in this professional skeptic role, they are likely to come across as hard nuts to crack. They are very likely to be less trusting and will need more proof before trusting. Be forewarned: they might even question your motives for seeking their trust, and in a way you might find insulting.

POWER AND TRUST

Imagine that you are very happy in your job at a small private company when the CEO of a larger, rival firm makes you an attractive offer to leave your current employer. The new position would offer more opportunities for growth, promotions, and travel, but your main concern immediately becomes whether you can trust the rival CEO. What are his true motives for contacting you? Does he assume you have company secrets to disclose? And what is this CEO's reputation for living up to his commitments? What if you decide to trust him and then he fails to follow through on his promises? Your current CEO would probably not take you back. You entertain suspicious thoughts, and may be reluctant to trust, for the simple reason that you are in a position of low power. If you offer your trust and that trust is betrayed, you will have little recourse. In more formal terms, you will have no way to penalize noncompliance. This is not true for your potential new CEO, who, if you misrepresented your experience, could fire you. You are in a lower power position and must calculate trust more carefully because you have less control and influence.

Power is the ability to act or to produce an effect. Powerful people are more able to influence outcomes and have the luxury of assuming proper intentions. When we perceive ourselves to be able to control an exchange, we tend to be more comfortable that we can manage risks and avoid negative outcomes. Depending on the degree to which negative outcomes seem remote or under our control, we are less anxious, more optimistic, and more apt to trust.

The disposition to trust is affected by a mix of all three trustor factors, so it is possible to have a high-power person who does not trust because he is risk averse or low in adjustment. John the micromanaging executive was such a person: he was powerful but also low in adjustment and low in risk tolerance, which contributed to his low disposition to trust. In the end, John ran a ship that was going no place very slowly. His lifelong fear of failure made it difficult for him to empower and trust his subordinates. His vice presidents, in turn, kept a very tight leash on their direct reports so that they were informed on everything and could avoid mistakes that would end up making John upset.

John's primary goal for his business unit was to grow market share, but the unit's performance suffered. John was too involved in tightly controlling his managers, and his talented managers were too busy obsessing over insignificant details, trying to anticipate John's idiosyncrasies, to focus on the bigger goals of their jobs. The day finally came when John was moved to a less responsible position.

INFLUENCING THE DISPOSITION TO TRUST

John's case underscores one practical reality: trust building can be difficult, if not impossible, with certain people, simply because of their dispositional factors. Trying to change a trustor's degree of adjustment or risk tolerance is like trying to change someone's personality: it is hard, very intrusive, and, in John's case, it was impossible because he saw it as other people's problem. There are times when we find ourselves in the position where we must adapt to the trustor's chronic distrust or accept a less productive or limited relationship with him or her. As we will see in the next chapter, it is sometimes possible to change some of the seven situational and relationship factors to offset or overcome the suspicions of a decision maker with a low disposition to trust.

But there are some ways we can affect trustors' dispositional posture more directly. For people with a low tolerance for risk, we can educate them concerning the risks involved. We can also help them understand that failing to trust due to low risk tolerance may in some cases actually increase their risk. We may on occasion be able to build a safety net to mitigate their risk and communicate this to them in a way that is comforting. These actions take patience on the part of the trustee and an ability to see and understand risk aversion.

In some cases, the trustee can affect the environment in a way that increases adjustment and risk tolerance. For example take Joanne, whose boss was highly critical, demanding, and harsh. Soon the atmosphere of conflict between them was fairly evident. Joanne's confidence waned as a result. She became more awkward in meetings and was not comfortable making decisions or taking decisive action. She was thinking of leaving, but reconsidered when her boss announced that he was being promoted and leaving the unit.

Over the course of the next year, Joanne's performance changed radically because her new boss was an exceptionally empowering, positive, and supportive leader, and Joanne knew he thought very highly of her. Joanne's early anxiety and lack of confidence were in part due to the harsh judgments from her boss, which caused her to unravel a bit. She was a different person under this more supportive leader. In a sense, she was partially dependent on her environment to feel confident in her job.

We are all products of our environment to some extent. It's a mistake to think that confidence resides only within a person and is unaffected by an environment of distrust. Most of us have some insecurity, and given a perfect storm of stress, uncertainty, and lack of support, most of us are capable of having lower self-esteem.

There is an exercise to conduct to understand the effect of the social environment on our level of confidence. It starts with your asking a room full of business executives, "By a show of hands, who in the room has worked on a team where they felt *competent* and confident?" Often a great many hands are raised. Then ask them, "Now, also by show of hands, who in the room has worked on a team where they felt *incompetent* and lacked confidence?" Many of the same hands would rise again.

Conclude the exercise by asking the group, "How could it be that so many people raised their hands twice? How could they feel powerful and confident in one situation and so lacking in confidence in another? Did they magically become stupid somehow?"

Of course not. Our sense of confidence, power, and influence is a function of our own view of ourselves but also of the environment around us. When we feel powerless, it is harder to trust because we feel less able to correct or recover from betrayal.

Trustees have some ability to directly influence others' disposition to trust by improving risk tolerance, helping build confidence, helping others be less self-critical, and, finally, increasing their power and influence over events. That being said, it is important to recognize that often the best approach to increasing trust is to change some of the situational and relationship factors in the DTM. These factors, which are covered in the next chapter, can help tip the scales toward trust even for people with a low disposition to trust.

FOUR

Situational Factors in the Building of Trust

Pretend for a moment that you are Bernie Madoff and are running the largest Ponzi scheme in history. What do you need in order to keep it going? You need a steadily growing supply of trust. Ponzi schemes collapse if too many investors lose faith and withdraw their money. To prevent that from happening, you need more and more investors to trust you with their money, just so you can continue to provide illusory gains to your longer-term clients.

Bernie Madoff did this for almost thirty years. He preyed upon the natural human inclination to trust, as all con artists do. By some estimates, Madoff defrauded his investors out of $10 billion to $17 billion.[1] If you look at the details of how Madoff managed to maintain such an enormous, high-profile fraud for so many years, you will see that he did it by masterfully exploiting each of the seven situational factors found in the DTM.

Madoff's various funds provided his victims with the illusion of steady returns on their money, year after year, in good markets and bad. Investors clamored for admission to some of Madoff's closed investment funds because such steady performance provided them with a profound sense of *situational security* and confidence in Madoff's *capability* and *predictability*. "I know all I need to know," said one wealthy investor in 2001, concerning Madoff's secretive investment practices. "I've been with him [Madoff] for three or four years and my returns have been about one percent a month, without fail."[2]

Madoff also traded on his *similarities* with his victims in order to win their trust. New investors were identified in wealthy social settings, thanks to word-of-mouth referrals. Many were members with Madoff of elite Florida and New York country clubs or belonged to what the *New York Times* called "a network of trust that began to stretch wider and deeper into the Jewish community."[3]

As a part of that community, Madoff maintained a high profile in New York philanthropic circles and welcomed his pet charities to place their investable assets with him. In a perverse way, Madoff used these charities to burnish his reputation for *benevolent concern,* even as he was looting their endowments. Because Madoff declined to charge his clients any money management fees, he further bolstered his reputation for benevolence and could also lay claim to a superior *alignment of interests* with them. Finally, everything Madoff did and said in public *communicated* the impression that he was nothing other than a wealthy and gifted

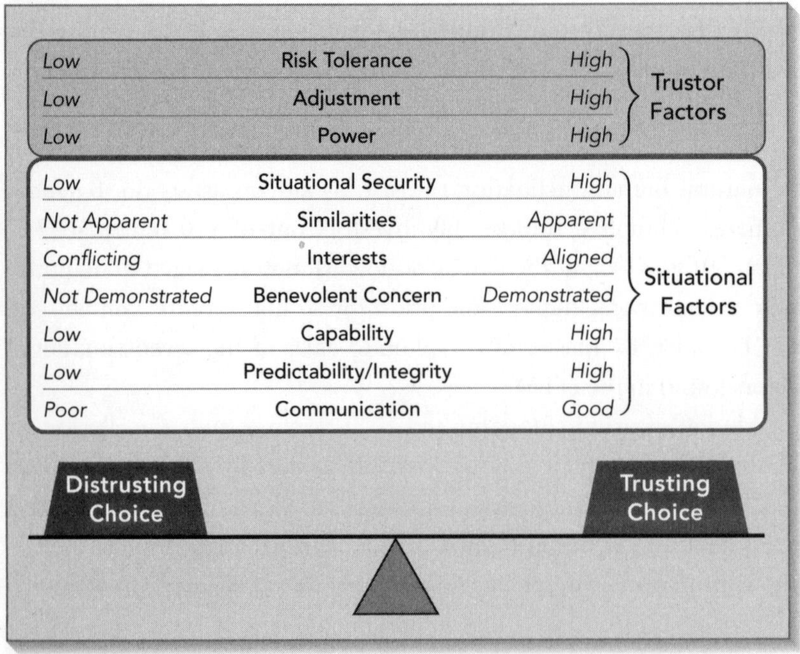

Figure 4.1 The Decision to Trust Model: Situational Factors

securities trader and a socially conscious philanthropist worthy of trust and admiration—right up until the day of his arrest in December 2008.

Ponzi schemes inevitably collapse or get discovered because they are based on fabricated elements of trustworthiness. Madoff's story illustrates how thoroughly he relied on the seven factors of situational trust to conceal a swindle of gigantic proportions taking place right under the noses of some of the most sophisticated investors in the world. Had these trustors examined these elements of trustworthiness in a more robust manner, they would have concluded, as many did, that distrust was the more prudent option.

The seven situational factors of the DTM, highlighted in Figure 4.1, offer the most powerful opportunities to both understand and build trust and trustworthiness.

SECURITY AND TRUST

When we are in situations where risk is high, trusting is more difficult, as illustrated in Figure 4.2. Our perception of situational risk is influenced by our knowledge and prior experience with the matter at hand and the distribution of the variability and severity of possible outcomes.

When risk is high, building trust often begins by trying to get the trustor comfortable with the risk itself, convince him of the need to

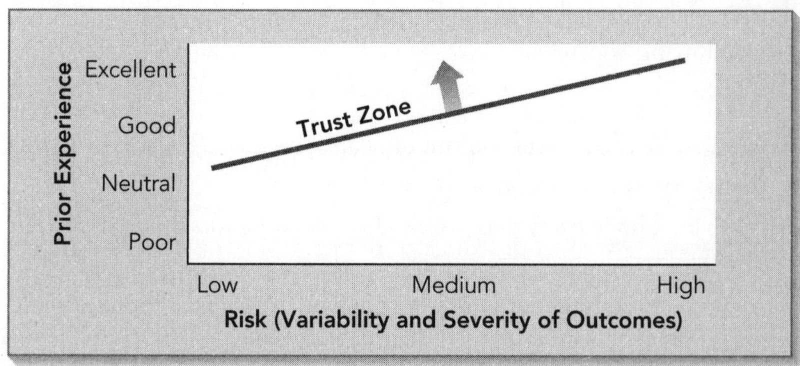

Figure 4.2 Risk, Experience, and Trust

take the risk to achieve some goal, or convince him of the cost of not taking the risk. The trustor, or decision maker, usually wants to know that (1) any resulting losses will be manageable, or (2) the potential gain from trusting far outweighs the risks, or (3) the danger of distrusting is greater than the danger of trusting.

IBM profited enormously from the first of these approaches to situational security because the company had a reputation for being able to apply vast resources to help clients recover from any information system crisis. IBM was the safer choice because it could limit possible damages. Many corporate IT professionals were fond of saying that when it came to installing expensive and complex computer systems, "nobody ever got fired for buying IBM." Some of IBM's competitors were just as good if not better, and many were less expensive. But if a complex systems project bought from a little-known computer company were to fail, the purchasing agent's judgment might be called into question. The safer bet, from the purchasing agent's perspective, was to hire IBM, the market leader, even if it cost the company more.

As shown in Figure 4.2, when we can reduce risk or improve experience, we enlarge the trust zone. Wherever the risks appear too great and present an undue obstacle to trust and exchange, it is the primary function of deal making to enhance situational security. Lawyers, salespeople, and finance professionals often spend a great deal of time negotiating over terms to mitigate risk, increase trust, and promote exchange. They try to "de-risk" a deal, usually through formal contracts that incorporate some of the following approaches:

Prototyping. The trustor will commit only after receiving a piece or a prototype of a deliverable from a trustee.

Joint analysis. The severity and probability of risk factors are agreed to in advance.

Risk-sharing. An agreement is made in advance to share the downside costs between trustor and trustee in a losing deal.

Phased risk. Risk to the trustee escalates on an agreed-on schedule of performance milestones as the relationship proceeds.

Hostage posting. The trustor wins hostage resources if the trustee fails to live up to agreements.

Stop-loss. The trustor can exit the relationship if a certain downside threshold is crossed.

Inspections. The hiring of independent monitoring or auditing resources is agreed to in advance to ensure compliance.

Insurance. An insurance policy is purchased from a third party in order to limit possible losses.

Arbitration. The trustee and trustor agree in advance to have future disputes settled by mutually agreed-on independent experts.

Each of these contractual terms can be seen as a functional substitute for one or another form of social or interpersonal trust. Another way to look at these terms is as a set of impersonal structures that allow a mutually beneficial exchange to begin at a low level of trust. They provide the opportunity for interpersonal trust to grow with positive experiences as the exchange relationship develops.

For example, in business-critical outsourcing projects, the organization doing the outsourcing is typically advised never to accept the provider's standard contract provisions for the transition project. The recommended procedure is to select two potential finalists, provide enough due diligence time for them to judge the situation, and have them develop an explicit transition plan that is phased (by geography, business units, or teams and not entire lines of business) in a way that a failure during the early phases could trigger the end of the entire contract. The quality of the transition plan and the extent of the risk reduction provided are key criteria for the final selection of the vendor.[4] These techniques have the effect of reducing risk and increasing confident reliance or trust in the initial stages of a relationship.

The nine contractual tools listed here are functional and impersonal by design, which is why their long-term usefulness is limited to initiating trust, not substituting for it. Anyone who has been in a partnership that has gone bad will tell you that in such a risky situation, a highly trustworthy partner is far more preferable than an ironclad contract. Events unfold in every partnership that are unforeseen and unpredictable, so it is always a good idea to be joined with someone who has proven that he or she will do the right thing and promote your joint interests if things go wrong.

SIMILARITIES AND TRUST

As noted in Chapter Two, research in the field of social identity theory confirms that despite our advancement in many ways, we are at heart still quite tribal.[5] This does not mean that we cannot build trust across tribes; it merely means that people with whom we can "identify" or whom we see as similar to us in some fashion have an advantage in gaining our trust—deserved or otherwise.

In the best and most high-trust organizations, great attention is paid to creating bonds of trust that go well beyond the impersonal contractual approaches noted in the preceding section. Instead, trust is built by focusing on personnel issues, including careful recruitment and selection of employees, professional training, and active culture building, all of which can help ensure reliable patterns of behavior in even the very highest risk situations.

Every inductee in the U.S. armed forces swears an oath to "obey the orders of the President of the United States and the orders of the officers appointed over me, according to regulations and the Uniform Code of Military Justice." This code compels soldiers to follow all legal orders from their officers and to face the possible death penalty if they fail to follow these orders in a time of war.

Training and socialization in the military are conducted in a way that forms strong bonds of trust in superiors and among troops so that trust can be assumed without calculation even in the most risky circumstances. This high level of social capital, combined with the serious consequences resulting from a decision not to trust, creates a "speed of trust" in the military that is unseen in most other risky environments. Within the military's most elite units are intense cultures that value trust above everything, including human life. All four members of a U.S.

Air Force Thunderbirds team were killed in 1982 while practicing a tight four-plane diamond-formation loop. When the lead plane suffered a brief mechanical failure at the bottom of the loop and slammed into the practice field, the three trailing planes crashed right along with it. The pilots had been trained to trust their leader and orient themselves visually only to the lead plane while ignoring their orientation to the ground. In precision flying, there is no substitute for trust, even if it may someday cost you your life.[6]

Strong workplace cultures at high-trust organizations are geared toward cultivating the natural human instinct to bond—that is, to form groups. Similarities and in-group status, if they are meaningful, can confer positive trust properties, or what has been referred to as identification-based trust.[7] This is why companies with a strong unifying culture enjoy higher levels of internal trust—particularly if their cultural values include candor, integrity, and fair process. Without a strong, shared culture to bind people together, they drift into silos of in-groups and out-groups that promote conflict rather than cooperation. For example, conflicts can arise between the entrepreneurial field sales group and the control-oriented headquarters or between the innovative marketing group and the reliability-oriented manufacturing group. Without a common workplace culture and identity, it's too easy for differences, instead of their similarities, to shape trust relations.

Research reveals that when we see others as being similar to us, we tend to like them more and see them as more likely to engage in reciprocity, which enhances trust.[8] Also, the "gossip effect"—word spreading in the network that betrayal has occurred—is seen by members as reducing opportunism, which acts to enhance trust.[9] People are instantly more trusting of people who are members of "their" group.

But sometimes the similarity effect causes misplaced trust. Strangely enough, human beings will often confer in-group status on meaningless bases. Research has shown that even when groups are formed on completely arbitrary or random bases, in-groups will discriminate against out-groups in order to maintain group cohesion.[10] The obvious downside of this effect is prejudice and misplaced trust. Imagine that you are looking to hire a consultant for a strategy assignment. The first candidate walks into your office wearing a robe; he speaks with an accent and has a degree from a university you've never heard of. When you meet the second candidate, she is dressed very much like you and speaks as you do. You learn that she also attended your alma mater. Most people would feel more comfortable hiring the second candidate, rationalizing that she could be counted on to act as they would in a given situation. When common identity status is conferred for trivial, superficial, or even imagined bonds, it can cause us to trust for the wrong reasons. When we confer trusted status to in-group members who do not deserve it, we lower our guard and put ourselves at risk. Recall the proverb "Lord defend me from my friends; from my enemies I can defend myself" as an eternal warning against allowing unwarranted in-group trust to lead you astray.

ALIGNMENT OF INTERESTS AND TRUST

One chief benefit of a compelling shared culture within an organization is that it promotes a common interest, namely, maintaining one's membership status. In fact, transparent and rational promotion of self-interest has been a dominant model of trust.[11] I trust you because our interests are aligned, and when you promote your own interests, it benefits me. Transparency is important because promoting self-interest with guile or deception is called opportunism, which promotes distrust.[12] Research shows that competing interests engender suspicion rather than trust.[13] Marketing and sales departments tend to trust and cooperate more because they both tend to be interested in increasing market share. In contrast, there is often more conflict between marketing and manufacturing because one group often wants more features and benefits (marketing), and the other wants simplicity and ease of assembly (manufacturing). Marketing may be most concerned with market share, and manufacturing most focused on cost control. Conflicting interests and mixed-motive situations, where there is marginal alignment, often create trust problems.

Unfortunately, not all managers are adept at aligning interests to promote trust. Unsophisticated managers will often assume that everyone in the organization has the same interests, but in reality people have both common and unique interests. A good leader engineers superordinate goals and common interests into the system to form the basis for cooperation and trust. The primary purpose of getting stakeholder buy-in to key decisions is to achieve a critical mass of commitment to common goals in order to enhance trust and cooperation. Trust will break down if people's interests are merely implied or assumed, and then appear to be violated through misunderstandings. Confusion of this sort only prompts people to question each other's motives, and trust soon begins to unravel.

One of the reasons that trust has broken down in business and society in general is that there are many situations where the complexity of misaligned interests is not acknowledged, much less dealt with. Mixed-motive situations exist when there are reasons both to support collective interests (cooperate) and to maximize self-interest (compete) at the expense of others. In many situations of social exchange, we may have as many as three kinds of interests at play: joint, independent, and even conflicting interests. Encapsulating and aligning these interests, which is essential to trust, is an increasingly challenging task.

For an example of complexity and the challenge of gaining the trust of multiple stakeholders, consider the case of Aaron Feuerstein, CEO of Malden Mills. In 1995, a fire destroyed his textile mill and the jobs of thirty-two hundred people in Lawrence, Massachusetts. Some advised Feuerstein to take the insurance money and manufacture his textiles overseas; others suggested that at his age (seventy-two), he should just keep the money and retire. Feuerstein promised his workers that he would rebuild the plant and save their jobs. Feuerstein kept his word and continued to pay his employees. The resulting debt eventually forced the company into bankruptcy. Feuerstein's benevolent protection of employees' interests, despite the cost to himself, gained the trust of the employees but lost the trust of the banks, which probably would have preferred that their interests be served. The company emerged from bankruptcy in late 2003. Feuerstein tried to buy back the company in late 2004, but was rejected by its board of directors, who were influenced by the creditors.

This story highlights the importance of aligning and integrating diverse interests in managing trust. The stakeholder map in Figure 4.3 shows some of the complex interests that Feuerstein had to navigate as CEO. Feuerstein clearly favored employee stakeholders over investors and even his own interests. Richard Fuld of Lehman Brothers and Stan O'Neal of Merrill Lynch favored executives and investors interested in stock appreciation over lower-level employees and the larger financial community that wanted secure employment. Serving one group at the expense of others leads not only to distrust but to risk to the sustainability of the firm, which must depend on multiple stakeholders for long-term survival.

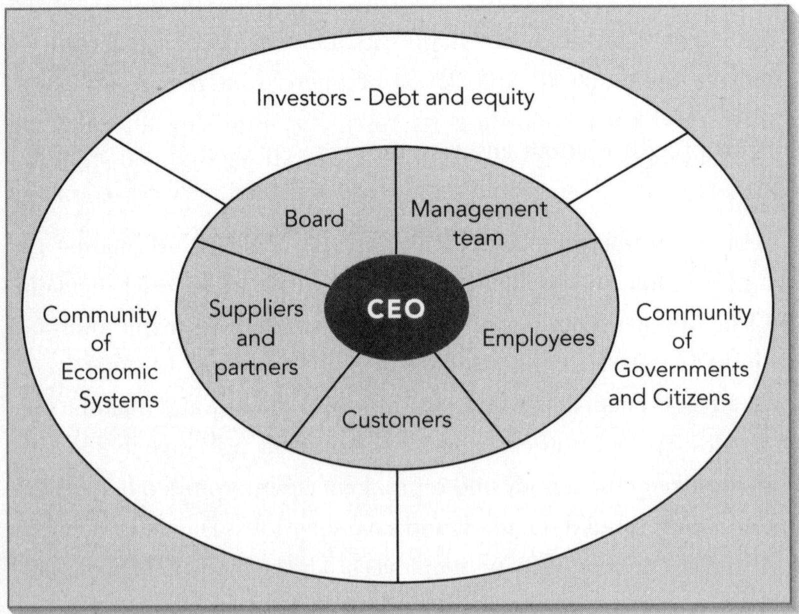

Figure 4.3 CEO Stakeholder Map

The most trusted leaders navigate this territory by carefully thinking in terms of integration and alignment of interests within the overall strategy of the firm. They then communicate with transparency and integrity, clarifying to stakeholders how interests will be aligned. One company that was having major trust and morale problems brought in a CEO from another firm that had a history of trust and excellent management development. The reaction among employees was interesting. One person summarized it well: "I do not always like what he says, but there is no question that he is a straight shooter. He tells you how it is and doesn't sugarcoat like the prior CEO did. He is a breath of fresh air in this company." The truth is that you cannot satisfy all stakeholder interests in the way that each of them would prefer. The best you can do is be clear about interests, decide whose interests will be primary or secondary, and be transparent about what trade-offs you are making and why.

Aligning interests as a means of increasing trust also operates on a more macro organizational level. Research indicates that making organizational decisions using a process that is seen as transparent, rigorous, and fair leads to higher levels of organizational trust.[14] Employees will support a manager's decision—even one they don't like—if the process by which the decision was made is seen as fair.

Fair process is about ensuring the representation of diverse stakeholder interests. For example, a large financial services company demonstrated fair process in deciding whether to close one of three major office facilities to reduce costs. The company formed a team representing all three locations and different functional areas to study the options. The senior managers conducted town hall meetings with potentially affected employees to explain what was being done and how it was being done and to get their reactions. This same company also instituted a fair process policy concerning termination of independent agent contracts. First, only the chairman's office could make this decision. Second, the agent had a right to a hearing, and at that hearing there had to be two other independent agents (selected by the agent being reviewed) and an outside consultant who was not an employee of the company.

BENEVOLENT CONCERN AND TRUST

Alignment of interests and fair process are comforting, but an even more powerful builder of trust is our belief that the trustee cares more about us than she does about herself. We can call this a benevolence or a character of service to others. A lack of benevolence creates distrust because it makes the trustee seem exclusively self-centered. Why would I trust someone who is only going to look out after his own interests unless our interests are always perfectly aligned?

People who balance advocating for their own interests with listening and acting to support others' interests tend to be seen as more trustworthy, for fairly obvious reasons. They demonstrate a respect for others and understand others' needs in a way that helps them find win-win solutions. Remarkably, in some circles of business, the idea of being benevolent has become a foreign concept. As an example, consider the following real exchange that took place in a trust seminar at a major company. When the idea that benevolence enhances trust came up, one participant took exception. He said, "There is no such thing as benevolent concern; there is only self-interest." The instructor responded, "Do you mean that Mother Teresa saves people in the streets of Calcutta because it gives her pleasure, that she is a hedonist?" He said, "That's right!" Then another manager next to him chimed in: "I go even further. I do not want my agents being benevolent or fair to anyone. I want them to screw the other party because if they do, I will benefit!"

This was a tough crowd. So the instructor conducted an experiment and asked the group to pair up and designate one person as A and the other as B.[15] Then he announced to the total group that every person A had won a lottery and would be getting $100 cash. Every person A had sixty seconds to decide how much, if any, of the $100 he would share with his partner. In a room of thirty people, only three of the A's offered their partner nothing. Most split the proceeds 50-50. The instructor then asked the group: "How is it that a group of people trained in business and economics could have made such a financially illogical decision to give away money?" In the conversation that followed, they admitted that the economically optimal decision to share little or none of the windfall seemed socially inappropriate and unfair. This experiment has been conducted by researchers many times in various parts of the world, with similar results. Most people feel some obligation to share when there is some relationship with the other party.[16] There is a basic sense of fairness and reciprocity that enables human beings to survive in social groups. We may explain this as benevolence motivated by long-term self-interest in maintaining group membership or a relationship, but we cannot deny that displays of benevolence facilitate trust and that an absence of benevolence breeds distrust in most social situations.

With a different group, the instructor took the point further. He presented the following scenario. You have a person working for you, Fred, whose performance has been terrific and who has really made a difference in your group. Your boss tells you that the head count in your group must be reduced. He feels strongly that Fred should go because he does not think highly of him. Do you comply with what your boss wants, to the detriment of Fred and the group's performance, or do you try to convince your boss that someone else is more suitable for being let go? Most people will say, as they did in this group, that you should try to persuade the boss, because it's best for your group and for Fred. But, the instructor asked, what if the boss responds with irritation that you're disagreeing with his opinion on Fred? What then? Among this group of thirty people, most agreed that you should fold. Some even admitted that when your boss expresses his opposition to Fred, you accept it and abandon Fred: "You throw him under the bus." Finally one person piped up, in a very firm and serious voice, "No! You stand by Fred because it is the right thing to do!" The group as a whole was a bit shocked at the divergence in values that was revealed in this conversation concerning benevolence and supporting others in the workplace.

Conversely, take as an example Ted, an investment banker at a Fortune 500 financial institution. Bright and aggressive with a great deal of self-confidence, Ted was an executive director leading a team responsible for all investment banking in the media sector. By all reports, clients loved Ted, and he had a great many contacts in the media industry. The problem with Ted, as described by his regional directors and members of his team, was that Ted was all about Ted. When deals came in, Ted positioned himself to maximize his income, even cutting out other members of his team to do so. The only "trust" that anyone had in Ted was that he would do whatever it took to maximize his income. (By the way, this is predictability, not trust as we have defined it.) Talented people began to leave or to defect to other teams within the bank. It got so bad that the bank leadership realized that if Ted did not change his approach toward others on his team, the bank's capability in the media sector would be eroded over time. Not surprisingly, Ted never really changed his behavior, and he was moved out a year later.

These examples from trust seminars conducted at major firms underscore the point made earlier: in many conference rooms and offices, there are very different views concerning the place of benevolence in business. No wonder trust scores have been declining so precipitously. In many places, it is "every man for himself." In other, high-trust firms, we find managers who demonstrate benevolent concern—who show employees that they will put themselves at risk for others if they feel it is the right thing to do. This engenders not only trust but also loyalty and commitment.

CAPABILITY AND TRUST

Benevolent concern is important, but it is only one piece of the puzzle. Some people might too easily conclude that when someone demonstrates that she is kind and benevolent, she can be trusted. This isn't true if she is deficient in capability or predictability. It is foolhardy to trust a person, company, or institution that has good intentions and a fine image but lacks the competence to deliver on its commitments. The degree of trust or distrust should correspond to the degree of competence or incompetence demonstrated by trustees.

Consider the example of a consulting firm whose reputation and image within its industry declined because its promises to clients far exceeded its capability to execute. This firm was led by an extremely intelligent and creative business strategist, Mike, who had never demonstrated much capability at implementation. This was not a problem in his consulting relationship because clients wanted his ideas and analysis, not his help in execution. It was, however, a disaster inside the firm that he was leading. Inside the firm, Mike would float from meeting to meeting with client teams and offer interesting ideas, but he never followed through, and he never appointed a chief operating officer to do so. Internally the consultants were chasing lots of ideas with little time to button things down and deliver on client commitments. Projects slipped time tables and were off target, according to clients. What made matters worse was that when Mike was operating with clients externally, he would make commitments without having any idea of how the firm would deliver on them. Mike was a brilliant man whom employees and clients liked but whom everybody came to distrust because he made commitments without building the capability to deliver.

Trust tends to follow perceptions of competence and capability.[17] For example, in 1973, 61 percent of Americans surveyed said they had a great deal of confidence on the U.S. military. In that same period, only 18 percent said they had a great deal of confidence in the U.S. Congress. By 2010, those expressing a great deal of confidence in Congress had fallen to 8 percent, but 59 percent said they had confidence in the military.[18] Why such different scores in confident reliance? The American public doubts the efficiency and effectiveness of Congress to get the right things done, but they do not doubt the capability of the military to protect the country. When Congress makes lofty promises and then fails to deliver because of partisan gridlock, trust erodes. In contrast, the military is careful about overpromising and has a good track record concerning its mission of protecting the country. It builds and maintains trust because it generally understands its capability, communicates accurately, and has the processes and methods to reliably deliver and establish a track record that warrants trust.

PREDICTABILITY, INTEGRITY, AND TRUST

Being capable does not build trust if the trustee is unpredictable. Your predictability relates to my ability to predict—on the basis of your words, your values, or your track record of past behavior—what you will do. If predictability is low, then trusting is hard, because it is difficult to rely on someone when you can't know with confidence what he is likely to do. Integrity (honoring one's word or practicing what one preaches) increases predictability. When someone with integrity tells you that she will do something, you have great confidence that her behavior will match her words. If for some reason a high-integrity person cannot honor her word, she will give you an explanation and an apology, and the problem will not recur.

Imagine a highly competent person who says he will do something but then mysteriously fails to do so. Perhaps he got distracted, he forgot, someone else influenced him, or he simply didn't feel like it. All of these reasons for nonperformance make him unpredictable even though he is capable of doing what he said he would do.

There is an entire category of people in leadership, government, and the professions who systematically breed distrust by overpromising and underdelivering. When we are having to deal with someone who has overpromised and underdelivered in the past, we may apply what I call the "distrust discount." We hear the person say, "I can deliver a thousand," and we say to ourselves, "Count on zero or five hundred." Figure 4.4 illustrates this matching of promises to the trustee's ability to deliver and how perceptions of trust or distrust arise. We can exchange with such people, but we widen our range of estimates of what will actually happen and prepare for the possibility of disappointment. In short, we exchange, but we don't really trust what they say, and it worries us if the stakes are great.

In their book *Execution*, Larry Bossidy and Ram Charan do a superb job articulating how high-predictability and high-integrity organizations and leaders operate.[19] These high-trust organizations have leaders who know their business very well, follow through religiously, deal in facts

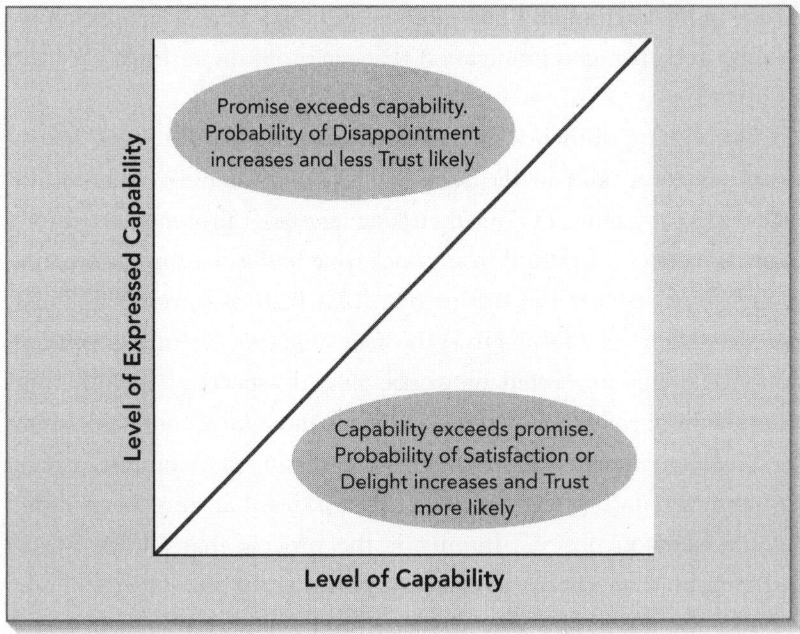

Figure 4.4 Actual Capability in Relation to Expressed Capability

more than opinions, and are clear and careful in their communication internally and externally. At the organizational level, they have processes for developing strategies, hiring the right people, and holding them accountable for performance.

COMMUNICATION AND TRUST

Of the six situational factors of the DTM—situational security, similarities, alignment of interests, benevolent concern, capability, and predictability—all but situational security are supported and underpinned by the seventh: communication. We locate similarities, define interests, express benevolent concern, clarify areas of capability, and improve predictability through excellent communication. At its core, a trusting relationship involves good communication, and it is through communication that trust is built. How do we know if we have similar values with someone and how do we find alignment of interests if we do not have open communication that seeks out these similarities and interests?

Establishing authentic benevolent concern requires some special communication skills in the area of empathic listening, what is also called active listening. This means asking questions, probing the trustor's hopes and concerns, paraphrasing back what has been heard, and taking enough time to hear the trustor out. This kind of communication is also valuable in establishing trust through similarities. Finding common values, overlaps in trusted networks, shared aspects of identity, and other bonds of connectivity require careful, thoughtful communication.

Building and maintaining an effective alignment of interests usually require a separate set of communication skills that have been called "inquiry and advocacy." Inquiry is the process that allows you to find out about another person's perceptions and knowledge, and why she sees the world the way she does and holds certain beliefs and opinions. Advocacy is the communication skill that enables a person to get another to understand his perceptions, data, beliefs, and opinions. Both of these two skills are essential to creating alignment and win-win solutions.

A professor at a university in California who had published some notable work found himself in high demand for his teaching and research at a number of universities around the country. He approached his dean one day to inform him that he was most likely going to accept one offer he'd gotten from another school that would *triple* his current salary.

The dean sat with the faculty member, congratulated him on his job offer, complimented his work, and began to ask the professor about his career and what he wanted from it. For almost an hour, the dean and the professor talked about the professor's aspirations and what he valued most in his career. At the end of the conversation, the dean asked the faculty member to give him a week to find out what the university might do to keep him.

To the professor's surprise, the dean returned to him a week later with a counteroffer. The dean could afford to provide him with only a modest salary increase. However, the dean also offered the professor an opportunity to devote more time to his research, something the professor valued even more than a higher salary. The professor ended up rejecting the higher offer and staying at his current school. When telling this story, he spoke admiringly of the dean for his positive and productive approach.

The dean had used genuine inquiry to understand the professor's needs, and had used advocacy to explain in candid terms how he could meet some of those needs and could not meet others. In order to find some alignment of interests, trustees must listen to uncover others' motives and find common ground. Equally important, but often overlooked, is the use of advocacy whereby the trustee clearly articulates his own interests so that the trustor understands them up front. When the trustee fails to express or assert her own interests, it can lead to a failure of compliance (she does what she wanted to do anyway, but does not say so), withdrawal (she gradually removes herself from the relationship), or resentment (anger at always doing only what the trustor wants).

Such frankness in communication is rare in a time when over-promising seems the norm. A client at a large global consulting firm once pointed out, "If my competitors overpromise and I am more careful to promise only what I know I can deliver, they will get the customer's business, and I will lose a sale!" He might be correct. However, if he were to look at the sale not as a single transaction but as the beginning of a longer-term relationship, he would see that it becomes important to ask whether one should start relationships with misrepresentations. People and firms that are the exemplars of trust go even further by using advocacy to actively manage the expectations of the trustor and ensure that the capability set is framed accurately. They will tell a trustor if they have not had experience with something, and they do not oversell their capabilities. High-trust people and firms communicate so as to convey an accurate understanding of what they can and cannot do for the trustor.

The truth is that entrepreneurs and others may begin with rosy promises in order to gain acceptance and establish a track record, but for the long term, it is more advisable to treat customers as intelligent rather than gullible and to communicate more accurately one's capability to deliver on commitments. This behavior makes for a more trusting and sustainable relationship, but obviously, there are risks along the way; in the short term at least, you may lose out to those willing to overpromise.

Communication that is clear and open is perhaps the most important trust-building tool available. Yet far too many people and organizations fall into a downward spiral in which miscommunication causes others to feel betrayed, which leads to a greater breakdown in communication and, eventually, outright distrust. For example, when serious allegations of sexual abuse by priests in the Boston area arose in the 1990s, Cardinal Bernard Law of the Boston archdiocese failed to communicate openly the nature and scope of the allegations. Then, as details emerged during legal proceedings surrounding the abuse, parishioners felt betrayed, and trust was destroyed. The word "cover-up" was frequently used in the media to describe Law's response to the crisis. His lack of candor caused people to feel that the truth was being obscured at the expense of the victims. Legal settlements eventually cost the archdiocese more than $100 million, and Law, who had once been very popular, resigned in disgrace in 2002. He issued a formal, impersonal apology for his "shortcomings and mistakes" and moved to Rome shortly thereafter.

Yet an extraordinary case of building trust through open, forthright communication was observed inside a Catholic church. One Sunday morning, a priest confessed from the altar that twenty years earlier he had had an inappropriate encounter with a woman employed by the parish. In an agonizingly uncomfortable homily, he candidly acknowledged his mistake, talked about how he had dealt with the issue, and asked the congregation for forgiveness. His offense was far less serious than Law's, and although it went against church doctrine, it was not against the law. However, his story shows that honest communication can go a long way toward building and repairing relationships and engendering trust. Over time, his parishioners came once again to regard him as a tremendously valuable and trusted spiritual leader. Openness has a way of inducing openness in others, and the decision to put faith and trust in others makes it more likely that they will reciprocate.[20]

Having now explored all the variables in the DTM, we can take a deeper look at some tools and techniques that show how the mysterious thing called trust can be made more practical and actionable.

FIVE

Tools for Diagnosing, Building, and Repairing Trust

With a deeper understanding of trust comes the realization that all people, groups, and organizations are untrustworthy at certain times and under certain circumstances. A senior executive leading a seminar on trust opened the discussion by telling the group that although she loved her husband and trusted him completely with their children, she did not trust him at all with the family's finances. As an expert on the DTM, using a multidimensional approach to trust, she was able to accept her husband as being neither totally trustworthy nor totally untrustworthy. She limited her assessment of her husband's untrustworthiness to home finances, on the basis of his past track record of very inadequate capability.

Can the husband in this case do anything to win his wife's trust with the family budget? Perhaps, but it may not be necessary for him to try. In this case, the senior executive and her husband were quite content to reduce interdependence and delegate authority in this matter, agreeing that she should handle all the finances. This agreement to distrust (not rely on) the husband regarding finances was a more efficient and lower-risk alternative to turning him into a financial expert. People use this approach in work teams as well when they allow the best public speaker to lead the team presentation rather than forcing the reluctant speaker to develop great communication skills when he prefers to use his talents to write the report.

But what if the senior executive leading the trust seminar distrusted her husband concerning raising the children? Furthermore, what if a CEO does not trust his chief operating officer? These cases cannot be solved by delegating control and reducing interdependence. There is too much overlap to divide labor, and the potential for conflict with unilateral decision making would be too great. Trying to build trust would be essential to maintaining a productive relationship, and proceeding with distrust would increase risk. There are four criteria with which to determine if taking the time and effort to build trust is warranted:

1. There is risk, uncertainty, and vulnerability in important matters.
2. Proceeding with distrust is too risky, is impossible, or has a very low probability of success.
3. There are no alternative higher-trust relationships that are practical.
4. The will and ability exist to change some elements of the DTM.

The question of when trust building is warranted is related to a larger issue of what kind of relationship is needed among parties in order for the exchange to be productive. The amount and nature of trust required for effective exchange vary depending on the situation. Imagine the strange look you would get if as you left your hotel in the morning, you told the doorman that you wanted to have a trust-building session with him later in the day. His strange look tells you that he knows that high trust is simply not needed in the relationship.

If we were to launch into building trust without considering the type of relationship we need, we would exhaust ourselves and build the wrong types of relationships in the wrong locations. The following list lays out some basic relationship options, ranging from trusting to neutral to distrusting or adversarial. It is possible, after all, to have a relationship with less than full trust. In these low-trust relationships, there is less open communication and more reliance on monitoring of compliance and on measured reciprocity. In trusting relationships, there is little need to monitor, and exchange could occur with general confidence in future reciprocity. The real question is: Would more trust facilitate the achievement of individual and collective goals? If so, we may need to build trust.

Trusting Relationship	*Neutral*	*Distrusting Relationship*
Supportive	Indifferent	Adversarial
Mutually cooperative	Indifferent	Competitive
Win-win	Neutral	Win-lose

TRUST BUILDING

As noted earlier, trust relations are dynamic. We frequently update and reassess our perceptions of trustworthiness on the basis of our experiences. Because conflict is part of life in general, and surely part of life in organizations, then the chances are that if we are not building trust, it is declining. Trust over the long term requires effort, maintenance, and sometimes even repair. The DTM is helpful because it enables us to diagnose precisely where effort can best be applied to enhance trust.

At the center of the process for building trust (illustrated in Figure 5.1) is communication. Trust building demands communication among the parties as they work through the process; otherwise it will break down. A hallmark of distrust is an impoverishment of communication, and this must be changed if trust is to be built.

The first step is to identify the situation and the relationship or relationships that could benefit from increased trust. Who are the trustees and trustors, and in what matters do we want to build trust? Before we invest time and effort, we need to be sure that we are targeting relationships where trust is needed and there is some prospect for improvement.

The second step is to more carefully define who the relevant stakeholders are in the relationship and to conduct a thorough analysis of trust relations using the DTM. In the most complicated cases, like that of the global financial system, this involves identifying multiple agents (banks, regulators, legislators, ratings agencies, and so on) and assessing the trustworthiness of key players in the system. In building trust within a team, perhaps the key relationship is between the team leader and the

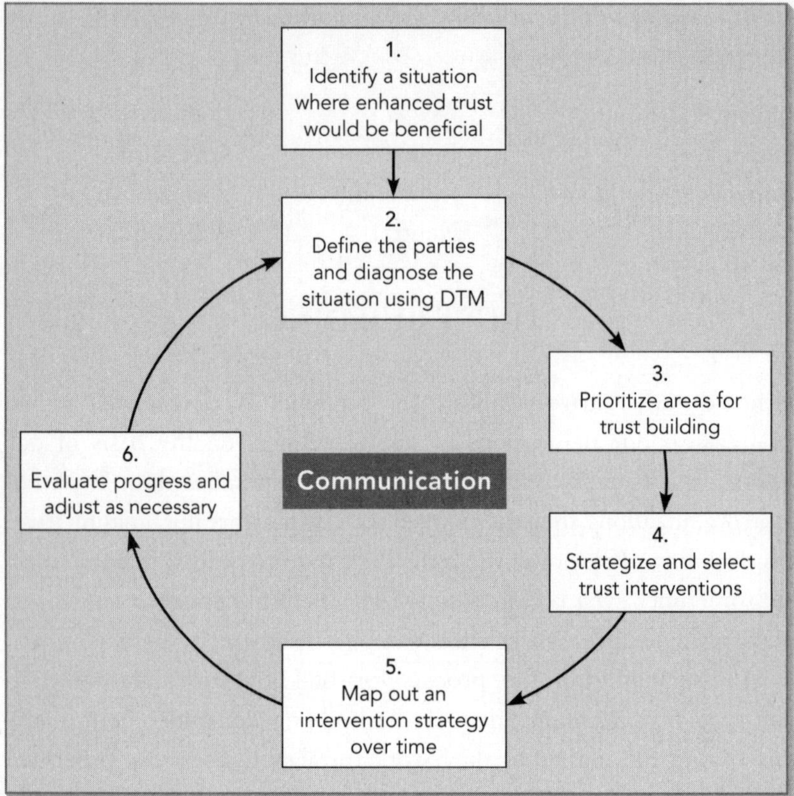

Figure 5.1 The Process for Building Trust

team as a whole or between team members. The point is to think about trust as being embedded in the larger network of relationships and about trust building as having some purpose. Creating a stakeholder map (illustrated in Figure 4.3) is essential in the most complex cases.

Once we are clear about where trust needs to be established, the parties should use a series of diagnostic questions (following this discussion) that are part of the DTM to do a robust analysis of trust among the relevant agents. Ideally both parties complete this exercise from the vantage point of a trustor who wants to enhance trust with a trustee. They then discuss their assessments with one another to improve mutual understanding and develop an accurate diagnosis. Sometimes this is not feasible because one party is more invested in trust building than the other, or perhaps trust is too low to even broach this type of conversation at this point. In this case, the assessment can be completed by only one of the parties, who engages the second party later. When the DTM is used at the team level, each member of the team does an assessment assuming that she is a trustor and that she desires to enhance trust in the overall team, considering all the other team members as trustees. Whether this exercise is done by one party, a pair, or a group, it results in a much clearer picture of why the state of trust is at its current level and of the most fruitful areas for trust building.

To illustrate, take a scenario where there are two partners and only one of the partners, partner A, is motivated at this stage to try to build trust. I am partner A, and I want to improve my trust in partner B (A is the trustor). I will go through the questions noted below and assess whether in this situation I am high or low in adjustment, risk tolerance, and power. I give each of these factors a rating. Alternatively, suppose I am partner A, but instead, I want partner B to trust me more (A is the trustee). In this case, I would try to rate the adjustment, risk tolerance, and power of partner B, the trustor. In both cases, whether I take the position of trustor or trustee, I finish the rating process the same way by assessing the last seven factors in the DTM as they relate to our relationship. Specifically, I assess how risky this situation is and the extent of similarities, alignment of interests, benevolence, capability, predictability, and communication among both parties.

Using the questions listed here for each category as a general guide, the party or parties rate the ten factors of the DTM on a scale from 1 (low) to 5 (high). For example, if you feel that your tolerance for risk is low or that there is poor alignment of interests, you might score that factor a 1 or 2; if you felt that the trustee was highly capable and predictable, you might score those factors a 4 or 5.

1. **Adjustment.** The trustor generally tends not to worry or fret about possible betrayal.
   - Is the trustor generally optimistic?

- Does the trustor rarely worry about what might go wrong?
- Is the trustor generally easygoing and not stressed about things?
- Does the trustor get over a minor loss or failure fairly well?

2. **Risk tolerance.** The trustor is generally comfortable taking risks and accepting uncertainty.
   - Is the trustor risk seeking?
   - Is the trustor comfortable not being in control?
   - Does the trustor accept uncertainty as a normal part of life?
   - Is the trustor comfortable moving forward before all details and arrangements are clear?
3. **Power.** The trustor has some power or recourse to punish betrayal.
   - Is the trustor in a high-power position?
   - Does the trustor have options to punish betrayal?
   - Does the trustor stand to lose less than the other party if failure or betrayal occurs?
   - Does the trustor have the support of people with some power over the other party?
   - Can the trustor control outcomes to a large extent in this relationship?
4. **Situational security.** The potential damage from betrayal among the parties is low or recoverable.
   - If the parties fail to deliver, will the damage be easy to recover from?
   - Are the parties involved experienced with these kinds of risks?
   - Are the risks generally manageable?
5. **Similarities.** The parties feel that there are similarities between them.
   - Do the parties have a common identity?
   - Do they have similar values?
   - Are the parties members of common groups?
   - Are they similar in personality, background, education, or interests?
6. **Interests.** The parties' interests are aligned.
   - Are interests among the parties transparent and well communicated?

- Are interests fully aligned rather than partially aligned or conflicting?
- Is alignment good among a broader network of related stakeholders?
- Are the parties concerned about the same issues?

7. **Benevolent concern.** The parties care about each other.
   - Do the parties listen with empathy?
   - Are they willing to support others' interests?
   - Do the parties care about each other?
   - Do they have a tendency to put others' interests ahead of their own interests?
8. **Capability.** The parties can reliably deliver on commitments and perform.
   - Are the parties competent?
   - Do their capabilities match the scope of their promises?
   - Will they ask for help if needed?
   - Do the parties have, or can they acquire, the required knowledge and skill in areas related to commitments?
   - Do they demonstrate good judgment?
9. **Predictability and integrity.** The parties' behavior is reasonably predictable.
   - Do the parties have a good track record?
   - Do they rarely overpromise and underdeliver?
   - Do their deeds match their words?
   - Do they tend to be consistent?
10. **Communication.** The relationship has open, timely, two-way communication.
    - Do the parties communicate frequently?
    - Are the parties open and accessible?
    - Do they share information in a timely manner?
    - Do they communicate needed information even if it will affect them adversely?
    - Are the parties good at listening and taking others' perspectives?

Once you have rated each of these ten elements of the DTM, step three calls for entering these figures into a prioritization sheet (see Appendix B, Trust Diagnosis Worksheet). In addition, for each element you assign a rating that estimates the potential *impact* of building trust in that aspect of the relationship, and another that estimates the relative *difficulty* involved in effecting change in that area. After being added across, the lowest scores in the far right column will point out the areas with the highest potential for building or restoring trust. These are areas that are weak in the trust relationship, are potentially very significant in their impact, and are relatively easy to implement. This prioritization process helps focus our limited time on trust-building efforts in the areas most likely to produce positive results that will, in turn, encourage more trust.

In some cases, the process stops here. The diagnosis may reveal so many high difficulty-of-change ratings that building trust is not a reasonable option. Then participants may find a polite way to continue the relationship in a cautious, low-trust manner or exit the relationship altogether. Even in such an instance, the process has served to crystallize the true nature of the relationship. Often this improved understanding also relieves stress by putting the root cause of distrust into clearer perspective.

Now that we have individually or, even better, collectively agreed on the two or three highest-priority areas for trust building, we can move into step four, action planning. Here we delve into the specific areas for intervention and make meaningful changes in the priority areas of the DTM to enhance trust. We can conduct a brainstorming session to identify interventions to build trust. Appendix C, Trust Interventions, includes a list of possible interventions for each dimension in the model that we can use to jump-start the brainstorming process. For example, if communication has been impoverished, we may need to set up weekly or monthly meetings and stick to them. Alternatively, if there has been a lack of predictability or of benevolence, we need to talk about this and agree on what behaviors would demonstrate predictability and benevolence in the future for this relationship. There are a host of concrete interventions that if implemented can increase trust. The challenge is to pick a limited number of actions that fit the trust situation as you have diagnosed it.

Step five recognizes that trust can take a long time to build at the outset, a short time to destroy, and a very long time to rebuild once violated. The goal is to develop a long-term developmental approach to executing interventions. Before we can make strides in significant impact areas like alignment of interests or increased predictability, we may need to work first on opening lines of trusted communication.

It is not rare to see people with low-trust relationships approach trust building making the same rash and overly emotional mistakes that created distrust in the first place. For example, it would be rash to start building trust with your boss by saying as the weekly group meeting breaks up, "We may have a trust issue; can we talk?" This would be awkward and stressful. Instead, you might set up a meeting and begin with a conversation about joint expectations concerning predictability, alignment of interests, or some other elements of trust that you feel are at the root of the issue. Alternatively, you could start with some inquiry concerning what your boss thinks is critical to trust. You would then use that feedback to aid in your diagnosis of the relationship and perhaps gently steer the conversation to one element that you think is missing in your relationship. Over time, when trust has been increased, you will be better able to tackle more emotional and potentially inflammatory issues. The idea is to take a longer-term and thoughtful approach to relationship development.

In step six, we monitor progress and adjust our plans in accordance with changes in the situation. As the trust relationship grows, new opportunities may present themselves for enhancing trust. If there is a lack of progress, it might prompt a review of the initial diagnosis or perhaps a decision to abandon the effort. As we take action to build trust, we should be open to learning more about ourselves and others, regardless of the outcome. Maybe the trust issues we sought to address were more significant than we imagined. Maybe the failure of the other party to live up to agreements is a signal that there is a fundamental lack of willingness or ability to grow trust. In any event, we must learn and adapt as time passes and the situation and the relationship change.

Step six feeds back into step two because the most trustworthy people and organizations see trust building not as "once and done" but as an ongoing process of earning trust. They are always looking for ways to improve their reliability to those who depend on them.

Because, as already noted, trust takes time to build, but can be destroyed very quickly, we will turn now to a review of some of the unique aspects of building trust after there has been some violation—that is, trust repair.

REPAIRING TRUST

Imagine you trusted, making yourself vulnerable to someone, and the person took advantage of that vulnerability to benefit himself. You invited him to meet your client, and he stole the relationship, or you gave someone responsibility with clear guidelines, and she violated them and caused damage. When we trust, our willing vulnerability, the faith we place in another, magnifies the pain we feel at any betrayal. The major difference between trust building and trust repair is that restoring a relationship after a violation entails having to overcome more negative emotion.

When trust is violated, the trustor changes his appraisal of particular dimensions of the trustworthiness of the other party: "He only cares about himself" (lack of benevolence) or "He says one thing then does another" (lack of integrity). Trust repair involves trying to reform the aspects of trustworthiness that are now in question. Figure 5.2 displays the thought process and options considered in trust violation and repair.[1]

Trust repair must begin with a sincere acknowledgment and acceptance of responsibility for the violation. Without these, there is little chance of building trust. As noted, trust repair also requires overcoming the negative perceptions and emotions caused by the violation. There is a steeper hill to climb in trust repair, as compared to trust building where there has been no violation. The exact nature and process of trust

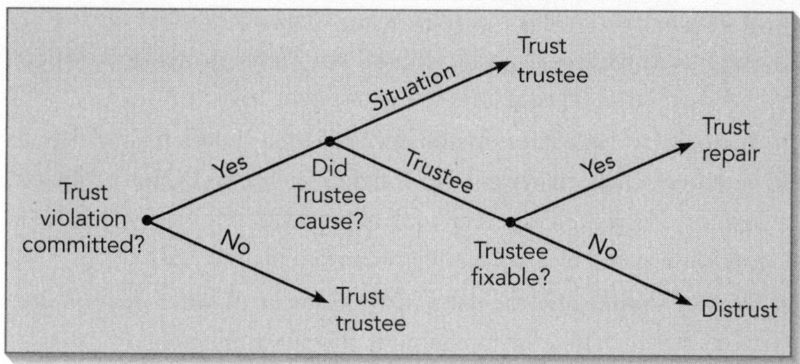

Figure 5.2 Decision to Repair Trust

repair will vary depending on several factors. More severe breaches, multiple breaches, and violations earlier in the relationship have been shown to be more difficult to repair.[2]

When there has been a trust violation at the interpersonal level, trust researchers have suggested that the appropriate actions are to (1) acknowledge that a violation has occurred, (2) determine the causes and admit culpability, (3) admit that the act was destructive, and (4) accept responsibility and the consequences.[3] For organizational trust repair, researchers have suggested that there are four stages: (1) immediate response: acknowledgment, regret, announcement of investigation, commitment of resources to prevention, and action against known causes; (2) diagnosis: timely, transparent, systemic and multilevel examination of violations; (3) reforming interventions: verbal apology and reparation, and implementation of recommendations from the diagnosis; and (4) evaluation: timely and transparent assessment of whether reforms have corrected the problem.[4]

Research concerning some specific trust repair remedies at the interpersonal and organizational levels can be summarized as follows:

- Explanations offered after deception must be adequate and satisfactory to help restore trust.[5]
- Apologies can help repair trust, and they work best when they are sincere, are offered early in the process, and include taking some responsibility.[6]

- Apologies work better than not apologizing because giving no response is judged as an indication that there was no guilt experienced and that there is little desire to repair trust.[7]
- Apologies work best for capability-based trust violations, and denials work best when the trustee is wrongfully perceived to have violated integrity. Unjustified perceptions of betrayal of integrity should be met with swift, credible, and vigorous denials.[8]
- Excuses should only be used in restoring trust when they (1) are credible, (2) include an assumption of responsibility, and (3) can be offered while maintaining the goodwill of the receiver.[9]
- Offering penance or some reparation, rather than simply apologizing or explaining is more powerful in restoring long-term trust. Open offers whereby the victim can define the terms are more powerful than specific targeted offers.[10]
- Organizational and system trust repair require interventions at multiple levels, congruence and integration among reforms, and ongoing evaluation to ensure that reforms are actually taking hold and working.[11]
- Implementing structural remedies that can be used to punish any future trust violations aid in trust repair. Remedies include rules, contracts, regulatory processes, monitoring systems, fines, and posting bond or hostage assets that can be forfeited in the event of violation.[12]

Although these techniques for trust repair have been shown to work, they rely on the adoption of a mind-set and skills that are critical for trust building and even more so for successful trust repair. We look at these enablers of trust building in the next section.

MIND-SET AND SKILLS FOR TRUST BUILDING

There are two overarching competencies that are most critical to successful trust building and trust repair: (1) a mind-set of clinical pragmatism rather than excessive emotionality concerning improving relationships; and (2) a communication skill set that enables one to initiate and conduct difficult conversations using inquiry, advocacy, compromise, empathy, and assertiveness in the proper balance to effect positive results.

The trust-building process requires clinical pragmatism in order to avoid unproductive emotionality. A low-trust relationship with someone important to you may leave you feeling stressed, victimized, and angry. These feelings can motivate you to address the problem, or they can paralyze you with resignation and resentment. The clinically pragmatic individual avoids taking personal offense at being betrayed or distrusted and will not pass hasty judgment on a betrayer's trustworthiness for all time. Instead he or she will look more objectively at the trustee and make an assessment of whether trust can be improved enough to continue the relationship. This mind-set is vital for repairing trust, and at its deepest level, it requires the capacity for forgiveness.

Fred Luskin has shown in programs at Stanford University that even unforgiving people can be taught to forgive. At the heart of forgiveness is the acceptance that humans are imperfect. As long as we must depend on imperfect people, we must also accept the fact that they will sometimes betray our trust. To repair or build trust, we must be open both emotionally and intellectually to the forgiving of transgressions. Responding to a violation of trust by consigning a relationship to low-trust status may not help anyone. In some situations, the betrayed person, the withholder of forgiveness, may suffer more lost opportunities. In this sense, never forgiving and refusing to trust may continue the victimization of the betrayed. Forgiveness can be seen as more of a gift to the betrayed than it is to the betrayer.

The second competency that is critical to trust building is the ability to handle difficult conversations well. Trust can be severely eroded when conversations are handled poorly. Let's say that some misunderstanding leaves you feeling disappointed in a trustee. You express this disappointment the next time you see the person, but you do so with a certain emotional edge in your voice. The other person takes offense but does not express it due to avoidance or in reaction to your emotional edge. Soon the lines of communication between the two of you have shut down, and the opportunity to address the misunderstanding in a productive way has been lost. The preferred approach would be to start out using inquiry to explore why the disappointment occurred. In this conversation, you might also employ an advocacy approach to help the other party see how his or her actions created a problem. If it's done well, addressing a problem of this kind can be an opportunity for two people to expand their level of mutual trust and understanding. If it's done poorly, these conversations can devolve into a cycle of distrust.

A great deal of the trust building and repair process requires high-level communication skills in a context where conflict is a possibility: exploration of interests and similarities, accurate expression of intentions, and the development of relational bonds that can enhance personal comfort. The essential communication skills required include the ability to engage in effective inquiry in which the parties suspend their own interests, opinions, and beliefs to understand the other party in an empathetic manner. Equally important is effective advocacy for one's own interests and articulating one's own beliefs in a way that doesn't put off the other party.

Inquiry helps us see an issue from another person's perspective, but only if we are able to suspend judgment and momentarily set aside the need to promote our own interests. How can we hope to build trust if we seem oblivious to or not in the least curious about the other person's point of view? And if we do not seek to understand a trustor, why should that person assume we would help advance his interests? At the same time, advocacy has an important role in asserting our place in the relationship. If we are not careful to assert our needs and ensure that some are met, we are likely to develop a sense of resentment and distrust. A lack of advocacy that turns into passive-aggressive behavior (avoidance, withdrawal) can erode trust as much as a lack of empathy or benevolence.

Skilled communication builds trust by enabling parties to pursue all available avenues of joint problem solving while making every effort to avoid allocating blame. Expert communication of this kind has the power to transform relationships and careers. For instance, a young executive named Pat was confronted early in her career with a supervisor who seemed to trust no one but himself. This supervisor was a source of frustration for Pat and all her peers. Some resented him and badmouthed him behind his back. Among all of them, only Pat resolved to do something about the situation.

Her first step was to ask the supervisor, Bill, for some time on his calendar when she knew he would be less stressed. At their meeting, after a few moments of small talk, Pat opened up a line of inquiry in a nonthreatening way: "Earning your trust and confidence is important to me," she told him. "I'd like to hear from you what I can do to increase your confidence in me." Bill seemed a bit surprised and replied that he had total trust in her already. "Thanks," she said, and then she probed further. "I know you feel under a lot of pressure for us to perform well and not make mistakes. I sometimes think that I could do more, and take some things off your plate, but you seem reluctant. How can I change the way I do things to make it easier for you to let me take on more and feel comfortable with doing that?" She and Bill came to an agreement: Pat would take on more responsibilities, but she would also make a concerted effort to keep Bill well informed enough that he was comfortable in giving up a measure of control.

Pat used a strategy of gentle inquiry to probe the source of the anxieties that made Bill such a controlling boss. She also used a gentle advocacy approach to let Bill know that she felt underutilized and that she wanted to take on more responsibilities. At the same time, she reassured Bill that she was on his side and wanted to help him be successful. In taking on this difficult conversation, Pat confronted a risky situation and was able to change the level of trust in the relationship. In the months that followed, Pat delivered on her end of the commitment, and their relationship grew and developed. Pat became Bill's most trusted adviser, which increased her influence in the unit. Eventually she became a C-level executive at this Fortune 100 company. Pat was such a master of sincere inquiry, effective advocacy, and joint problem solving that she was able to turn this potentially negative situation with her supervisor into a trusting, career-building relationship.

LARGER-SCALE BETRAYAL AND REPAIR

Much of the discussion in this chapter has focused on trust building at the interpersonal level, but the DTM works in building trust at the organizational level as well. One difference is that in nearly all organizational trust repair situations, multiple interventions must be made in different areas of the organization in order to sustain a reinforcing effect of increasing trust. When the oil giant Texaco was faced with a costly scandal involving racism among senior executives, restoring trust in the company required a wide array of trust interventions.

A group of minority employees filed a racial discrimination suit against Texaco in 1994, charging that black employees were being paid less than white employees for equal work. Two years later, a secretly recorded audiotape of a group of senior Texaco executives discussing the case was leaked to the public. The executives were heard denigrating black workers in coarse language. Excerpts of the tapes made all the evening news broadcasts, and within days Texaco's stock value had dropped by $1 billion.

Texaco's then chairman and CEO Peter Bijur recognized the gravity of the situation and knew he needed to act quickly to repair the public trust that had been broken by the tapes. He led a brilliant process of trust repair and trust building. Bijur made an emphatic public apology (open communication, benevolent concern) and hired an outside counsel (eliminate conflicts of interest) to investigate the matter.

Then Bijur settled the discrimination lawsuit. He agreed to pay out over $100 million to current and former Texaco employees who were minorities. He set aside millions more for diversity training and created a special board of directors committee charged with evaluating its effectiveness. That step demonstrated that Texaco was willing to place a high value on diversity and would create a corporate culture built on shared values. Those who didn't belong—specifically, the three senior executives heard speaking offensively on the tape—were ousted, by termination, retirement, or suspension (demonstrating similarity by sanctioning not living the values). To make the company's actions more predictable for employees, Bijur hired a respected judge to evaluate Texaco's HR policies, and the company changed those that were deemed unfair or not transparent (reforming systems and capabilities). Moreover, senior executives were sent to all company locations to apologize for the humiliation to which black workers had been subjected (benevolent concern, open and candid communication).

Collectively, these actions made it easier for disillusioned workers to place their faith in the company again. Trust wasn't restored overnight—there is no quick fix for broken faith on this scale—but concerted efforts to correct the sources of distrust eventually paid off. In 1999, Bijur received an award from a national African American group for commitment to diversity, and in 2000 Texaco received praise from Socialfunds.com for being a "model for challenging corporate racism."

The dimensions of the DTM that Texaco's interventions addressed are presented in Figure 5.3. Bijur was a masterful leader in restoring trust. In the next chapter, we explore in more detail what it takes to be such a leader.

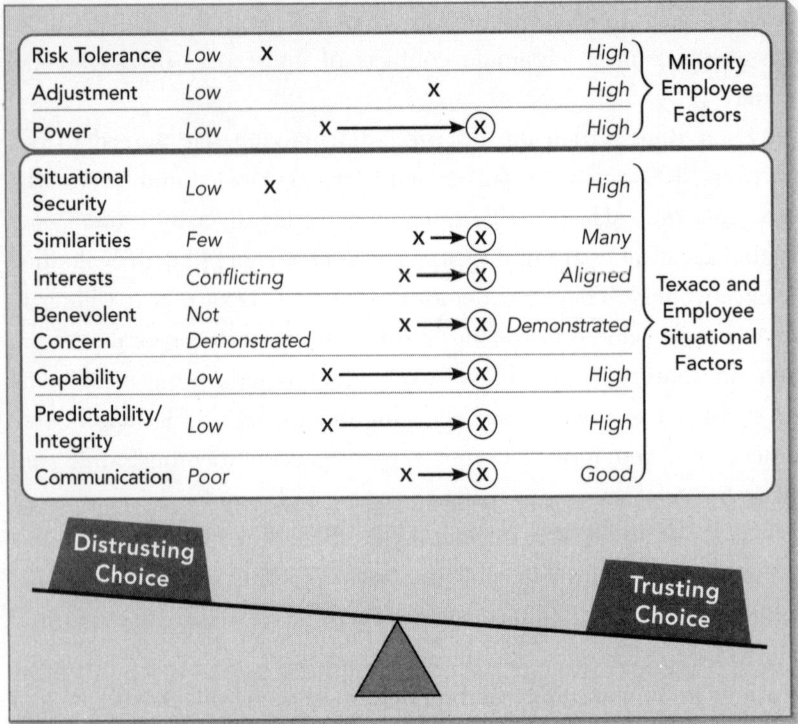

Figure 5.3 Restoring Trust at Texaco

SIX

Trust in Leadership and Management

When there is uncertainty, risk, and vulnerability, we hope that those in positions of power will help ensure fair outcomes. This longing for a benevolent, all-powerful ruler has been part of the human psyche since Plato wrote of Utopias led by philosopher-kings. Although it may be unreasonable for us to expect leaders to solve all our problems, at a minimum we want to be able to trust them. We therefore find it particularly unnerving when we are in a risky situation and must depend on a leader we do not trust.

Trust in leadership is critical in that it sets the tone for the rest of the organization. When the leader is trustworthy and expects this behavior from others, trust cascades throughout the organization and can, eventually, become embedded in the culture of the enterprise. Trust in one's direct leader has been shown to influence willingness to follow, time spent on task, organization citizenship behavior, willingness to share sensitive information, job performance, job satisfaction, organizational commitment, goal commitment, belief in information, and organizational trust.[1] For those wishing to build trust in organizations and institutions, there is no better place to start than by enhancing trust in leadership.

In assessing the trustworthiness of leaders, we ask ourselves, *Who is this person? Does she tend to speak the truth? Does she seem to care about others?*

Is she responsible and predictable? To what degree do I feel comfortable that she will do the right thing? Our assessment of the leader as a person and of her leadership style and our trust in her, or lack of it, influence how or whether we follow her.

Consider two radically different scenarios of leader-follower relations: low-trust coercion versus high-trust empowerment. In the low-trust coercion scenario, you have seen clear cues that the person is out for his own interests, hides information, and says one thing but does another. You follow this person perhaps because you see no other options or because you fear retribution if you fail to comply with his wishes. You follow, but cautiously, while trying to protect yourself from harm. The time and energy you spend protecting yourself from betrayal seems wasted but necessary. The situation also creates stress because you never really know if or when this person might betray you. Is this really a leadership style, or might it be better labeled coercive control? Whichever label we choose, this approach creates a careful and distrusting style of followership.

Al Dunlap, the former CEO of Sunbeam and turnaround artist sometimes referred to as "Rambo in Pinstripes" or "Chainsaw Al," is an example of a low-trust coercive leader.[2] Brought in to turn Sunbeam around, Dunlap from the start pitted stakeholders against one another: community and employees versus shareholders. This was in part due to the fact that Sunbeam's new private equity shareholders were interested in a short-term increase in the stock price.[3] Dunlap relished this short-term shareholder orientation, even commenting that he never wanted to see the word "stakeholder" in an annual report and that there was only one constituency that mattered—shareholders who paid for their stake.[4] This certainly created a misalignment of interests with the community and employees.

Dunlap's management style was aggressive, even angry, and he intimidated those around him. One of his staff described his coercive style well: "Dunlap created a culture of misery, an environment of moral ambiguity, indifferent to everything except the stock price. He did not lead by intellect or by vision, but by fear and intimidation. The pressure was beyond tough. It was barbarous."[5] After massive cost and job cutting, the stock price went up, only to fall later. David Fannin, a lawyer who worked for Dunlap, described him as a "capricious and egotistical hothead" and working for him as being like an "abusive relationship." Dunlap was eventually fired by the board over the phone, and Sunbeam was forced to restate its profits. In September 2002, Dunlap was forced to agree to a demand by the SEC that he would never serve as officer or director of another public company. It was clear that with Dunlap at the helm, ethical and moral considerations and the long-term interests of communities and employees were subordinated to the financial returns to the private equity owners and to Dunlap.

In the high-trust empowerment scenario, the leader projects clear signals that he cares about others and takes their interests into account even if it hurts him. He communicates in an open and straightforward manner and encourages others to do so without retribution. Followers can count on the leader's behaving in a manner that is consistent with his words. Those around him feel confident that he will balance stakeholder interests and do the right thing in a situation that involves some uncertainty and risk. In this case, people follow with more confidence and less anxiety. Followers still seek to avoid harm, but feel that they have someone they can count on. This helps them relax and focus more on the task at hand with less second-guessing and concern.

At the opposite end of the spectrum from Al Dunlap is Chester Cadieux, the founder and former CEO of QuikTrip. Cadieux created a culture in which employees and customers were the first priority. At QuikTrip, it was a priority for Cadieux to ensure that employees shared in the wealth created by the company.[6] Cadieux's book about the company's success is a tale of acknowledging other people's contributions. Where Dunlap was feared, Cadieux was revered.

If you consider the quality of followership, not merely results, it seems clear that it is impossible to be a strong leader if your followers do not trust you. The data concerning trust in leadership are troubling. The Edelman Trust Barometer, a measure of credibility in leadership, appears in Figure 6.1.[7]

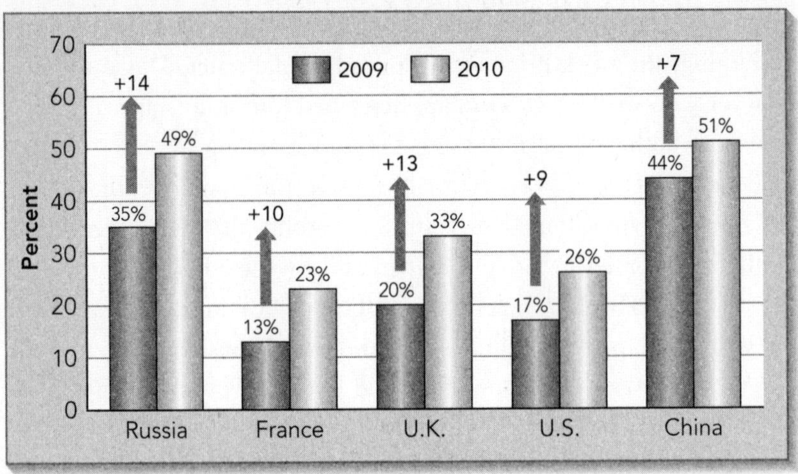

Figure 6.1 Percentage of People Who Said Hearing Information from a CEO Would Be Very or Extremely Credible. © Edelman, 2010. Used with permission.

None of these credibility scores are high, and some (United States, United Kingdom, and France) are disturbingly low. But an even more compelling story lies behind these data: assuming that these figures reflect the perception of a majority of employees, consider how much stress and anxiety are being produced because millions of stakeholders find themselves in vulnerable situations where low-trust leaders will affect their futures.

Although the declining trust scores noted in Chapter One are cause for concern and the low scores on CEO credibility are somewhat alarming, there is hope. Decades of research have yielded a great deal that can help leaders sustain trust even in the increasingly dynamic and complex environments that they and their followers find themselves in. In many ways, the challenge is to focus on actionable areas that leaders can incorporate into their behavioral repertoire. Drawing on the DTM and the factors that research shows are associated with trust, the rest of this chapter offers ten very focused and high-impact areas for leaders to enhance trust and a list of specific leadership practices for manifesting high-trust leadership.

BUILD RISK TOLERANCE IN THE FACE OF GROWING RISK

High-trust leaders understand that followers with a low tolerance for risk will need more support and assurance in risky situations. The term *adaptive leadership* is often used to refer to this leadership role of helping people contain anxiety so that they can operate effectively.[8] To do this, the adaptive leader brings the risks involved to the surface and helps people understand them, share them, and cope. Addressing followers' anxiety in risky situations by providing risk mitigation strategies, information, support, and productive ways to channel anxiety tends to enhance comfort, trust, and exchange.

A leader's ability to enable people to share and manage risk has a direct impact on the level of trust within an organization. If the leader's behavior suggests that accountability for success or failure is at the team level rather than at the individual level, people are encouraged to support one another, and this increases everyone's tolerance for risk. In contrast, when a manager's behavior suggests that accountability is only at the individual level, people look out for themselves and tend to offer less support to others. Rather than sharing and managing risk together, people will adopt an "every man for himself" mind-set, and focus on protecting their interests even at the expense of the whole organization.

Two consulting firms with which I have had experience provide a sharp contrast in the ways in which leaders manage and mitigate anxiety within organizations. One firm had a fairly brutal public shaming routine whereby consultants who had brought in the least amount of new business in the previous quarter were taken to task in front of their peers. The leader's philosophy was that fear stimulated the proper effort needed to generate sales. The result was a culture in which people did not share leads or any sort of information at all, and consultants would work just hard enough to avoid being the one shamed next quarter. There was fear, little social support, and low trust. In the other firm, the leader was not concerned about which consultant brought in each particular piece of business; instead, her focus was on overall productivity and on making sure people were working together to seize market opportunities. The anxiety associated with new business was shared, and people worked with a high degree of cooperation and trust to achieve goals as a group.

Although it would be naïve to suggest that inducing fear does not increase focus and effort in the short run, fear is unsustainable as a long-term driver of performance. People burn out and resent the manipulation associated with the use of fear as a motivator. The best people leave these types of fearful, low-trust environments because they are often presented with better options. Data from the Great Place to Work Institute show that higher-trust organizations have about half the voluntary employee turnover of the average company (as measured and defined by the Bureau of Labor Statistics).[9]

INSPIRE SELF-CONFIDENCE, ESPECIALLY IN LOW-ADJUSTMENT PEOPLE

Jack Welch demonstrated an understanding that confidence is affected by the environment when he said, "Giving people self-confidence is by far the most important thing that I can do. Because then they will act."[10] Albert Bandura, a psychologist at Stanford, spent most of his career studying the factors that affect confidence, or what he called self-efficacy—the belief that one can act to achieve a goal. He identified four factors that build a positive sense that one can accomplish a task:[11]

1. Past success at the task
2. Seeing others succeed at the task
3. Having a generally positive mind-set
4. Receiving encouragement and validation from others

This last factor underscores that our sense of confidence comes not only from our talent and success but also from the confidence others express in us. The way managers and peers act toward others can affect their confidence level.

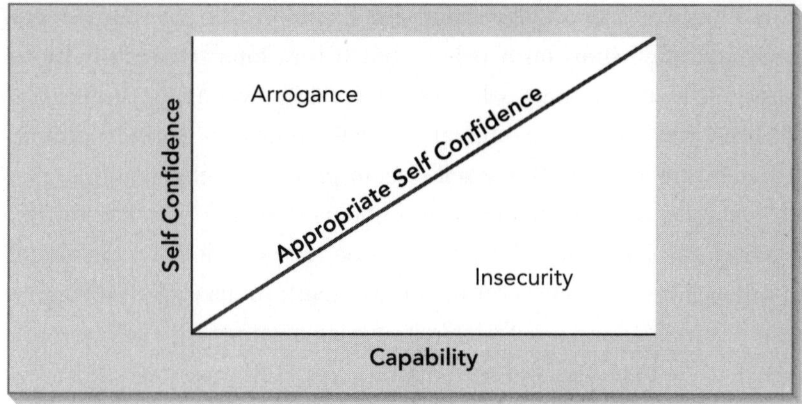

Figure 6.2 Appropriate Self-Confidence

A good leader helps those around her achieve an appropriate level of self-confidence. The ideal is for self-confidence to equal capability. The diagonal line in Figure 6.2 shows this graphically: below the line, when capability is greater than self-confidence, there is unwarranted insecurity or self-doubt. If this is motivating without inhibiting action, it may be a good thing. However, unwarranted doubt indicates a lack of self-trust that can lead to inaction, procrastination, and generally poor performance.[12] Above the diagonal line, where self-confidence exceeds capability, is arrogance. Arrogance can be defined as unwarranted or misplaced confidence. It leads to an erosion of trust with others, who will eventually learn that the person promises more than she can deliver. We might think of it as a mathematical equation: confidence minus capability equals arrogance.

All of us are capable of at least temporary self-doubt in situations of great uncertainty and risk. Former U.S. treasury secretary Hank Paulson offered an extremely candid and humble account of the financial crisis. In the midst of the crisis, this highly successful former chairman of Goldman Sachs found himself so beset by stress, so upset and unsure and fearful, that he threw up between meetings. He called his wife asking for her prayers and help.[13] Imagine the fear a junior analyst feels when, in a difficult situation, the boss decides to crank up the pain level with threats and criticism. This fanning-the-flames-of-fear approach might produce certain short-term results, but it isn't long before it leads to workers who are cautious, self-protective, and unwilling to trust others.

Leaders cannot manufacture self-confidence from nothing. Although the job of building self-esteem primarily belongs to parents, leaders and managers can enhance confidence and mitigate insecurities. Doing so can have a significant impact on the behavior of members of an organization as well as on the entity's performance. To the degree we feel confident and comfortable in our environment, we will be more likely to trust ourselves and trust others.

BALANCE OUT INEQUITIES WHERE YOU HAVE ALL THE POWER

Research in psychology shows that people in uncertain and stressful environments respond better to stress and recover from it better when they have more control.[14] Leaders who empower people by giving them some control increase trust. Conversely, micromanagers who refuse to delegate and empower signal that they do not trust, and they create powerlessness, which makes others less trusting.[15]

Chapter Three featured the story of a micromanager named John, who was demoted because he didn't trust his direct reports to help him run his ten-thousand-employee unit. John was moved to a less demanding position, you'll recall, because his mania for controlling his employees spread like a contagion throughout the unit. Everyone was micromanaging, slowing down the decision making and reducing productivity in order to accommodate John's craving for control.

An example of a more effective leader, Ray, was a senior executive at a Fortune 100 consumer products company. Ray was a general manager of a division that had revenues of $200 million and included a number of major brand names. Ray and the CEO had decided to explore licensing some of these trademarks to other companies to be used on related products, enabling the company to increase sales. This was a risky venture because it involved trusting other companies to protect the image of this company's valuable brands.

Rather than trying to run this complicated business himself, Ray depended on a promising young MBA in his organization who had an excellent reputation as a product manager. He called this MBA into his office and told him that he was going to be responsible for all the licensing for the premier brand in the division, a trademark that had been an iconic brand for over 150 years. After this meeting, this product manager was highly motivated to live up to Ray's trust; he was heard to say to a colleague, "I had better not screw this up."

Ray placed trust in subordinates by empowering them, and just as John's management style spread distrust and inertia throughout his division, Ray's style promoted a culture of trust, delegation, and high productivity. His management approach not only helped his subordinates trust their staff but also helped establish relationships of reciprocal trust throughout the organization, at all levels. High-trust leaders distribute power to competent people and encourage them to do the same. The result is an organization where power and influence flow to where they are most effective rather than always migrating back to the corner office.

ADD SECURITY TO INSECURE CIRCUMSTANCES

Some of the decline in trust in leaders is due to the immense challenges of managing in a complex and intensely competitive environment. Between September 2009 and January 2010, IBM surveyed 1,541 CEOs and senior managers in sixty countries and thirty-three industries about change and complexity.[16] The results showed that relative to their current state, 69 percent of those surveyed expected significantly more volatility, 65 percent expected significantly more uncertainty, and 60 percent expected significantly more complexity in their environments. Less than half felt prepared to deal with the increased complexity.

Leading in a world of complexity and change demands taking responsibility for strategic adaptation of the firm to ensure current and future success. This requires a paradoxical combination of execution skills fused with abstract, creative, and strategic thinking. Effective leaders shape the organization to match the speed and complexity of the environment that it must navigate. They act as sense makers to accelerate understanding and orchestrators to enable speed of adaptation within the organization. When performed well, this kind of leadership gives people confidence that they can prevail even in turbulent environments.

Given the speed of change and complexity in most modern organizations, leaders often have very little room to create a sense of security in the workplace. But sometimes they make things worse by projecting a false security rather than addressing the real challenges. This was the case with a large global company that had major trust issues; it was clear that employees did not trust senior management. Every time senior management addressed employees, there would be cynical comments and even laughter when people were behind closed doors. Morale and turnover were so bad that the board replaced many of the senior leaders. One of these new leaders, who had come with a good reputation from a well-managed competitor in the industry, quickly increased security simply by being candid. People consistently described this leader as a "breath of fresh air in this place" and said, "We do not always like what he says, but we know he is giving it to us straight. We can work with that."

High-trust leaders will candidly admit the risks and try to help followers understand them and learn what they can do to manage them. By acknowledging potential dangers openly and showing empathy, leaders deepen relationships and create a greater foundation for trust. Recall the story of Sue and Joe in Chapter Two. By acknowledging the risk to Joe and by helping him sort out possible solutions, Sue was not only able to increase trust with Joe individually but also with all of the associates who talked to Joe on his way out the door. They heard him sing Sue's praises as a leader, for helping him make a difficult choice in a difficult situation.

CULTIVATE SIMILARITIES AND SHARED VALUES IN A DIVERSE WORKPLACE

Creating a stronger sense of unity and identity in a company or workplace requires a leader who is willing to take on the role of chief social engineer. In part, the culture of an organization develops from the inferences people make about what is important, which are based on observations of the leader's reactions. When the leader emphasizes the values of subordination of individual interests to those of the group, supporting one another, fair process, transparency in communication and decision making, and timely and open communication, the organizational culture promotes trust.

This all sounds very nice, but it requires tough decisions that not all leaders seem able to make. Jack Welch said that GE made a tremendous leap when the company began to identify and remove "Type 4" managers—people who get results but do not live out the company's values—and then inform the entire company of why these managers had been asked to leave. Of the Type 4, Welch said, "This type is the toughest to part with because organizations always want to deliver, and to let someone go who gets the job done is yet another unnatural act. But we have to remove these Type 4s because they have the power, by themselves, to destroy the open, informal, trust-based culture we need to win today and tomorrow."[17] He believed that only by taking this drastic action could he persuade stakeholders and employees of GE that the company took its values seriously and intended for the entire organization to stick to them. Leaders must be the primary engineers of a culture whose values promote alignment, pride in the team, transparency, and other elements of the DTM that are the bedrock of organizational trust.

KEEP INTERESTS ALIGNED AMID COMPETING AND CONFLICTING LOYALTIES

One of the most important things a leader does is to get people to integrate their individual interests with the interests of the enterprise. How leaders define and communicate the collective interests, and reward those who promote them, will determine to a large extent whether trust and collective action are present.

During a conference call with the CEO of a $10 billion manufacturing firm, one of the CEO's direct reports complained that two of their business units were feuding with one another. The CEO replied, "Tell them to look at the name on their paychecks. It has the enterprise's name on it, not their business unit. That's where their primary loyalty should lie." Leaders face a constant battle reminding their subordinates that it's not enough to optimize each business unit so that the company is nothing but a series of fiefdoms or silos. This particular CEO expended considerable effort creating a set of community-of-practice groups in the organization to enable dialogue and sharing across organization lines. He also began a quarterly business development and marketing council populated with key people from each division, to enable integrated pursuit of critical opportunities across markets. The secondary benefit of all these actions, of course, is that they also give people a chance to identify themselves as members of groups with similarities.

High-trust leaders also create rigorous and fair processes to help people understand the mission, strategy, and tactical priorities of the enterprise. They also ensure that these priorities are communicated and translated throughout the organization. Most organizations do this in their strategic planning processes, and in high-trust organizations, strategic planning is characterized by three important elements: first, all employees are involved at some level in the planning process; second, when the planning begins, people are willing to participate in a robust and candid negotiation of priorities, across functions and business units; and, third, during and after the process, everyone engages in a rigorous communication of priorities and goals across hierarchical, functional, and geographical boundaries.

At QuikTrip Convenience Stores, CEO Chester Cadieux made sure that all leaders and managers were keenly aware that they were responsible for ensuring that every employee understood the company's strategy, as laid out in the company's strategic plan. In interviews and focus groups that I conducted at QuikTrip, employees in various departments and at various levels all described the company's strategy in nearly identical terms. The company's strong performance and famously low rate of employee turnover are due in part to the fact that all employees have largely internalized the same set of strategies and goals. In a real sense, they are one team all rowing in the same direction.

DEMONSTRATE BENEVOLENCE IN A BOTTOM-LINE WORLD

Most of us expect our leaders to be benevolent and to "watch out" for their followers. We won't trust them if they don't. In 2008, the chief executives of many financial institutions—including Citigroup, Barclays, Goldman Sachs, Morgan Stanley, and Royal Bank of Scotland—chose to forgo their bonuses that year as a way of demonstrating benevolent concern for their companies and the other stakeholders. At the same time, many of these CEOs advocated for the right of their employees to *keep* their bonuses for the year, despite knowing that this would raise a firestorm of criticism from the public, which had just put in billions of dollars of taxpayer money to shore up the financial system the banks had contributed to nearly destroying. Yet the CEOs stood firm against the criticism, arguing that the employees were due bonuses under the company's rules and procedures and that those employees were not primarily responsible for the financial crisis. Their sacrifice, of bearing public scorn, was well noted by their employees.

Whenever leaders demonstrate more concern for others' interests than their own, they enhance trust throughout the organization. Conversely, when leaders act opportunistically, to the detriment of others in the organization, they sow distrust. Acts of generosity are even more powerful and meaningful when they are performed outside the public spotlight. When benevolent concern is seen flowing unforced, directly from the leader's personal values, it gives everyone a sense of comfort about the leader. Behaviors produced by someone's interior values are seen as more reliable guides to how he will act in the future.

This idea of benevolent leadership is an old one; it seems to have lost favor in some realms, and this may in part explain the loss of trust in so many arenas. For many years, the U.S. Army has had selfless service as one of its values: "Put the welfare of the Nation, the Army and your subordinates before your own. Selfless service is larger than just one person. In serving your country, you are doing your duty loyally without thought of recognition or gain. The basic building block of selfless service is the commitment of each team member to go a little further, endure a little longer, and look a little closer to see how he or she can add to the effort."[18]

When leaders expend effort engaging in fair processes and go out of their way to exhibit true humility, empathy, and concern for the welfare of others, they engender a sense of trust and loyalty in their followers. In his book *Good to Great,* Jim Collins refers to "Level 5" leaders who are driven but humble in demeanor. Their primary motivation is not self-gratification but building an institution that is much bigger than themselves. This devotion to others, to the larger mission at one's own expense, breeds trust and, very often, the reciprocation of that devotion: loyalty.

PROVE AND IMPROVE YOUR CAPABILITY IN AN AGE OF COMPLEXITY

A famous incident during a 1949 forest fire in Montana underscores the need to build confidence in leadership well before a group faces its most difficult challenges. A fire chief named Wagner Dodge was leading his team of fifteen smokejumpers into an area known as Mann Gulch when the wind shifted and a massive wall of flame headed their way. Dodge had analyzed the intensity of the fire, the wind conditions, and the speed at which the fire was traveling much more accurately than his crew. He knew that they could not outrun the fire. He quickly lit a small fire in front of them, an escape fire, in order to create a pre-burned area of ashes that would deprive the oncoming flames of fuel. All the men would be safe if they remained lying down in this vegetation-free area and allowed the huge wall of flame to pass. Dodge ordered the crew to drop their tools and lie down in the ashen area he had just burned away. One of the crew was reported to have shouted, "To hell with that; I'm getting out of here." The men did not trust their leader with their lives on the line. They ignored their leader and desperately attempted to outrun flames that were advancing at more than six hundred feet per second. Dodge survived, and all but two of the others died.[19]

Subsequent analyses of the Mann Gulch tragedy indicated a number of problems. First, although Dodge's analytical skills in assessing the fire were good, he did not communicate frequently or explain much about changing conditions to his fairly inexperienced crew as the situation unfolded. As a result, they had no way of gaining confidence in Dodge's ability to handle the situation. Second, at a critical moment, Dodge did not communicate clearly how the burn patch would be used. Survivors reported that they could not understand Dodge's direction at this key moment as the fire approached. Third, Dodge was operating with a flawed approach to fire safety. Today's practice is to ascertain the location of safety zones and escape routes in advance and continually update the crew about them. Current practice is also to appoint one person to do nothing but study the movement of the fire, a job that Dodge had juggled among others at Mann Gulch. Dodge was later sued by a senior firefighter whose son was killed at Mann Gulch, claiming incompetent leadership.[20]

The metaphor of fighting fires is increasingly relevant to business. There is risk, the conditions are changing rapidly, and we are looking to leaders for some sign that they know what they are doing and that we will prevail if we stay focused. In my analysis of more than twenty organizational surveys that include measures of trust, I found that low scores for confidence and trust in senior management frequently accompanied low organizational trust scores. When I studied these results to find their root causes, they typically showed perceptions among employees that senior management was not taking the necessary actions or decisions to warrant high trust in the organization (low performers kept in key jobs, protection of status quo, failure to confront issues, and so on). As we will see more clearly in the next chapter on organizational trust, the most common trust issues today are connected to managing change well in turbulent times.

Beyond the competencies related to the DTM, such as communication, alignment of interests, and the like, to project confidence in turbulent times, a leader must be able to

- Think strategically about the future and anticipate change
- Break changes down into manageable initiatives that can be implemented over time
- Stay focused and execute, but also demonstrate agility
- Mobilize groups of people in a change process
- Use organization levers (structure, culture, systems, strategy) to manage the "organization," not just the "business"
- Put the right people in the right jobs to manage change and execute
- Develop and maintain good relationships

This list of competencies has been summarized by Yukl into three broad domains of behavior: (1) task-oriented behavior to ensure efficiency and reliability, (2) relations-oriented behavior to build strong human relations and resources, and (3) change-oriented behavior to ensure timely adaptation to changes in the environment. Leaders effectively use both direct means (themselves) and indirect means (other people, programs, initiatives, and organization levers) to ensure that things work and that the part of the organization they lead is seen as capable.[21]

A final capability, and perhaps the most critical to maintaining trust, is the leader's self-awareness and humility concerning admitting his or her own weaknesses. In his autobiography, Jack Welch said that he recommended Jeff Immelt to succeed him at GE, in part, because he felt that Immelt was "comfortable in his own skin."[22] When a leader is comfortable enough to acknowledge areas where he or she is *not* competent and then compensate for that area by sharing or delegating responsibilities, he or she builds trust. Conversely, a leader who is blind to the limits of his or her capabilities breeds distrust.

All of these capabilities need not reside in one leader, but overall the CEO must ensure that they exist in his or her leadership team. Like Dodge, when leaders operate with flawed strategies or fail to make sure that their capabilities are known and trusted by their subordinates, the odds of distrust and of being abandoned by their troops go up.

PRACTICE PREDICTABILITY AND INTEGRITY IN A SEA OF UNCERTAINTY

A challenge in leading today is that stakeholders expect high performance, vision, and transformational change, preferably wrapped up in a trustworthy, reliable, and predictable package; but the turbulence and complexity in the environment make this a struggle. In many cases, CEOs destroyed trust (Enron, Arthur Andersen, Lehman Brothers, and others) because ethical principles were violated in an attempt to take shortcuts in the struggle to achieve goals. Andersen shredded documents, Lehman Brothers misled its directors concerning risk management, and Enron manipulated equity analysts. Short-term performance or survival took precedence over integrity and long-term trust.

At the heart of trust in leadership is the integrity and authenticity that come from clear values that guide behavior. When we have internalized our values, we know when we have strayed and are acting without integrity. It feels wrong, and this discomfort causes us to stop, examine our conscience, and discern what is right. There is a reason that all major religions advocate some periodic examination of conscience (Christian penance, Judaic atonement, and Islamic recollectedness). An active examination of conscience makes values and principles living guides and creates a comforting coherence in our behavior for those who follow.

Robert McDonald, a West Point graduate and CEO of Procter & Gamble, espouses what he calls "value-based leadership." Two of the values that he suggests are critical are purpose and character. Purpose is belief in the mission and ethics of your firm. Character is acting with integrity and personal responsibility.[23] Bill George, former CEO of Medtronic, advocates authentic leadership, which requires clarity of purpose, clarity of values, and concern for relationships. He suggests that high performance comes by combining authentic leadership with the empowerment of others and an effective style for using power.[24]

Leadership modeling is essential to creating a firm of high-integrity leaders. GE has done an excellent job of using leadership modeling to promote both high performance and high integrity. The demands for performance at GE are legendary, but GE leaders are also expected to model integrity, and they know that if they do not, there will be serious consequences. Jeff Immelt, the CEO of GE, begins and ends each annual meeting of the top managers at GE with an affirmation of the company's integrity principles: "GE's business success is built on our reputation with all stakeholders for lawful and ethical behavior. Commercial considerations *never* justify cutting corners."[25] Each employee at GE must sign the "Spirit and Letter" integrity document, and the first value in the GE code of conduct is "be honest, fair and trustworthy in all your GE activities and relationships." What makes this real to employees is that Immelt has backed it up by terminating some talented and valuable senior managers whose business units failed to live up to the standard.[26]

COMMUNICATE, COMMUNICATE, COMMUNICATE

A talent for public speaking is a very valuable tool for any leader, but public speaking is not the same as communicating. Some of the most untrustworthy leaders have been great public speakers. The invention of radio in the twentieth century was partly responsible for allowing great orators like Stalin, Hitler, Mussolini, and Mao Zedong to manipulate and exploit their followers.

The following are six keys to leading with trust from a communication standpoint:[27]

1. Share information
2. Tell the truth

3. Admit mistakes
4. Give and receive constructive feedback
5. Maintain confidentiality
6. Speak with good purpose

Most of these ways of communicating to build trust are self-explanatory, but "speaking with good purpose" requires some clarification. When a leader speaks with good purpose, he or she communicates constructively and directly to the people involved. To be constructive means to communicate with positive intent to resolve the issue. To be direct means that we do not go around people and create an environment of gossip. To tolerate communicating "behind people's backs" and creating rumors feeds suspicion and distrust.[28] The caveat to this, which will be covered in more detail in the chapter on trust across cultures, is to make sure that direct communication is culturally appropriate. Some cultures (for example, in India and Japan) sometimes prefer indirect communication as a means to create a face-saving opportunity when there is potential for conflict.

Research supports the view that using direct communication by consulting with followers and expressing support for them is the leadership style most closely associated with trust building.[29] This approach, along with being willing to receive feedback, creates an important element of trust: establishing that you are approachable. Approachability facilitates dialogue, listening, and support, which are more important to building trust than great oratory and manipulation.

■ ■ ■

Beyond these ten ideas to build trust in leadership are many more practices that address specific aspects of the DTM. These are listed in Table 6.1. Although being a trustworthy leader is not easy in the complex, multi-stakeholder world we live in, the path is more straightforward when we understand the foundational elements of trust.

Table 6.1 Leadership Trust Practices

If this factor is low...	Then you should...
Risk Tolerance	• Position more risk-tolerant people where most of the company's risks are. • Celebrate failure of outcome if the process of managing projects is excellent. • Communicate to people that you see the size and resources of the firm as advantages used to enable risk taking. • Reduce people's risk with some safety net.
Level of Adjustment	• Hire leaders who are confident. • Express confidence in people (when confidence is authentic). • Attack ideas but never the person. • Praise in public; criticize in private. • Recognize that for some people, building trust takes longer. Be patient.
Relative Power	• Give people voice and influence whenever possible. • Have an open door policy or some other feedback process to receive upward communication. • Avoid the use of coercive power that forces people to comply without other options. • Demonstrate that leadership decisions are not arbitrary but are based on fair process and serving collective interests.
Security	• Off-load risk by using the enterprise-wide resources and portfolio as a diversification tool. • Lower your expectations of trust from the trustor when security is low. • Expect to invest time in building comfort. • Share risk. • Create safety nets where possible.
Similarities	• Create a "one firm" focus. • Embed cultural values that promote trust (integrity, benevolence, power sharing, serving stakeholders, and so on). • Create identity and meaning in being part of the "enterprise," beyond geographical, business unit, or functional identity.
Interests	• Be clear about whose interests you are serving when acting. Take others' interest into account and find a win for them where possible. • Align people with the strategy and vision—superordinate goals. • Shape a culture that reinforces doing "the right thing" for the enterprise and penalizes those who do not (without inducing excess fear). • Lead with a fair and transparent process.

Table 6.1 (*Continued*)

If this factor is low...	Then you should...
Benevolent Concern	• Take actions that demonstrate a genuine concern for others. • Serve others' interests even if, on occasion, you bear some loss (and find a tasteful way to show that by your choice, they won more than you did).
Capability	• Demonstrate your capability and competence tangibly and humbly regarding the matter in which you want trust. • Increase your understanding of what it takes to deliver on expectations. • Obsess over finding the right person for the right job, and work to make sure that the system within which people operate is functional. • Build the firm's capability to execute strategies. • Take action on problems or with people who impede consistency of execution.
Predictability and Integrity	• Do what you said you would do, and if you cannot, explain why. • Model underpromising and overdelivering. • Explain the "whys" of decisions. • Describe the values that drive your behavior, so that others see consistency rather than randomness. • Adopt a rigorous daily process of self-examination of conscience.
Level of Communication	• Increase the frequency and candor of your communications. • Occasionally engage in non-task- or work-related relationship-building activities (lunch, a sporting event, and so on) that enable you to relate to others outside your respective roles. • Be sure the same message cascades down throughout the organization. • Hold others accountable for communication. • Emphasize listening, consultation, and support in communication. • Promote direct communication and discourage gossip.

SEVEN

Trust in Organizations

Few would disagree that organizational trust is important and useful, but the challenge lies in how to create trust and sustain it in an environment of change, risk, and uncertainty. At the heart of this challenge is the difference between treating the symptoms of distrust as opposed to addressing the systemic root causes. High-trust organizations embed trustworthiness into the very fabric of their organizational architecture and behavior, not merely in one or two places or subsystems. Nearly all of the major corporate scandals from Enron to Lehman Brothers occurred in firms that had ethics training and codes of conduct. Trust must be fundamental to how the organization operates as a whole.

Survey research that my colleagues and I conducted involving more than fifteen hundred people from twenty different companies in North America, Europe, and Asia showed that trust issues in organizations go well beyond ethics, codes of conduct, or honesty.[1] In the survey, corporate employees were asked to identify the source of their most frequently encountered trust issues at work. The following are the top five issues cited by respondents (and the percentage of respondents who mentioned each):

1. Organization change and instability (20%)
2. Lack of support for execution (19%)
3. Fairness in management, recognition, and compensation (13%)
4. Lack of communication (13%)
5. Lack of confidence in leadership and strategy (13%)

This research makes it clear that trustworthiness or its absence emanates from the basic underpinnings of how the organization operates and that building trust requires much more than ethics classes or codes of conduct.

Organizational trust exists when stakeholders—the people who have a stake in (are affected by) the actions of the firm—feel they can confidently rely on the organization to do the right thing. Stakeholders include investors, employees, suppliers, customers, and the wider communities affected by the firm. The Edelman survey results shown in Figure 7.1 show the precarious state of trust in business organizations.[2]

Surveys and interviews that I conducted from 2005 to 2010 with more than one thousand employees and executives provide a vantage point to understand what high and low trust feel like inside an organization. Those fortunate enough to work in high-trust organizations speak of them as places that are "fun," "supportive," "open," "transparent," and, above all, "successful" and "productive." In these high-trust organizations, employees exercise their ability to make decisions and take

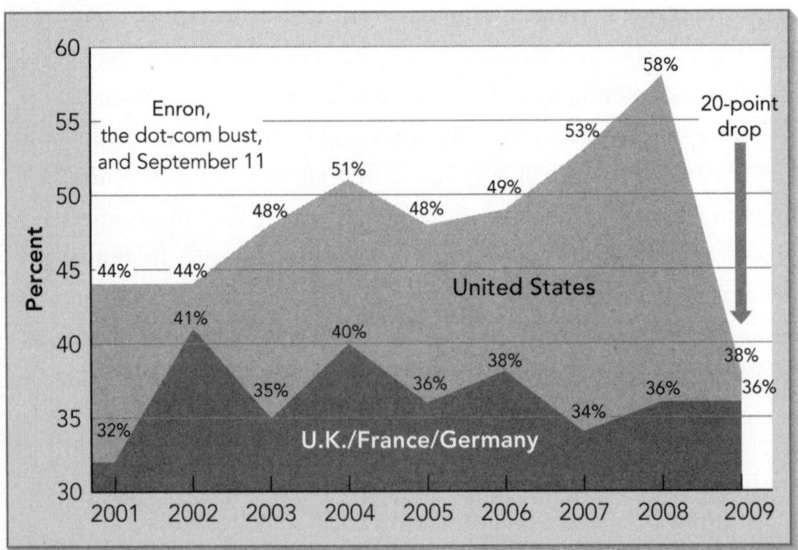

Figure 7.1 Precentage of People Who Trust Business to Do What Is Right. © Edelman, 2010. Used with permission.

risks while feeling secure that others want them to succeed. They feel that their efforts will be fairly supported and that their results will be judged fairly.

When respondents describe low-trust environments, their responses come fast and furious in what feels like a flood of cathartic emotion as they describe a "stressful," "divisive," and "unproductive" experience. The following list reflects many of the comments made by trust seminar participants describing what it is like to work in high- and low-trust environments:

High-Trust Environment	Low-Trust Environment
Fun	Stressful
Supportive	Threatening
Motivating	Careful
Challenging	Divisive
Open	Unproductive
Productive	Tense
Transparent	Secretive
Comfortable	Competitive

Given these results, it comes as no surprise that a host of empirical studies have shown that higher levels of organizational trust lead to many benefits:

- Lower negotiation costs, reduced conflict, and higher performance[3]
- Improved collaboration[4]
- More sharing of information[5]
- Higher stakeholder satisfaction[6]
- Longevity of relationships[7]
- Higher employee satisfaction and long-run stock price[8]
- Greater organizational committment, lower turnover, and higher job performance[9]

Studies of the Fortune 100 Best Companies to Work For in the United States have shown superior financial returns when compared to the S&P 500, and these results have been confirmed among the corresponding lists in Denmark, the United Kingdom, and Brazil.[10]

BUILDING ORGANIZATIONAL TRUST

Creating and sustaining a high-trust organization requires two things: (1) an understanding of the elements of organizational trustworthiness and (2) an understanding of how to embed elements of trustworthiness into the architecture of an organization. As shown in Figure 7.2, seven factors in the DTM answer the first requirement. To the degree that these seven elements of trustworthiness can be embedded in the organization, stakeholders will be likely to decide to trust. (We will look at these elements later in the chapter.)

The second requirement concerning embedding elements of trustworthiness into an organization draws on concepts of organizational design, which we can approach using a practical example. Procter & Gamble (P&G) is a global firm that has one of the most impressive records of external recognition of any corporation since 2000, including recognition by *Fortune*, Dow Jones, and others as one of the most "respected," "admired," "innovative," and "sustainable" companies.[11] Over the long term, the company has also largely escaped corporate scandals that have plagued other firms. One of the reasons for this is that P&G goes well beyond having an ethics policy or code of conduct and has embedded elements of trustworthiness into its management infrastructure and organizational processes. P&G's management infrastructure includes

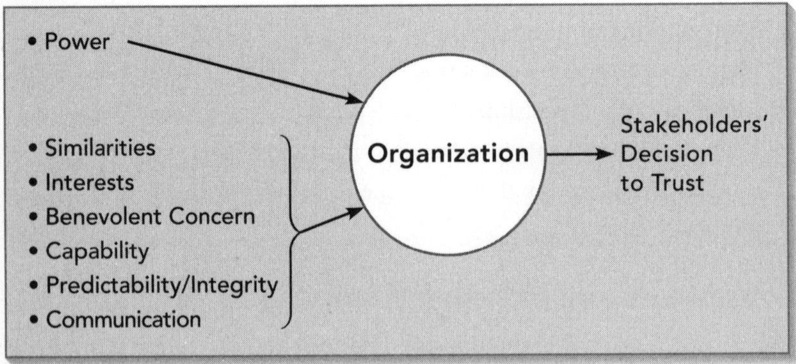

Figure 7.2 Embedding Trust in the Organization

clear strategy that is responsive to its environment, effective leadership, a culture that reinforces trust-producing values (for example, excellence and integrity), and structure and organizational systems that reinforce cooperation and adaptation. P&G also has in place world-class product development, manufacturing, distribution, marketing, and research and development processes that reliably meet internal and external stakeholder expectations. Excellence in management infrastructure and organizational processes creates the foundation of trustworthiness.

The Organizational Performance and Trust model illustrated in Figure 7.3 enables us to generalize from the P&G example to understand how to embed trustworthiness into the architecture of any organization. The model draws on the work of Burke and Litwin and Tushman and Nadler, who have developed models of how organizations function and how they change.[12] The model illustrates how developing trust with a broad range of organizational stakeholders demands effective management infrastructure (at the top of model) and effective value-added processes (at the bottom of the model). When companies like P&G embed trust-producing elements at all levels of this model, they create internal trust. When they perform reliably over time, firms earn a reputation of trust with their customers, investors, and even those representing communities of future stakeholders (that is, future generations). At world-class high-trust organizations like P&G, there is a chain of trust that runs from deep inside the organization all the way to its products on store and consumer shelves. And like all chains, this chain of trust is only as strong as its weakest link.

Customer trust can eventually lead to what marketers refer to as brand loyalty, whereby trust is assumed when, for example, we see the P&G logo. But this external trust rests on the foundation of internal trust. Toyota, which is still considered by many to be a world-class company and for many years had stellar quality and customer satisfaction ratings, learned this lesson the hard way when weaknesses in its management infrastructure led to trust issues among U.S. customers. Recalls in some parts of the world concerning vehicle acceleration were not communicated globally, putting some customers in the United States

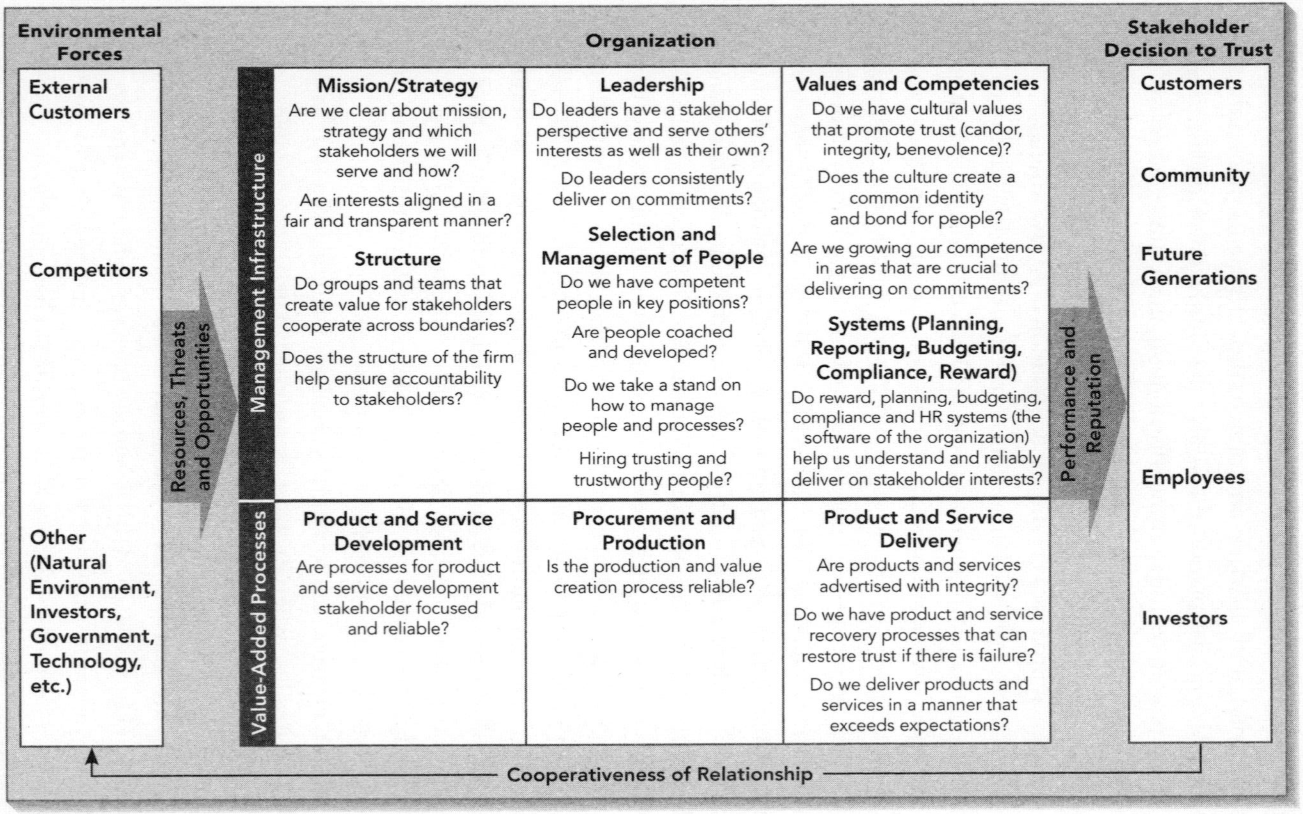

Environmental Forces

External Customers

Competitors

Other (Natural Environment, Investors, Government, Technology, etc.)

Resources, Threats and Opportunities

Organization

Management Infrastructure

Mission/Strategy
Are we clear about mission, strategy and which stakeholders we will serve and how?
Are interests aligned in a fair and transparent manner?

Structure
Do groups and teams that create value for stakeholders cooperate across boundaries?
Does the structure of the firm help ensure accountability to stakeholders?

Leadership
Do leaders have a stakeholder perspective and serve others' interests as well as their own?
Do leaders consistently deliver on commitments?

Selection and Management of People
Do we have competent people in key positions?
Are people coached and developed?
Do we take a stand on how to manage people and processes?
Hiring trusting and trustworthy people?

Values and Competencies
Do we have cultural values that promote trust (candor, integrity, benevolence)?
Does the culture create a common identity and bond for people?
Are we growing our competence in areas that are crucial to delivering on commitments?

Systems (Planning, Reporting, Budgeting, Compliance, Reward)
Do reward, planning, budgeting, compliance and HR systems (the software of the organization) help us understand and reliably deliver on stakeholder interests?

Value-Added Processes

Product and Service Development
Are processes for product and service development stakeholder focused and reliable?

Procurement and Production
Is the production and value creation process reliable?

Product and Service Delivery
Are products and services advertised with integrity?
Do we have product and service recovery processes that can restore trust if there is failure?
Do we deliver products and services in a manner that exceeds expectations?

Performance and Reputation

Stakeholder Decision to Trust

Customers

Community

Future Generations

Employees

Investors

Cooperativeness of Relationship

Figure 7.3 Organizational Performance and Trust Model

at risk. This created perceptions of trust violation (lack of transparency and concern for customer safety) among Toyota owners and the U.S. Department of Transportation.[13] Since this happened, Toyota has taken some impressive steps to change its organizational culture and infrastructure. It has increased its decentralization of decision making concerning recalls and communication of safety issues.[14]

EMBEDDING ELEMENTS OF THE DTM INTO THE ORGANIZATION

The challenge to creating a high-trust organization is installing elements of trustworthiness throughout the system. For example, creating an alignment of interests and demonstrating benevolent concern require changes in leadership behavior, culture, performance appraisals, and compensation systems that are congruent and reinforcing. Otherwise we fall victim to thinking that one intervention (an ethics program, code of conduct, change of leader, and so on) alone will cure trust issues. We will now cover the seven factors in the DTM that are essential to organizational trust and how to embed them into organizational systems.

Power and Organizational Trust

Recall that powerlessness breeds distrust. When managers are not empowered to do their jobs, one commonly sees a climate of self-protection and distrust pervade an entire organization. A high-tech company run by a control-oriented founder was typical of such organizations. The founder had a low disposition to trust and held a tight grip on the company for forty years. He had to approve every significant expenditure, frowned on collaboration, and actively pitted managers against each other. He created a corporate staff whose role was to control operations and gather information about any potential betrayals on the part of the business unit leaders. The company was successful when it was smaller, driven by the intensity of the founder and his ability to hire talented people. As the company grew, however, the founder became a bottleneck. His fear of giving his talented managers the power and autonomy to collaborate with one another made it impossible to pursue larger, more complex contracts. Eventually the board removed the founder.

In organizations where power is shared and distributed, everyone tends to feel that he or she has more influence because authority flows based on the merits of an idea or position. Survey research that I conducted at NASA in the late 1980s confirmed a strong correlation between empowerment and trust across all NASA locations.[15] This correlation is observed in other firms as well. When there is trust, you find empowerment; when there is distrust, people tend to feel powerless.

In high-trust organizations, employees feel that they can influence events. If they feel strongly about something, they have people they can talk to. Processes are available enabling them to make their views known. Meritorious points of view tend to be heard and acted on. This degree of openness gives employees an authentic sense of empowerment and vastly increases the odds that they will decide to trust the organization. They have no illusions that their company is perfect, but they have confident reliance that if they are wronged or betrayed, they will have some recourse.

Maintaining the sense that justice exists within the power structure is critical to building and maintaining trust. Bill was a senior vice president at a $7 billion retail company. He had a very tight relationship with the CEO, with whom he had worked from the start of the company, and everyone knew it. This was a problem for Bill's direct reports, however, because Bill was violating company policy and engaging in abusive behavior. All of Bill's direct reports were afraid to tell the CEO, fearing that his loyalty to Bill would exceed his commitment to company policy.

Torn about what to do, Bill's direct reports confided in a management consultant during a trust seminar. They expressed concerns because they had raised these issues directly with Bill in the past, with no change in behavior. Now they feared that if they went over Bill's head to the CEO with their complaints, they, not Bill, might get the axe.

They eventually decided to trust the CEO, however, and several of them approached him as a group and detailed Bill's abusive behavior.

Ideas for Embedding Trust Through Power Sharing

- Create an empowering culture
- Promote managers who share power and retrain or demote micro-managers
- Engage employees and prove that you will listen and act
- Use process techniques to provide voice, such as upward feedback, open door policies, and employee surveys
- Use authoritarian decision making only when it enhances trust (for example, when it avoids unproductive conflict among people or creates necessary speed in decisions); use participative or collaborative decision making most other times

After discussing the matter with the management consultant, who confirmed the accuracy of the abusive behavior reports, the CEO had a heart-to-heart talk with his good friend Bill. They both agreed that it was in the best interests of the company for Bill to retire.

Word quickly got around the company that the CEO had backed his managers, and the company's values, over the interests of his longtime friend. He had acted in the best interest of his employees and other stakeholders by removing an abusive senior executive. The CEO's reputation was burnished as someone who could be relied on to "do the right thing" for the company. The story left other employees feeling empowered: they felt they could trust that they would be safe if they themselves looked out for the company's interests.

Similarities and Organizational Trust

In high-trust organizations, employees share a strong bond of identity. Goldman Sachs, Google, Microsoft, Ernst and Young, Nordstrom, the Mayo Clinic, and other high-trust firms on the Fortune 100 Best Companies to Work For list provide their employees with an invaluable sense of pride and common purpose. Membership in such organizations can feel like a privilege, which in turn imbues members with a sense of duty to uphold the organization's defining values. When these values include trust-promoting principles (excellence, empowerment, integrity, fairness, transparency), they enhance trust from the top to the bottom of the Organizational Performance and Trust model. Members' bonds of loyalty to those values, and their willingness to spread the values to new members, will help make trust compelling and contagious.

Google's ten corporate values define the meaning of membership and promote trust:[16]

1. Focus on the user and all else will follow.
2. It's best to do one thing really, really well.
3. Fast is better than slow.
4. Democracy on the web works.
5. You don't need to be at your desk to need an answer.
6. You can make money without doing evil.
7. There's always more information out there.
8. The need for information crosses all borders.
9. You can be serious without a suit.
10. Great just isn't good enough.

People at Google are passionate about users, love a fast-paced work environment, and are generally obsessed with the democracy of information. Google's announcement that it was considering leaving the China market due to censorship and attempts to hack into human rights advocates' accounts reflected its intense commitment to its corporate values.

> These attacks and the surveillance they have uncovered—combined with the attempts over the past year to further limit free speech on the web—have led us to conclude that we should review the feasibility of our business operations in China. We have decided we are no longer willing to continue censoring our results on Google.cn, and so over the next few weeks we will be discussing with the Chinese government the basis on which we could operate an unfiltered search engine

within the law, if at all. We recognize that this may well mean having to shut down Google.cn, and potentially our offices in China.[17]

At high-trust firms, underlying dimensions of trust have become embedded into the culture from years of rewarding these behaviors and penalizing people when they violate these principles. Over time, this leads to a form of social engineering whereby these values become deeply embedded expectations for how members of the institution will behave. As an example, MITRE has a carefully crafted socialization process for new employees. The company spends a great deal of time making sure that the on-boarding process for hiring new people works effectively. The security department, the information center, and the help desk all send welcome emails and make phone calls to ensure that everything is working for the new employee. Great care is taken to assimilate new employees into the high-trust culture and to nurture their sense of identity as part of MITRE.[18] At Microsoft, new employees attend a course after their second month on the job where they can discuss their experience so far and help them find their fit in the company.[19]

Zappos, an online retailer, makes hiring people who share the company's values so important that it even pays people to quit if they don't believe in what the company stands for. There is a standing offer on the table to all new employees during their four weeks of initial training: "If you quit today, we will pay you for the amount of time you've worked, plus we will offer you a $2,000 bonus." If the employee takes Zappos up on the offer, management knows that he or she was a bad fit.[20] Zappos rewards people for opting out when they can't get excited about the company values, knowing that it would cost the company far more than $2,000 in the long run to keep an employee who wasn't a good fit or committed to the firm's values. When companies are able to get their members to buy into and demonstrate the right values, they create a supportive environment that is ripe for collaboration and trust. Although leaders are critical to effecting this social engineering, once the culture has been embedded, it is maintained and perpetuated by the employees themselves.

Ideas for Embedding Trust Through Shared Values and Identity

- Periodically conduct a values clarification exercise (for board and senior management team)
- Become a values-driven organization
- Take socialization very seriously and reinforce it with leadership behavior, rewards, and recognition systems
- Foster pride in in-group identity
- Avoid excessively loose cultures that lack meaning and identity
- Adapt and adjust values carefully and deliberately to ensure relevance

Alignment of Interests and Organizational Trust

Where interests are aligned in an organization, there will tend to be more trust; however, achieving alignment in complex organizations can be a challenge. Is manufacturing aligned with marketing? What about alignment between headquarters and the business units? How about up and down the hierarchy? Complex organizations are often a chaotic network of individual and group interests that compete and cooperate for recognition, resources, and power all the time. In this chaotic network, decisions get made that help some people and groups and hurt others. The outcomes of these decisions signal whose interests matter most, but the process also signals to people who matters enough to be included.

At its core, the alignment of interests begins with a philosophy of the firm: fundamental judgments are made about why the firm exists (purpose and mission) and its obligations to stakeholders (customers, shareholders, employees, communities). Trade-offs are difficult to make without clarity of values. Imagine that everyone in your family had some urgent personal need that required more money than you had. What would you do? What and who would receive money? When you can't have it all, you are forced to make trade-offs. How you make those trade-offs determines who should trust you. If you are not clear about what you value most, it is hard to make decisions and hard for others to determine whose interests you will serve.

A classic case demonstrating the importance of clarity of values occurred in 1982 when Johnson & Johnson (J&J) faced a crisis with its Tylenol pain reliever.[21] Bottles of Tylenol, the company's most reputable brand, were found laced with cyanide due to an error that occurred outside of J&J. The company chose to recall, at a cost of $100 million, all Tylenol from stores across the country. At the time, the FDA did not want the company to pull the product for fear of creating a panic. J&J's chairman, James Burke, ordered the recall anyway. Burke believed he needed to follow J&J's forty-year-old credo that customers come first, employees second, communities third, and shareholders last. To this day, J&J leadership is very explicit that the purpose of this credo is to guide decision making throughout the organization.

Achieving brutal clarity about a hierarchy of values around which to align interests requires a good deal of dialogue among the board and senior management. Very few boards have processes in place to produce the depth and clarity of values that exist in high-trust firms like SAS, whose CEO Jim Goodnight lost millions of dollars when he and the rest of the board and management team chose not to go public because they felt it would adversely affect the culture that had been created.[22]

There are a variety of different approaches to developing a set of organizational values. A "stakeholder" approach suggests that the firm is a coalition of interest groups (employees, stockholders, customers, debtors, communities, future generations, and the environment) and that the organization should consider these interests fairly in making decisions. The "shareholder" approach suggests that the firm exists to maximize the wealth of its owners, whose interests should be primary. Increasingly, firms are recognizing the risks and difficult sustainability of the shareholder primacy model and are adopting the broader stakeholder approach. These firms are engaging in more discussions to sort through unique, joint, and conflicting interests in order to sustain the commitment of a more diverse set of stakeholders. An excellent example of this is McDonald's, which through its partnership with the Environmental Defense Fund since 1989 replaced polystyrene foam with paper and made many other changes to serve joint interests.[23] Techniques of integrative negotiation are helpful in this process. Whatever approach is chosen, the key point is that interests cannot be aligned properly without clarity of values and mission.

There are two dimensions of every major decision that stakeholders use to infer the firm's values: the *outcome* of the decision and the *process* of the decision (how it got made). Regarding outcomes, when AzKoNobel, a Netherlands-based paint and chemical company, announced that 50 percent of the bonus of six hundred of its managers would be based on sustainability (reduction of greenhouse gas emissions, water consumption, waste and energy inefficiencies, and employee injuries) as measured by its ranking on the Dow Jones Sustainability Index, this sent a clear message concerning company values. Similarly, John Thain's decision at Merrill Lynch to spend $1.2 million to redecorate his office suggested that the company's highest value was status and luxury for those at the top, rather than frugality with shareholders' money.[24]

But the process of decision making, particularly perceived fairness, is a major factor affecting the alignment of interests and organizational trust. For example, when a Fortune 500 company had to make a decision concerning which of five plants it needed to close, the company formed a task force with representation from each of the plants and a number of functional groups. The sponsor of the task force was a senior executive who instructed the group to make a recommendation to the executive team about how to reduce capacity and cut costs. The formation of this task force was promoted and discussed in the quarterly employee publication. Employees were given the names and contact information of the task force members who represented them and were encouraged to seek out these people to ask questions or provide opinions. The group studied the question over a three-month period and presented their recommendations to management. Management then made a decision and held town hall meetings throughout the company to explain their decision to close one of the plants. Although many employees did not like the reduction in force or the shrinking of the company, they all supported the decision, appreciated being consulted, and expressed high trust in the process and the company.

When an organization uses what is considered a fair process in its decision making, stakeholders feel more trust and confidence that their interests will be considered. Stakeholders commonly consider three elements of decision making essential to fair process.[25] First, they are engaged in the process and offered the opportunity to provide input. Second, they are reassured that their opinions have been considered. Third, when the decision is made, it is clearly communicated, and expectations are clarified. Fair process does not require that all stakeholders be involved in every part of every decision. It doesn't mean that enormous efforts are dedicated to justifying or apologizing for decisions. Fair process means that reasonable attempts are made to respect stakeholders' interests throughout the course of decision making. These three elements create transparency in decision making and enhance the degree to which there is likely to be alignment of interests and trust.

For most companies, many important decisions are made through the strategic planning process; it presents an opportunity to align interests and enhance trust. Ensuring that members perceive fair process in goal alignment requires thoughtful strategies for involving people and communicating the "what" and "why" of strategies. High-trust companies have clear methods of delineating superordinate goals and creating alignment among the goals of interdependent groups. Alignment is driven down to functional and operational levels, where priorities and resource allocations are negotiated and "synched up." In high-trust companies, the strategic and operational planning processes are rigorous so that there is less confusion about whose interests should be served and why.

Three critical elements of the strategic planning process of high-trust organizations are (1) the systematic involvement of people in planning, (2) robust and candid negotiation of priorities across functions and business units, and (3) rigorous translation and communication of priorities and goals across hierarchical, functional, and geographical boundaries.

Ideas for Embedding Trust Through Aligning Interests

- Create an alignment map that illustrates links to company values
- Expect leaders to translate strategy
- Hold leaders and their people accountable for articulating alignment down the line
- Make fair and transparent decisions and connect them to company values
- Involve people and communicate the "whys" of strategy and decisions
- Hold management accountable for being stewards of stakeholder interests
- Define the values of the firm that will guide decisions and trade-offs

Systematic involvement means that all stakeholders have some role in the process of developing strategic priorities, but it also entails avoiding the paralysis and lethargy that can ensue when everyone has to be involved in everything. Rigorous translation comes when the firm has an effective communication process to deploy strategies and goals throughout the organization. The Principal Financial Group produces what its leaders call the Big Map, which they use to communicate to employees where they fit into the major strategies and initiatives that are going on at the company. Alignment can even be a daily discipline. For example, at Alston and Bird, a global law firm, all departments participate in a ten-minute daily "top echelon" meeting to make sure there is a focus on common goals.[26] These companies have succeeded in translating the mission and strategy right down to entry-level employees and helped people see and feel how interests are aligned.

Benevolent Concern and Organizational Trust

When stakeholders believe that the organization cares about them, they will be more likely to trust. It is interesting to ask: When do organizations demonstrate altruism for stakeholders that goes beyond self-interest? During the global financial crisis, the accounting firm PricewaterhouseCoopers, like other companies, was hurting. Many clients were desperately trying to reduce costs and demanding lower audit fees. Consulting fees were drying up. Many times the question of whether the company should conduct layoffs came up. Each time it opted to reduce other expenses, and partners took less income. The firm was one of the few that largely protected staff during the downturn. At great sacrifice and risk, it demonstrated its concern for staff.

Early on during the war in Iraq, American soldiers were being killed by roadside bombs at an alarming rate. Generals in the field were clamoring for a solution, but the purchasing bureaucracy in the Pentagon couldn't seem to move any faster. Knowing that every day more soldiers were dying, a few large defense contractors in the United States put millions of dollars at risk without contracts from the Department of Defense to speed production of mine-resistant vehicles and get them to Iraq to save soldiers' lives.[27]

A cynical interpretation of these examples is that the companies were acting out of long-term self-interest, not altruism. This may be true, and when companies do think long term about stakeholders, perhaps altruism is more often aligned with their interests than is opportunism. Nevertheless, whether they are acting out of long-term self-interest or out of altruism, when companies sacrifice for the welfare of others, it creates goodwill and contributes to developing trust throughout the organization.

A lack of benevolence damages trust. I witnessed this firsthand at a global investment bank from 2005 to 2009, when a new CEO tried to change a venerable firm that some suggested had become a clubby but underperforming bank. He aggressively changed leaders throughout the company and initiated major layoffs. The stock price rose, and the board decided to award the CEO a generous bonus. In what would become a glaring problem for the bank, the announcement of this huge bonus hit the press at the same time as the company's announcement that thousands more would lose their jobs and that the company had just

Ideas for Embedding Trust Through Benevolent Concern

- Consider benevolence to stakeholders in strategy and mission deliberations
- Practice serving others over self, especially if you are in a high-power position
- Offer employees noncoerced options to team and do charitable work
- Focus more on long-term stakeholder relationships

made record profits. Even the most hardened capitalists and proponents of maximization of shareholder value within the firm questioned the fairness of the firm's decisions. Many at the firm would later report that it was at that moment that they realized they had better look out for themselves because the bank would not. There had been too many decisions that showed a remarkable insensitivity to employees' needs and interests. Many of the best people left, and eventually the CEO was forced out when the stock tanked. At the end, the CEO left the bank a very rich man, at least in financial terms.[28]

Every decision an organization makes serves someone's interests. Powerful players usually do not have to rely on benevolent concern as a source of leverage, so benevolent concern is more important to those with less power. If the organization says it cares about employees, shareholders, and customers but acts to enrich management at their expense, it invites distrust. Ask the laid-off employees and the poorer investors in this investment bank.

Capability and Organizational Trust

In their book *Execution,* Larry Bossidy and Ram Charan describe the essence of capability- or competence-based trust in organizations.[29] They suggest that the discipline of execution includes leaders who are on top of their businesses, a clear strategic plan, budgetary and operating plans that allocate resources and accountability, candor throughout the firm, and rewarding the doers and dealing with the poor performers.

Some companies deliver reliably on their commitments because they are clear about stakeholder needs, they are careful not to overpromise, and they have reliable people, processes, and structures to consistently perform. Others invite distrust and lack of confidence because they perform sometimes but let stakeholders down at other times. Consider the example of two companies in the same industry. They were both retailers, one with stores on the East Coast, the other with stores on the West Coast. In planning meetings, the top executive team of the West Coast company would agree to take certain actions, but when they would meet again, it was rare to find that they had actually delivered on their commitments. Excuses would be offered and accepted. Their stores reflected this same lack of consistency. Some were clean and offered friendly service; others were dirty and had rude employees.

With the East Coast company, things were very different. Everyone knew that when the team agreed to do something, it would be done, unless some rare circumstances came up. This same attention to detail and consistent execution were evident in their stores. They were universally clean, and they executed the same high standards of customer care.

In the early 1980s, both companies were about the same size and earning similar profits. By 2010, the East Coast company had grown to be twice as large and four times as profitable as the West Coast company. More important for our discussion, in customer and employee surveys, the East Coast company earned higher trust and satisfaction scores. Both companies wanted to be successful and manifested benevolent concern toward stakeholders, but only one company backed up its good intentions with consistent competence.

Building organizational capability is complicated and takes time, which explains why some organizations become trusted and others want to but just can't seem to get there. The Organizational Performance and Trust model (Figure 7.3) can help in thinking through the steps to capability-based trust. First, we have to know the challenges that

Ideas for Embedding Trust Through Capability

- Become great at executing strategy
- Develop a culture in which you deliver on promises
- Continuously upgrade and improve capability
- Build capability in advance of demands
- Be brutally honest about weaknesses
- Make it a religion to conduct after-action reviews at the conclusion of projects

confront the organization and the interests of the stakeholders of the firm. We gain this information from an effective strategic plan and planning process. Next, we must have the management infrastructure and processes in place to deliver on commitments to stakeholders. Creating the requisite capability in management infrastructure and organizational processes requires a candid and rigorous assessment of the organization and its ability to navigate its environment. QuikTrip conducts such an assessment annually by talking to employees and customers and using senior management and the board to take a tough look at whether the organization is up to the task. The firm never stops trying to improve and is brutally honest, with no sacred cows. Employees and customers have confidence in the organization's capability, and it shows up in low turnover and high customer loyalty.

Predictability, Integrity, and Organizational Trust

It is interesting to ask how it is that some companies offer stakeholders coherence and predictability whereas others seem to say one thing but do another. Even well-intended organizations can preach one thing and practice another. For example, at a board meeting of a nonprofit organization that helps children, the people in charge of fundraising suggested some heart-tugging advertising to encourage people to give more during the year-end push. The problem was that what they wanted to advertise was not really what this nonprofit delivered. There was a mismatch between what they said to donors and what they said among themselves regarding their mission.

High-integrity companies have ways of catching these lapses. It seems that in recent years, as the pace of change has quickened and as disruptive innovation reinvents industry boundaries and assumptions, being consistent and predictable has gotten harder. High-trust companies ensure their integrity by employing firm-wide values-based management.

Publix Super Markets, a Florida-based supermarket chain, has won awards for high trust and consistent customer service.[30] According to the American Customer Satisfaction Index, the chain since 1994 has ranked among the best supermarkets in the United States when it comes to satisfying its customers. Even more impressive is that it is an employee-owned supermarket, and the shareholder return for these employees significantly exceeds the averages of the S&P 500 and a peer group of supermarkets. The company's mission is to be the premier food retailer in the world. This is listed on its Web site and in its training materials, but, much more important, employees in stores consistently demonstrate this mission in a way that shows they are invested in it.[31] Publix has managed to achieve excellent customer service by embedding into its structure a coherent set of values around serving customers, and ensuring buy-in among its employees. The mission is the company's true north, not just a slogan.

In low-integrity organizations, behavior that runs counter to espoused organizational values is tolerated or overlooked. The culture in these companies is at odds with the espoused one. Employees find this incoherence discomforting. They begin to lose trust in senior management, who promote one set of values while allowing another to prevail. At one such company, the salespeople operating globally knew that what really mattered—regardless of the company's ten-page code of ethics—was making your sales numbers. This company had a senior ethics officer who was marginalized over the years because the top management did not have the courage to reconcile the firm's espoused values with the behavior of its win-at-any-cost sales culture. The ethics officer was not surprised when it was later found that U.S. corruption laws were circumvented when salespeople used bribes to obtain contracts. Contrast this example with that of General Electric (GE), which has demonstrated its willingness to terminate even high-performing, commercially successful managers who violate the company's code of conduct.[32]

Companies, like people, are imperfect and get off track, so integrity over the long haul requires an ongoing self-examination and discernment process to make sure that what is preached is actually practiced. GE has people at various levels in the organization who examine ethical standards and update GE's code. It also has a "common-sense review" to examine its adequacy concerning disclosures.[33] Both GE and American Express have ombudspersons at locations around the world to provide employees a risk-free way to voice concerns about violations of company principles.

Google uses company meetings, annual surveys, and employee blogs to ensure that there are opportunities to catch violations of its standards. Beaverbrooks Jewelry in the United Kingdom trains people to "tell the total truth faster" to promote productive candor in the workplace. Microsoft Europe has enhanced its ability to ensure that deeds match words by embedding openness and honesty in its culture. Granite Construction used a "culture audit" to assess the degree to which it was practicing what it preached, particularly concerning sustainability and its Project Enduring Legacy, the goal of which was to move the construction industry to a more environmentally friendly way of operating.[34]

Because it is impossible for people, groups, or companies to be "perfectly" trustworthy, a company that truly acknowledges a betrayal and repairs it will build confidence. Although much maligned in the press and by Washington as the poster child of Wall Street's excess after the financial crisis of 2009, just two years later, Goldman Sachs drew on its core values of anticipating change, excellence, and protecting its reputation to conduct what some researchers labeled the most comprehensive and transparent trust reform process of any bank after the global financial crisis.[35] At the May 7, 2010 shareholders meeting,

Ideas for Embedding Trust Through Predictability and Integrity

- Measure the degree to which your espoused culture is practiced
- Practice values-based management
- Make honoring one's word a central part of the culture
- Create mechanisms to confront hypocrisy

Goldman Sachs announced the formation of a business standards committee to reexamine and clarify client relationships and responsibilities, review how the firm identifies and manages conflicts, examine how the firm's public disclosure and financial reporting can be improved to enhance transparency, and examine how to strengthen training and professional development to reinforce personal accountability and professional ethics. The committee would report to the board, and its report would be made public. The ability to recover after a failure, even a trust failure, is an increasingly important aspect of organizational resilience in a changing world where perfection is not possible.

Communication and Organizational Trust

One fairly reliable sign of a high-trust company is that it overcommunicates. A major element in creating confident reliance on the organization is an ongoing dialogue in which stakeholders understand the "why" behind the firm's intentions and actions and develop realistic expectations for the future. Investors, employees, and customers won't feel that they can trust if they are left in the dark.

High-trust companies deploy important messages throughout the hierarchy, and people hear about them directly from senior management or from their direct supervisor. Leaders take seriously their role as translators of critical information in the organization. A failure to communicate critical messages to employees is simply unacceptable. They also hold employees accountable for informing themselves about the organization's plans; that is, communication is a two-way street.

Google has a weekly TGIF event where senior managers get people together and present news on events that have happened that week. The most important part of a TGIF session at Google is the question-and-answer period. Senior management wants employees to know that they should feel comfortable asking management anything. At Genentech, managers in the technology group hold "office hours" reminiscent of their academic heritage, during which employees can walk in and engage with managers. When the organization takes the time and effort to ensure timely and full communication to stakeholders, it demonstrates two other elements that are just as essential to organizational trust: respect for stakeholder interests and benevolent concern.

Griffin Hospital in Derby, Connecticut, builds trust among stakeholders with a robust set of communication techniques that include

- Annual "State of the Hospital" employee meetings
- Monthly leadership conferences attended by the top sixty managers
- Monthly department meetings for purposes of sharing information from the leadership conference
- A daily online newsletter
- A published bimonthly newsletter
- Periodic letters from the hospital president to employees' homes on topical issues
- A community newsletter

Through excellent communication, the hospital had established a relationship of trust and respect with employees and the community. Then, in November 2001, Griffin's leadership was put to the test when the hospital was the site of an anthrax-related death. Patrick Charmel, the president of Griffin, came under pressure from FBI investigators to withhold information from employees and the public about the incident. Because Charmel knew that this would breach the trust he had developed with his workers, he chose to deny the FBI's request for silence. Charmel assembled two hundred shift personnel and disclosed what he knew about the incident. He was aware that the

Ideas for Embedding Trust Through Communication

- Overcommunicate
- Hold leaders accountable for helping people understand the "why" behind company values and decisions
- Use multiple media channels
- Put senior management in the room with people
- Encourage "ask anything" sessions
- Do not shoot messengers

news would leak out to the media and that the FBI wouldn't be pleased, but with courage and open communication, Charmel emerged from the crisis with increased trust among employees and his community.[36]

Given the dynamic nature of the economy, customers, markets, and technology, the challenge to building a high-trust organization is formidable. Sustainable organizational trust requires much more than clever advertising or attractive pay packages. It requires systematically embedding elements of the DTM into the organization's strategy, culture, processes, leadership, and systems. It takes years of effective leadership, development, and change to build such a high-trust, high-performing organization. Fortunately, there are examples of firms that have done so. With an understanding both of how organizational systems function and change and of the dimensions of the DTM, firms can build trustworthiness and create a virtuous cycle that increases not only social capital but also financial capital.

EIGHT

Building Trust Within Teams

Have you ever been dependent on a group or team of people in which there was no trust? You knew that others would affect your success or failure, but they could not be counted on. Deliverables were late, of poor quality—or not completed at all. I hope that you have also been part of a group or team in which there was high trust. You knew others had your back, which relieved some of the stress. You didn't have to be the hero every day; someone would always step up and help the group succeed. Less stress, and teammates with whom to celebrate the success—what could be better?

Organizations create working groups, task forces, and teams to accomplish goals that require diverse talents and capabilities. Collaboration within groups allows for specialization, the division of labor, and coordination, but attempting to collaborate without trust can be a nightmare. All high-functioning teams, whether they compete on soccer fields or corporate C-suites, depend on some form of trust for their success. Members of high-trust teams share information easily, extend support to one another, take up difficult tasks required by the group, and waste less time worrying that other team members will let them down.

The discussion of trust in this chapter is generally applicable to groups ranging in size from three to twenty people. A great deal of the work in organizations takes place in groups of this size, yet their small size ensures that group effectiveness is highly reliant on individual personalities and interpersonal relations. Unlike larger organizations, a team can be vulnerable to a few bad actors who, in short time, change its dynamics and erode trust. This makes the task of building trust in groups very challenging—and potentially very rewarding.

The terms *group* and *team* are often used interchangeably, but working in a true team requires much greater focus on trust issues than working in a group. The word *team* implies a high degree of interdependence among members. One definition of teams is that they are bound by a common measure of success and failure; they win or lose together.[1] By this standard, many top executive teams are groups and not teams, because they tend to their respective areas of responsibility in a fairly independent manner. Real teams have more interdependence, integration, and common identity than do working groups. Members of working groups may aspire to work as a team, but doing so requires more attention to how the team functions as a whole rather than to the work of its individual members. This requires more cohesion, cooperation, interdependence, and trust.[2]

The process of building trust within a team can be uncomfortable for some members, yet it often yields surprising and unexpected benefits. A common exercise in team building is to ask each member of the team to express publicly what he or she "appreciates most" about each of the other team members. This exercise proved to be enormously helpful for the top executive team at one particularly high-performing company because it revealed to them that they were a working group and not a real team. This team had an unspoken rule: "If you do something well, you should know, and if you do something wrong, you'll hear about it." Once a supportive trust-building environment was created through the appreciation exercise during a team-building event, one of the executives offered a stark revelation about himself. Earlier that year, he said, the stress of his job had brought him close to a nervous breakdown. The rest of the group was shocked. None had seen any signs of his suffering. In fact, most regarded him as the most competent and self-confident member of the group.

After the group got over their shock, the members had to confront what this revelation said about them all as a team. This member had been burdened almost to the breaking point earlier that year, yet he had not asked for help, probably because he had expected none. They all realized in that moment that they were not really a team in the full sense of the word. Instead, they operated as a group of generally independent executives with fairly low cohesion and social support. They trusted each other to some degree, but not enough to be personally vulnerable with each other, which is the kind of support that is felt in a real team. Once the strongest executive in this group felt that he could trust his teammates enough to confide in them about his emotional crisis, the others became more willing and able to express vulnerability and request help. Over the next two years, this group of C-suite executives became a real team.

TYPES OF TEAMS AND FORMS OF TRUST

Golf and tennis teams operate differently than football or basketball teams, so they require different group dynamics. The same is true with different types of work teams. Trust building within a team should start with a careful consideration of the type of team involved. In some groups, trust is vital (there is a lot at stake, and vulnerability exists); in others, it is of less consequence (the stakes are low, and there are marginal or temporary members). It is important to understand the answer to such questions as: *Why has the team been formed? How long will it be together? What is the nature of the interdependence among members? How critical is the task of the team? How much will success and failure affect team members and their stakeholders?* Thinking through these issues will help the team leader build the kind of trust that will be most helpful and avoid overkill—trying to create high trust when it is not needed and nobody has the time or desire to build it. Teams can vary in at least four ways that are relevant to trust:

1. Life span
    - Teams with long life spans, like top executive teams, typically need to share information and coordinate so that trust helps performance.

- Because teams with long life spans have more experiences together, they are more likely to come into conflict; periodic retreats or meetings may be needed for intensive relationship development and (if needed) repair.
- Teams with short life spans are often less invested in trust building, but if risk taking and interdependence are critical, trust may need to be accelerated.

2. Task interdependence and criticality
   - When the overall team task is highly critical and uncertain, trust among members is also more critical.
   - When interdependence among members is high, trust is critical.
   - When there is low specialization and interdependence, trust building may be less critical.
3. Member identification
   - When team members are temporary or marginal (because they are members of other teams), violations of trust will be more difficult to penalize.
   - When members are intensely identified with the team, cohesion within the team may increase, and exclusion of outsiders may erode trust outside the team.
4. Location
   - Teams with co-located members can build and repair trust more easily.
   - Virtual teams require a more deliberate trust-building process centered around communication practices and making careful use of the few occasions where members are physically together.
   - Virtual teams are at more risk when they have members who are not trusting or not trustworthy.
   - Virtual teams require more structure and attention to communication and to building and maintaining relationships.

THE DTM FACTORS MOST CRITICAL TO TRUST WITHIN TEAMS

Once we have understood the nature of the team and the degree and type of trust that may improve performance, we can begin to embed some appropriate elements of trust into the team, as depicted in the model in Figure 8.1 and discussed in the remainder of this chapter.

Trustor Dispositional Factors: Risk Tolerance, Adjustment, and Power

Taking all three trustor factors together helps us understand trust within the team from the perspective of an individual team member. Each person who joins the team comes to the trust decision with a slightly different perspective. Each team member varies with regard to risk tolerance, adjustment, and perceived power. There is the reticent team member, the dominant team member, and the team member who follows the trend of the group. What is important to recognize is that

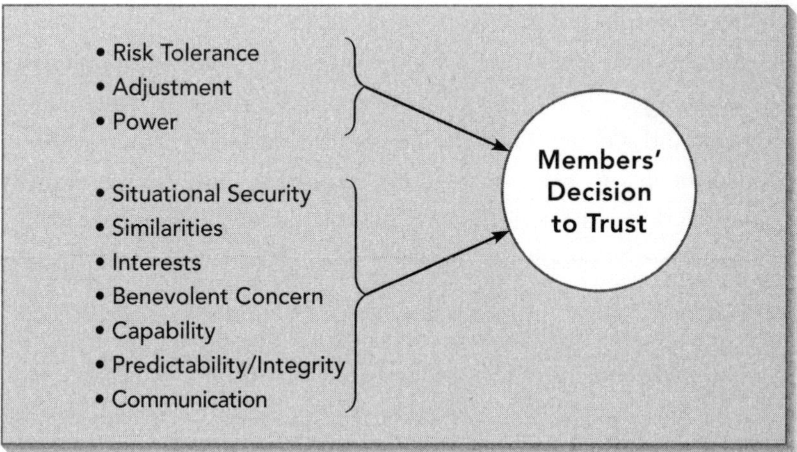

Figure 8.1 Embedding Trust in Teams

each team member may need more or fewer assurances within the team to feel comfortable trusting others.

A team leader hoping to build high trust in the team must have a sense of the members and what they may need for trust. Low-power people who are risk averse and low in adjustment will struggle more in trusting others and making themselves vulnerable to the group. In such cases, it is very helpful to have a leader or other person in the group who serves as "caretaker" for the group. Ensuring that all members have a means of contributing and are supported enables a group dynamic that contributes to trust and positive synergy among the team members. Often the people who are most helpful in building trust and making the team work well are never fully appreciated for this key role, because the focus is on individual performance rather than on how the team as a whole is functioning. Productivity would in many cases be increased if leaders focused less on individual stars and more on people who make star teams. It is naïve to expect all team members to trust on the same schedule and with the same type of assurances, so members who can guide and facilitate trust within the team are invaluable. Conversely, members who erode group trust and synergy, even when they are great individual contributors, can hurt overall team performance.

In teams that have complex interdependent tasks, team members who cannot come to a decision to trust will impair the development of team trust and synergy. Most often teams are formed to gather a diverse group of talents to work on complex problems. Because the team is deliberately formed for diversity, the team assigns different roles and responsibilities to people on the basis of their knowledge and talents. So the subject matter expert (SME) in marketing does marketing, and the manufacturing SME does manufacturing. The team must therefore trust members who are leading their area. If we ask the marketing guru to justify every action he takes in marketing, then we are forcing the team to be marketing experts, and we are not leveraging his expertise. In high-performing teams, the marketing person brings to the group only those issues that he thinks are important enough to warrant some consultation with the whole group. But what happens if someone on the team simply cannot trust any SMEs?

Ideas for Embedding Trust Through Trustor Disposition

- Create a group dynamic that encourages social support
- Reward team members who make others more effective due to increased comfort in the group
- Populate the team with people who can trust (unless suspicion is essential to the team's task)

It is sometimes the case that the division of labor and building of trust break down not because of the incompetence of a team member but because of an inability to trust on the part of another team member. The team member with the low disposition to trust always wants to know what the other team members are doing and "help them do their job." The inability to trust stalls the team development process. For this reason, team leaders should be careful about having too many people with a low disposition to trust on the team, and they should be cautious about putting them in leadership roles. It may be productive to have a skeptic, or the devil's advocate, on the team, but if this orientation permeates the entire group dynamic, trust development will stall.

Situational Security

We established in Chapter Four that increased risk makes the trust decision more difficult. The "common enemy" scenario is an exception: external threat to a group can actually promote internal trust.[3] In its most frequently occurring form, a team of people begin to confide in each other and support each other more because they agree that "we all hate" the same person or group. The object of scorn can be a team member, a competitor, or even the team leader. The classic film *The Caine Mutiny* depicted such a form of within-group trust and cohesion; the crew's common goal was to rid itself of the abusive captain of the ship.

To the degree that the external threat is real, using it to enhance trust is effective and often leads to good trust decisions by members of the group, because not trusting in such a situation can be riskier. This is

Ideas for Embedding Trust Through Situational Security

- When an external threat is real, use it to build cohesion
- Locate risk at the group level more than at the individual level
- Manage anxiety of group members and offer more social support when situational security is low

certainly the case among military units in a time of war. If team members are imagining or exaggerating the threat, it may be a manipulation that can induce bad trust decisions, causing group members to follow unreliable agents. This is a mechanism often employed by leaders of cults.[4]

In many respects, forming a real team is an excellent way to increase situational security by sharing risk and increasing social support. This underscores why for risky and critical tasks, having a high-trust real team is invaluable.

Similarities

Trust building through shared identity is very common among teams. In fact, an entire industry exists of manufacturers of clothing, coffee mugs, plaques, and other symbols celebrating common team experiences. These symbols are displayed as a sign of exclusivity, solidarity, and pride. When bonds of identity are strong within a group, they enhance trust through a shared sense of pride in membership, desire to maintain in-group status, and unspoken understanding that betraying a teammate would be met with sanctions if not expulsion. As we will see in the next chapter on trust across groups, sometimes this cohesion can be misplaced and leads to exclusion of other key members and groups that are necessary for overall success.

Aligned Interests

Certainly you have heard the expression "There is no 'I' in team." This is false. In every team, there are people, and people's individual

Ideas for Embedding Trust Through Similarities

- Make it mean something to be on the team (identity, values, pride)
- Develop a limited number of core values that are rewarded and that cannot be violated without some penalty
- Manage in-group cohesion so that it does not prevent adapting to critical externalities that could threaten productivity or survival

needs, interests, and personalities do not evaporate when they join a group. The truth is much more interesting. In most teams, there is a complex interplay between individual interests, subgroup interests, and the interests of the team as a whole. In the best teams, there is a melding process whereby members develop collective interests that coexist with individual interests. Team leaders must facilitate team members' willingness to integrate self-interest with group interests for the good of the whole. The team leader must encourage members to make trade-offs among these interests so as to facilitate the work of the team.

One of the most important tasks of the team leader is to facilitate a process whereby team members become clear about and accept the goals of the team. This does not mean that team members do not advocate for their agenda or interests. Rather, it means that they remain open to adjusting to the will of the group and have the integrity to leave the group if they cannot support its ends. To stay in a group and be unable to support its decisions invites distrust.

During a team-building exercise among C-level executives at one major company, a vice president of operations made the observation that one of his colleagues, the general counsel, did not always participate in decision making and then frequently failed to support decisions that they had made as a team. The general counsel replied that his role required him to be independent of the team, that he was duty-bound to the board of directors and exempt from certain team expectations.

The exercise exposed how the general counsel saw himself: as an outsider with interests that were not necessarily aligned with the rest of the team. After this meeting, the CEO began some candid conversations with the general counsel. Within six months, the CEO had decided to replace him. The new general counsel was more proficient in navigating his loyalties to the team and the board; and within a short period of time, the team was more cohesive and performing at a higher level. Behavior that serves the individual or subgroup interest but hinders the goals of the team as a whole must be confronted in a positive manner, preferably by the entire team, but at the very least by the team leader.

Data comparing outstanding teams to typical teams showed that outstanding teams scored over 30 percentage points higher on measures of clarity and commitment to goals.[5] Airbus increased cohesion and made major strides in competing with Boeing by establishing a clear central goal: beat Boeing! Figure 8.2 outlines a process that successfully helps teams build clarity and commitment to goals and enables trust through alignment of interests. The idea is to start by defining the team's explicit goals, then to identify a clear set of strategies the team will employ to accomplish these goals. Roles and responsibilities can then be assigned so as to leverage the diverse talents and abilities of the group members. The final step is to achieve clarity about how each member will help the team function well as a whole. This final step is

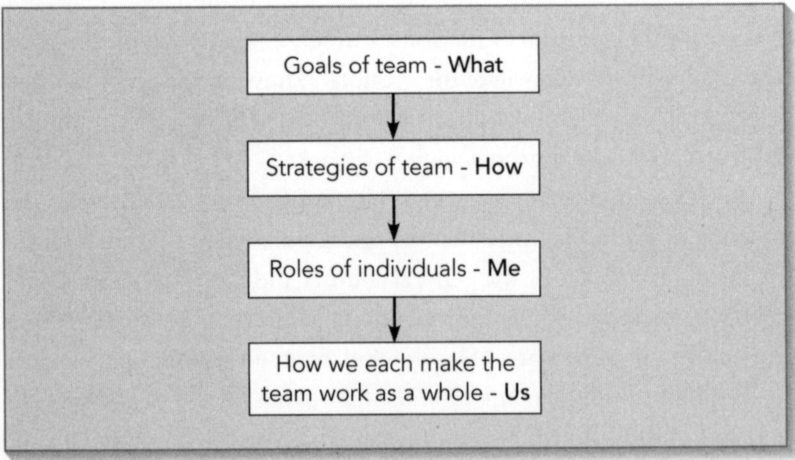

Figure 8.2 Team Goals, Roles, and Responsibilities

critical to establishing a focus on the team as a whole, not simply on the performance of individual members.

An alignment process of this kind is particularly difficult to execute when there is built-in marginality among team members. Teams often lack cohesion because members must balance other commitments, have been assigned on a temporary basis, and may also be on other teams. At an executive leadership seminar for a global pharmaceutical company, participants belonged to a pan-European marketing team with members from a half-dozen different countries. None of them reported directly to the team leader, and the team leader himself spent no more than 20 percent of his time on the project. Not surprisingly, the team leader struggled to keep team members committed to the work of the team. As a practical matter, there is a tipping point in the level of commitment within some teams. Once commitment slips below a certain threshold, team progress is impeded, and an erosion of trust is likely.

This issue of managing alignment is rampant today given so much multitasking and so many global matrix organizations. Imagine trying to make progress on a European marketing team when one or two key members miss 60 percent of the conference calls, meetings, or deadlines. A team leader who allows such behavior invites dissension and distrust into the team. To maintain trust, there should be a transparent negotiation of boundaries, laying out how multiple commitments will be managed so as not to derail the work of the team. Other options are to define the level of commitment needed at the start of the project as a condition of joining, to have delegates appoint a deputy who can fill in for them, and to establish a procedure up front for changing members who cannot fulfill obligations.

Benevolent Concern

The phrase *group chemistry* is fitting for teams because the interplay of personalities in a group is very much like mixing chemicals: you can't always predict what reaction will result. In teams, benevolent concern reflects itself in the team members' balance between concern for self and concern for others on the team. If one team member refuses to be

Ideas for Embedding Trust Through Aligned Interests

- Conduct periodic alignment exercises to create a connection between team goals, individual roles, and team behavior
- Allow members to voice dissent (productively and not of unlimited duration) about group interests and decisions
- Find productive ways to engage in dialogue about behaviors that are displayed which violate group interests

flexible and adjust to the needs of the team, a chemical reaction of the toxic variety can take place in which others follow suit and the whole team effort is put at risk.

Team cohesion develops over time in a sequence that Tuckman referred to as storming, forming, norming, and performing.[6] In reality, these stages overlap a good deal, but what underlies the evolution of a group is the way in which members adjust to each other and to the group as a whole. At the heart of this adjustment process and trust in the team is benevolent concern. It is the concern for the good of the group that is the defining characteristic of a "team player." The team leader must try to select members of the team on the basis of this characteristic and then reinforce its value within the team. When a team member puts his or her own interests ahead of the interests of the team, it is only a matter of time before the social capital required for mutual adjustment is lost.

In groups of five or so people, a member who lacks benevolent concern for the team can erode synergy and trust in the team. For example, in a consumer products company, a vice president formed a special team to study and recommend solutions for a major strategic problem. Six people from various parts of the company were specially selected and taken out of their regular jobs for a year. As the team began to progress with its work, one member became increasingly rigid and uncooperative. The team grew frustrated and dysfunctional because of this unyielding team member, and members withdrew and stopped

Ideas for Embedding Trust Through Benevolent Concern

- Emphasize the criticality of respectful mutual adjustment to creating a high-trust team
- Consider removing "non–team players" from the team even if they are stars
- Use flexibility and benevolence as selection criteria in addition to technical competence and experience

accommodating for the good of the group. When the vice president stepped in to diagnose the problem, he learned that the difficult member had not been selected for the group for the proper reason. He had been nominated for the position by his mentor in the company, someone who thought that this assignment would be helpful in his professional development, without any thought to his suitability for the role. The vice president didn't have the prerogative to single out one member and kick him off the team, so he did the next best thing. He offered each team member the option of quitting the team, no questions asked. The problem member was the only one who took the option, and the team was saved. The team went on to become a cohesive and high-performing group whose work received great recognition from senior management.

Capability

Imagine a team in your favorite sport. This team has a group of players who are true team players: they communicate well and cover for each other's weaknesses. As the season goes on, they try to maintain their team cohesion, but they lose far more games than they win. Often they seem outplayed and overmatched. What will happen to trust within and outside the team in such a case? It will break down.

Teams with a task to accomplish require the competence and capability to succeed in that task. Good personal relationships and good intentions will go only so far in building trust if there is no progress being made on the task. To build and maintain trust within and outside the team, the team must acquire, rent, or develop the required capabilities to match the challenges it faces over its life span.

There are three critical dimensions of team capability: individual member competence, team competence, and competence in team self-management. At the individual level, if the team leader sees avoidance or too many "workarounds" due to a team member's lack of competence, the leader will need to resolve this situation, because workarounds can lead to a lack of trust. A good team leader acts as a coach to help team members develop the capabilities they need to operate effectively in their role. Improving such skills as communication, handling conflict, or managing meetings can improve individual and team performance as well as trust. Smart leaders manage to integrate such efforts into the work of the team by delegating responsibility to the whole team or initiating a peer development dynamic in the group.

Other times, capability building involves development of the entire team. As new obstacles and challenges emerge in the team's work, new capabilities must arise to deal with them. A drug development team approaching the clinical trials phase may need to bring in a resource that is an expert on regulatory requirements. A software development team that is about to launch a product globally may need to bring people in from Asia or Europe in order for the team to execute the product introduction effectively. By proactively building capabilities of the team over time, the team leader helps the project maintain momentum. In particular, maintaining trust inside the team and with stakeholders outside the team requires that the team leader match team capabilities with project demands.

Finally, to build and maintain trust within the team, members must have effective means of regulating and managing themselves. This is particularly true if building team capability requires changing team members over time. Leaders must make sure they are helping the group ask and answer questions related to group trust: Are we communicating well? Do we make decisions effectively? Are we adjusting roles among ourselves? Is leadership shared appropriately? Are we developing each other? Are we supporting each other? In high-trust teams, adjustment takes place at both the individual level and the group level.

Group dynamics are such that if these questions are not asked, teams can become dysfunctional over time, and trust will break down. Conducting an annual team check-in or team-building session can often ensure that this does not happen. For example, in one Fortune 500 company that had a practice of holding annual team retreats, the senior management team discovered that what they thought was a ten-member team had in reality morphed into a two-camp structure with one group of three running things and another group of seven vice presidents feeling disenfranchised. The seven vice presidents were geographically scattered, and over time, the three C-level executives had more and more staff report directly to them, including vital departments, such as analytics and strategic planning. These executives were making more of the decisions and doing most of the management of the company, even though they continued to meet with the larger group and project the idea that "we manage this company as a team." All it took was an anonymous survey in the annual trust-building exercise to reveal the truth. Whereas the three C-level executives stated that they thought the team was running great, all of the vice presidents, in one way or another, expressed the feeling that they had been disempowered and taken out of the loop, and were now part of a "working group," not a real team with full trust, cohesion, and commitment among members. All three of the C-level executives were shocked that the vice presidents felt this way. One announced to the entire group, "I don't know about you, but I do not want to be part of a 'working group.' I want to be part of a real team." During the course of the next two days, this team agreed on changes in structure and operating procedures so that it could become a real team. The productivity and commitment of the team improved over the next two years.

Effective teams develop competence in seven key areas of self-management to enhance trust; they must have the ability to

1. Understand and adapt to external stakeholder challenges
2. Define and redefine roles and responsibilities

Ideas for Embedding Trust Through Capability

- Be careful not to allow social cohesion to inhibit capability and the achievement of goals
- Add capability to the team as task challenges evolve
- Make "winning" and achievement part of the team's ethos

3. Engage in difficult conversations with each other and to do so productively
4. Engage in efficient and effective decision making that involves the right people at the right time
5. Devote real-time attention to group dynamics and to the synergy or lack of synergy among members and in the group as a whole
6. Import and export people, skills, and knowledge to ensure effective functioning over time
7. Conduct effective after-action reviews to assess how things went versus how they were intended to go

Predictability and Integrity

One of the most critical norms in high-performing teams is that people live up to their commitments. In weaker teams, agreements are made, but there is little trust that what was said will actually be done. High-performance teams develop a culture and ethos that include not letting others down and delivering on one's commitments. When new members join a high-performing team, they are socialized to think before they make commitments and to understand that failure to deliver on commitments is likely to be looked on unfavorably by the team.

A task force group at a global automobile company was working on how to position one of their vehicle models in the market. The team involved representatives from manufacturing, sales, marketing, and service because all these functions affected consumer perception of the brand. With so many people involved, meetings were long, and involved

Ideas for Embedding Trust Through Predictability and Integrity

- Make honoring commitments to team members a cornerstone of team values
- Practice the skill of gently and respectfully challenging colleagues when they say one thing and do another
- Create group mechanisms to test whether team commitments can be met. If not, revise promises and communicate proactively

a host of issues and agreements. But after each meeting, the task force leader would put out a detailed memo summarizing conclusions, what had been decided, and who had agreed to do what by the next meeting. At the start of the next meeting, the leader reviewed this accountability list to ensure that everyone had lived up to his or her commitments since the last meeting. This was a high-trust team that, over time, knew that they could count on making progress—because people were doing what they said they would do.

Most teams exist in a messy, fast-paced world in which unexpected events can intrude on a team member's ability to deliver on a commitment. In such a case, members of high-performance teams are expected to explain what happened—without excuses, but with an apology for violating the team norm, out of respect for the team. They also take responsibility for avoiding violations of trust in the future.

Communication

Life in a group—whether it is a venture team, a top executive team, or a family—is largely about the quality of relationships; effective communication is therefore essential. Communication within a team affects the clarity of roles and expectations, the openness and transparency of relationships, and members' feelings of comfort and support. The dialogue techniques of inquiry and advocacy reviewed in Chapter Five are invaluable tools for building trust within teams.

Particularly when involved in fast-paced, challenging, and ambiguous projects, team members must clarify their roles often in order to maintain clear and common expectations for each other. Open communication can help members adjust to working together and deal with diversity in personalities, motives, and interests. An ability to explore these differences without passing judgment can aid in finding effective work strategies to deal with conflicts before or after they happen. Sometimes simply getting out of the confines of roles and connecting with another group member on a more human and personal level can facilitate relationship development and trust. Team members who establish the most trusting relations know that making a human connection is critical. When all communication is only about accomplishing tasks, an opportunity for relationship development and trust building is lost. When a conflict occurs, the parties will be less resilient in facing it. It is amazing how much more trusting and productive team members can be when they can see each other as whole people rather than merely as agents performing a role.

Where team members are highly interdependent, one of the more critical aspects of trust is sharing information and coordinating. Information must be shared with the team in a clear and timely manner if it will affect colleagues' work and the integration of that work into the team's output. Members require not only good communication skills but also respect and concern for others' interests; this further underscores the importance of benevolence to being a good team player.

As communication improves among a team and as the team grows, relationships can develop, which increases "affect" or trust based on relationship. As trust increases, so too does the degree of emotional support team members feel from the group, which in turn increases their confidence and capacity to deal with setbacks.

Building trust within teams can backfire if the cohesion and trust that develop do not allow members to achieve with others outside the team. This is the age-old problem of functional silos that inhibit value creation in organizations. The barriers of group national culture can

Ideas for Embedding Trust Through Communication

- Once a year, conduct a team-building exercise. If you think there are no issues and you can skip it, think again.
- Develop non-task and personal connections with team members, particularly where there is high interdependence.
- Develop excellent dialogue and conflict resolution skills in the team.

also function as silo-type walls that inhibit collaboration across groups. The next chapter offers some help on building trust across groups and national cultures.

NINE

Building Trust Across Groups and National Cultures

In 1998, the largest trans-Atlantic merger ever began with a breach of integrity, when the CEOs of both Daimler-Benz and Chrysler misled people by positioning the acquisition of Chrysler as a "merger of equals." This integrity breach then grew into major distrust as the failure of collaboration between Chrysler and Daimler-Benz led to more than $30 billion in losses. In fall 2000, the CEO of DaimlerChrysler, Jürgen Schrempp, was quoted in a German publication as saying that the "merger of equals statement was necessary in order to earn the support of Chrysler's workers and the American public, but it was never reality." He went on to say, "Me being a chess player, I don't normally talk about the second or third move. The structure we have now with Chrysler [Daimler-Benz in control and Chrysler as a division] was always the structure I wanted. We had to go a roundabout way, but it had to be done for psychological reasons." The English translation appeared in the *Financial Times* the next day and created a firestorm of distrust at Chrysler and a lawsuit by Kirk Kerkorian and other Chrysler shareholders.

We can use the DTM to break down this failure of trust and collaboration. Beyond the lack of transparency (poor communication and integrity) were more fundamental problems. The Mercedes engineering mentality of quality first and cost second did not integrate well with Chrysler's cost consciousness (value conflicts, lack of similarity). The bureaucracy at Daimler-Benz's German headquarters stifled Chrysler's risk-taking cowboy style (low power). There was also no superordinate integrative vision (poor alignment) or process (lack of capability) to determine how the two companies would achieve synergy together. They spent millions of dollars on cultural sensitivity training, but never addressed the deeper issues of distrust among key American and German managers (poor communication). Finally, the German workers resented the fact that the American workers earned more than they did, in some cases four times as much (poor alignment, lack of fairness). After the merger, Daimler-Benz's lack of clear direction sent Chrysler into a period of paralysis. Executives from both companies threw very public barbs across the Atlantic using the press (poor communication). A Mercedes-Benz division chief said he would never drive a Chrysler, and a Chrysler vice chairman pointed out that Jeep earned higher consumer satisfaction ratings than the Mercedes M class.

Many of the senior managers who had made Chrysler successful, retired or went to Ford or GM. Schrempp was fired in 2005. Having purchased Chrysler for $36 billion in 1998, Daimler-Benz sold an 80 percent stake in Chrysler to the private equity firm Cerberus in 2007 for a mere $7.4 billion.[1]

The DaimlerChrysler case is an example of a failure to create value through effective management of collaboration and trust across cultural, hierarchical, and organizational boundaries. The cultural forces within these separate organizations were directed toward self-protection rather than cooperation and integration. The result was that the merger of two formerly proud and successful companies was far less than the sum of its parts. This lack of synergy across groups can afflict exchanges beyond interorganizational mergers or joint ventures. It can be seen from the top of the silo walls of functions, divisions, geographies, or business units within organizations where there must be collaboration across group boundaries.

What happened at DaimlerChrysler makes perfect sense given what we covered in Chapter Four about trust and group psychology. Even groups that are formed on a random basis will develop an in-group bias. This bias can easily turn into competition and distrust unless efforts are made to establish strong superordinate goals and actively build trust and cooperation among the groups. In the absence of such trust and cooperation, groups are unlikely to achieve goals or create value.

Figure 9.1 illustrates this value creation dilemma using the integration of functions and processes inside an organization as an example. The most critical value creation processes in nearly all organizations are cross functional in nature; integration and value therefore require cohesion and trust *across* teams and *within* teams.[2] Silo walls of functions, divisions, geographies, or business units can produce failure even though each participating group is of world-class quality. In fact, increasing cohesion within a group can actually impede productivity when it inhibits trust and cooperation across the groups that are central to value creation. For this reason, sophisticated team leaders know that they must spend as much time attending to integration and trust with adjacent interdependent groups as they do on developing trust within their own group.[3]

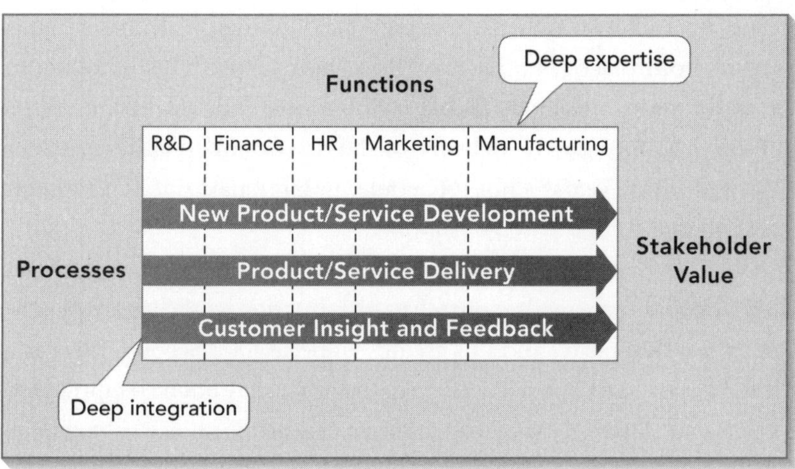

Figure 9.1 Trust Across Functions and Processes Within an Organization

COLLABORATION, TRUST, AND PERFORMANCE

The desire for organizations to operate in an integrated, borderless fashion across functions and geographies is not new. What is new is the increase in pressure to operate effectively across organization boundaries in order to improve adaptability, growth, and efficiency. IBM managed to reduce expenses by billions of dollars through consolidating functions on a global basis and learning to work in a more integrated fashion across geographical, functional, and business borders.[4] Cisco has been successful in improving its ability to leverage the R&D and marketing functions across its various business units. Best Buy has created added value by integrating customer segment teams with the formal merchandising function and by enabling floor salespeople to cooperate with the personal shopping specialists in the stores.[5] Many other organizations have used cross-group cooperation and trust to cut costs, create more value for customers, and grow profits, thereby putting more pressure on competitors to increase the effectiveness of collaboration across units.

Not all such efforts have met with the same degree of success experienced by IBM. In a departure from past supply chain approaches, Boeing assembles its 787 Dreamliner in Washington from segments flown in from places like Kansas, Italy, and Japan. This amounts to one of the most ambitious global collaborative manufacturing efforts in history. Unfortunately, delivery of the first commercial Dreamliner fell at least three years behind schedule, in large part due to problems managing the complex web of suppliers.[6]

Collaboration across groups requires trust for a few reasons. First, when we collaborate, we put ourselves in a situation where we are dependent on another party, and this creates vulnerability. Second, there is a risk that the support one party offers to the other may not be reciprocated or rewarded. Third, there is uncertainty because the choice to exchange with another group usually involves conceding a measure of control and depleting resources, and sometimes makes achieving one's own goals more problematic. Finally, it is often unclear how profit or credit for success will be shared among internal organization collaborators.

When we trust, not only are we more willing to collaborate, but the collaboration works better because we share information, support each other, and find ways to increase synergy as we join forces. If you do not trust the other group, or if you do not trust the larger organization to appreciate and reward your efforts at collaboration, then the safe choice is to find a reason not to collaborate. Research on the failures of collaboration in organizations indicates that many groups are successful in finding reasons not to collaborate, to the detriment of their enterprises.[7]

Collaboration takes place whenever two or more groups help each other complete a task or achieve a goal. It is possible to collaborate without trust, basing the relationship on contracts and monitoring, but this approach is time-consuming and costly. When there is trust, there is confidence that mutual interests will be served by success in the long run, without the need for formal contracts to govern all transactions.

Figure 9.2 identifies four distinct styles of cross-group interaction, each of which is based on a particular relationship between assertiveness (serving one's own interests) and cooperativeness (serving others' interests). In collaboration (the upper right quadrant), a party shows high concern for his or her own interests and for the interests of the other. That is, the person is willing to adjust to the other but also active in promoting his or her own interests. When two groups use the collaborative style in their exchange, it tends to build trust because there is more benevolence, alignment of interests, and open communication. When one or both groups use the accommodative style (low assertiveness and high cooperation), it can also build trust because it signals benevolent concern. Studies show that on the left side of the matrix, where parties are competing and avoiding, there is less trust.[8] When group exchange is characterized by avoidance (low cooperativeness and assertiveness), there is less investment in relationship building and an impoverishment of communication, which hinders trust. When groups use the competitive style (low cooperativeness but high assertiveness), the least trust exists because it signals to the other party that there is a desire to win at the other's expense. Teams that avoid each other or

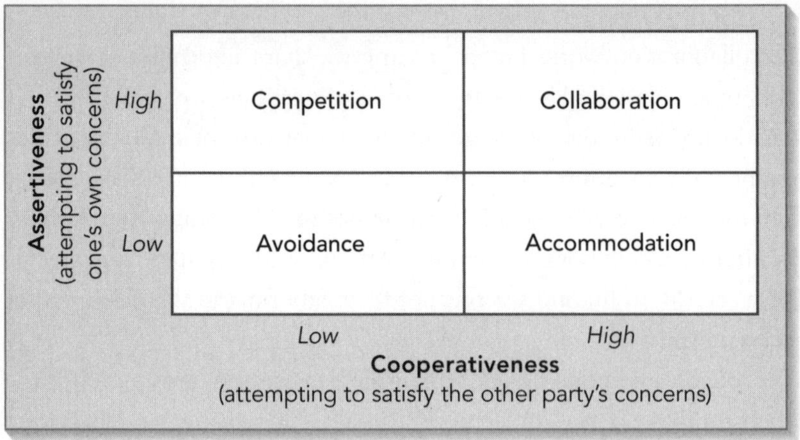

Figure 9.2 Styles of Social Exchange

compete with each other can exchange, but they rarely share or support enough to achieve synergy. Without trust, one plus one does not equal three and, in the worst cases, can amount to less than two if the failure to collaborate hinders both parties in achieving both individual and collective goals, as was the case in the DaimlerChrysler debacle.

Distrust can also result when parties use conflicting styles, as when one party collaborates and the other competes. In such a case, the openness and sharing on the part of the collaborator are often exploited by the competitor. After the first betrayal, most collaborators quickly retreat to competing to protect their interests. As we use the DTM to build trust across groups, we are trying to move both parties to the upper right quadrant in Figure 9.2.

DTM FACTORS MOST CRITICAL TO TRUST ACROSS GROUPS

The center of Figure 9.3 shows the six factors in the DTM that are most helpful in moving groups toward the collaborative style. Building trust across groups can help an organization, or a web of organizations, use

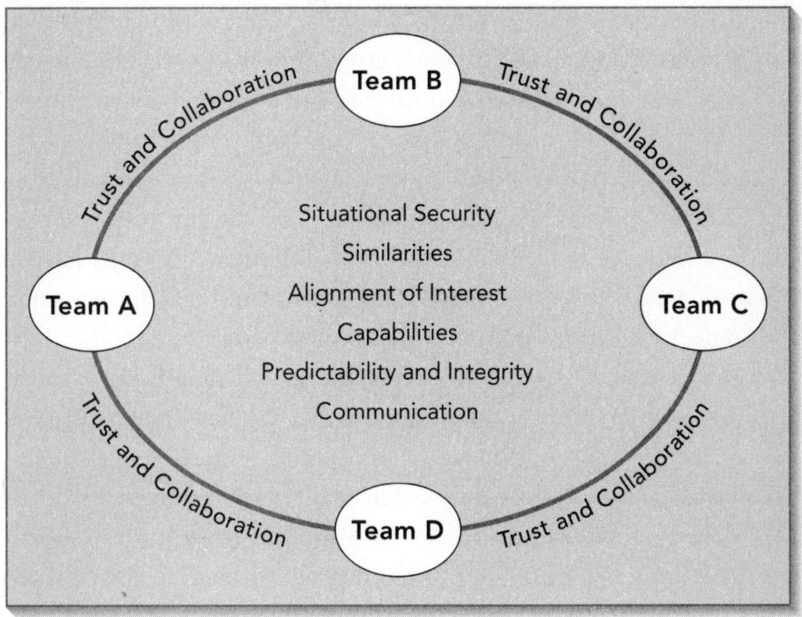

Figure 9.3 Building Trust Across Groups

collaborative networks to grow in markets that are complex, risky, and rapidly changing.

Situational Security

In Chapters Two and Four, we noted that when groups are under threat, they tend to close ranks and become more internally cohesive and less open to outsiders. This insecurity, and the resulting closing of ranks, can inhibit cross-group trust. Increasing situational security, a trust-building method that is often difficult or impractical in other situations, has worked quite effectively in promoting trust across groups.

In many cases, collaboration among groups within an organization is forced because there is no other practical option. There may be one accounting function or quality control group, and choosing to go outside the organization is not permissible. In other cases, there is a choice whether to collaborate with an in-house or an outside group for research, design, or some other capability. Although it may seem odd, group leaders often prefer to contract with an outside firm rather than partner with a capable in-house group. The reason is that in many ways they have more security and control when dealing with an outside group. Outside vendors are typically more under contractual control, whereas internal partners may invite risks of becoming embroiled in organizational politics and internal dissent. You can fire your external partner a lot more easily than your internal partner, who may have a relationship with your boss or your CEO. You also cannot sue your own company when an internal partner violates trust.

For example, the business development unit at a major manufacturing firm lost an important contract to a lower bidder, in part because the bid team had relied on an outside business research firm that recommended a costly design that made their bid uncompetitive. Only during an after-action review did the bid team leaders realize that the in-house research group would have led them to the cheaper design options that had been chosen by the winning bid group. This in-house research group had felt slighted that the bid team had chosen an outside contractor they considered a competitor. They did not offer help with the bid, nor were they asked for help. The reason the bid team cited for not using the internal research group was that they were too bureaucratic and enamored with their own procedures. They were seen as using the competing style (high assertiveness and low cooperativeness) noted earlier. This lack of trust and effective collaboration hurt both internal groups and the overall enterprise. As the company further explored the failure to collaborate, it uncovered that the core problem between these two groups was a desire for control due to insecurity.

Trust in this context can be facilitated by increasing situational security. If the larger institution wants to encourage collaboration among groups, it must reduce the risks of collaborating and increase the risk of avoiding or competing when it hurts the overall enterprise. As the president of one global manufacturing company told his managers in plain-spoken terms: "If you do the right thing for the enterprise and

Ideas for Embedding Trust Through Situational Security

- Restructure the incentives: reward collaboration that creates value; penalize decisions not to collaborate that reduce customer or enterprise value creation
- Clarify when collaborating can reduce risk and when it may add complexity and increase risk
- Allow risk to be transferred from the subgroup to the enterprise level if it can increase productive collaboration

the customer, I assure you that you will have my support. If you hurt the customer or the enterprise by doing the wrong thing out of self-interest, you will not have my support." His message was that when there was important cross-functional work to be done, collaborating for the right reasons would not entail nearly as great a risk as choosing to remain in a group silo. Ultimately, for such a message of situational security to be effective in changing behavior, the leader must be trusted to follow through on his or her word.

Organizations can create some structures that reduce the situational risks of cross-group collaboration. For example, they can establish some guidelines that help leaders think through when to collaborate and when to compete internally, balancing all stakeholder interests (in-group, out-group, customer, enterprise). Also, they can define rules for cost and revenue sharing and create incentives that promote internal synergy and partnering across the enterprise. In one organization, the CEO introduced a special bonus for leaders if they could demonstrate one collaborative project that they had conducted with a group from another part of the company. In such companies as Cisco and Harrah's, metrics are tied to customer satisfaction, which can only be achieved through cross-group collaboration.[9] Some companies even offer special categories of awards for successful cross-unit collaboration.

Similarities

To the degree that people in teams or groups subscribe to similar unifying values and a sense of common organizational identity, they will be more likely to collaborate. Promoting a common sense of identity is critical particularly when the groups' short-term interests conflict. The trick in building trust is to make similarities salient and allow differences to recede.

Imagine that the marketing group at a consumer products company wants to introduce a "new and improved" formula for one of its products. Marketing wants the new product to get to store shelves faster, but this will require the logistics department to move and dispose of the inventory of old product. The groups' interests are not well aligned because in order for the marketing people to succeed, the logistics people will have to work overtime and incur higher costs. Unless the members of the logistics department feel part of "one team" with similar values and goals, they are likely to resist cooperating in a scheme that will hurt them but benefit marketing and the overall enterprise.

The problem of a lack of common identity creating trust issues can often be seen most clearly among firms that have grown through acquisition. In one company, I found a lack of cooperation that was due to distrust among legacy subcultures—fifteen years after the initial acquisition. People were even labeled as "legacy XCO" personnel more than a decade later. In another firm, the CEO was particularly adept at creating trust from shared identity. He always made it a priority after an acquisition to change all the signs to display the parent company name as quickly as possible and to make the change a positive experience for the employees of the acquired company. The CEO also instructed the senior vice president of human resources to make sure that the leaders of the new company were invited to the next running of the parent company's senior leader development program as part of socializing them to the company. This company's acquisition strategy was designed to bring new capabilities into the firm, and it therefore relied on cooperation and trust among the parties to integrate these capabilities.

Ideas for Embedding Trust Through Similarities

- Create a "one firm" culture and be careful about unproductive subgroup cohesion
- Find a common problem to work on together to develop bonds
- Get everyone, everywhere to adopt a "do the right thing for the client or customer" mind-set as *the* decision rule

Powerful superordinate goals, common ways of thinking, and the use of language and symbols can help groups cooperate beyond silo walls. At Publix, the goal of becoming the best retailer in the world brings people together. At Cisco, an obsession with customer centricity is embedded in the culture and prevents the silo walls from taking priority. At JetBlue, the language used to describe roles ("crew member" and "coach") reinforces the idea of total teamwork.

Alignment of Interests

Conflicting interests are often inevitable, as with the marketing and logistics departments discussed in the previous section, and there are limits to what can be achieved through fostering the idealistic sense of common purpose. The common incentives typically seen in venture teams, for which employees are pulled from their former tribes (marketing, production, and so on), go a long way to increasing trust and collaboration. But this means of establishing trust and cooperation through the alignment of incentives and tight integration of goals is rarely seen outside of venture teams. Most groups work across multiple projects with multiple partners, and there is a necessary diversity and flexibility of priorities and incentives.

Sometimes managers react to the complexity of competing demands and mixed-motive situations with frustration. They lament that "if the incentive systems were aligned, we would have effective collaboration." This frustration misses the more important point. Incentive and reward systems move too slowly to be of much help in driving collaboration where it is needed to compete in changing markets. What is needed is a more dynamic and flexible approach that enables the group to make the right decision concerning whose interests should be served when there are competing agendas.

This alignment, collaboration, and trust challenge was evident in many conversations that took place during an executive program for the top 5 percent of the leaders in a company that wanted to build growth capabilities through internal and external collaboration. In one session, the participants were bemoaning the fact that the company's budgeting and reward systems impeded opportunities to grow through collaboration across business units. They said it was easier to partner with outside firms than it was to partner internally. The CFO who was teaching in the program was in the back of the room listening to the conversation. Finally out of frustration he said to the group very passionately, "It's a leadership problem, not a budgeting or reward system problem! We need you leaders to figure out how to make collaboration happen when it makes sense. That is why we call you leaders!" He was correct, but he failed to recognize the more subtle point that one of the reasons groups did not help each other was that many did not trust the senior management team to fairly recognize them for doing the right thing if it might hurt their chances to achieve their individual goals. The noncollaborators believed that the coin of the realm was still hitting "their" targets, not maximizing customer or firm value.

To build and maintain trust, leaders need to be able to promote the interests of their group but also have mechanisms in place to explore other stakeholder interests. A variety of interventions can enable this exploration. In one case, a global manufacturing company explicitly taught negotiation techniques from a cross-functional and cross-business-unit perspective. Participants were taught about the different collaborative styles and how to define independent and common interests, and encouraged to look at internal partnerships from the perspective of long-term growth capability. Cisco has a council structure that creates a cross-functional focus on customers and markets.

Ideas for Embedding Trust Through Alignment of Interests

- Use the strategic planning process to promote compelling superordinate goals
- Promote leaders who develop partnerships across groups
- Create cross-organizational councils or interest groups to connect people

Members of the councils must be at the director level or higher and be able to make decisions to allocate resources. The councils meet to share information across group boundaries for the benefit of customers and the enterprise.[10] Enterprise-wide marketing and business development groups, used at a number of companies, fit this approach to alignment. These techniques run the gamut from informal to more formal alignment. More formal approaches usually link into the organizational structure in some way. For example, in one company, the enterprise-wide business development council that decides which major pieces of business will be pursued is chaired by the CEO. Once this body blesses a priority and assigns a leader, every group in the company gets behind it.

Capability

Having intentions to collaborate and serve the larger interests of the enterprise is helpful, but building capabilities for effective borderless behavior is necessary as well. When capabilities that would promote collaboration across units are not present, silo-type behavior continues. A rather stunning example of this occurred in the production of the Airbus A380 aircraft. EASD, the European consortium, lost $6 billion and fell behind delivery schedule by two years when three hundred miles of wiring had to be scrapped because they did not "fit" into the airplane. The French and German manufacturing sites had been using different versions of the design software. In the postmortem analysis,

Ideas for Embedding Trust Through Capability

- Develop a knowledge management system to help people network.
- Create HR systems that make sharing people easier.
- Develop integrating groups across functions and geography and business units (for example, strategy councils and enterprise-wide venture or BD councils). Provide resources and decision-making authority to these groups.

it was determined that it was not the different versions that led to the problem but the fact that when the design specifications could not be sent electronically, there was no human process between the two facilities to ensure integration. Imagine the shock when the groups realized that billions of dollars of work became useless because they had no process to communicate and integrate across groups on such an enormous project.[11]

The alignment capabilities noted in the previous section, such as organization-wide interest groups or councils or enterprise-wide marketing or business development councils, can enable dialogue across boundaries. Other capabilities that enable collaboration are knowledge management systems for easily determining who has common interests or expertise, and financial systems that make it easy to transfer resources and share credit. Another vehicle for collaboration is the community-of-practice group, in which people from different functions or business units within the enterprise come together virtually or face-to-face.

Some companies have even begun to build capability for collaboration into their physical spaces. For example, Genzyme has designed its space in Boston to have small offices but larger and more attractive common areas to facilitate conversation.[12] There are terraces, interior gardens, and open space where groups of people can congregate.

Predictability and Integrity

Cross-group collaboration poses particular trust problems with regard to predictability and integrity because groups sometimes don't understand each other well enough to have clear expectations, much less meet them. One group does different work, worries about different issues, and perhaps even has a different worldview than the other group. For example, the research and development team may value innovation and think long term, whereas the manufacturing group may think that reliability and efficiency this quarter are paramount. Differences in values and expectations can lead to perceptions that the other group is unpredictable or lacking in integrity, or is somehow wrongheaded or deviant. Often what this really means is that "they" do not have integrity because they fail to follow "our" rules and expectations.

Sometimes trust breaks down simply because we are caught up in promoting our own needs and fail to truly understand what is most important to our partner. Why should another group trust us if we do not understand its needs? As an example, due to these kinds of problems, a well-respected bank with a large wealth management practice bungled an opportunity to bring more capabilities to its clients and sell mortgages. The mortgage group asked the client advisory teams to promote the bank's mortgage products with their clients. The advisers cooperated and were so successful that the flow of mortgage applications overwhelmed the bankers. The mortgage group could not process the mortgages in a timely manner, and in some cases the advisers' clients lost their real estate transactions because they could not meet closing dates. Clients were angry, and the advisers had to spend enormous energy repairing client trust. The advisers felt betrayed when the mortgage group did not live up to its commitments.

A group that is asked to join in a collaboration, like that of the advisers in the bank example, has a right to be skeptical from

Ideas for Embedding Trust Through Predictability and Integrity

- Get to know how other groups think and behave, and why
- Don't define predictability and integrity only from your group's vantage point
- Early on in the relationship, obsess over delivering on commitments

the start. It takes great management skill and conscientiousness to get collaboration right the first time, because collaboration often introduces certain unknown factors. The mortgage group, for instance, had no idea how successful the advisers would be in selling its mortgage products. Collaborators should start out by managing very carefully, building in redundancy and taking care not to raise expectations above what can be delivered with certainty. In the early stages, there is no better way to build cross-group trust and offset initial skepticism than to establish a strong track record of delivering on commitments. The leaders of the mortgage group were more focused on short-term growth and achieving their targets than they were on building long-term trust with the advisers.

When working across groups, all parties must carefully define what predictability and integrity mean to them. To the wealth management advisers, the most critical aspect of predictability and integrity was making sure that they could deliver on commitments they had made to their clients. This client trust was the foundation of their relationships and the key to their livelihood. When the mortgage group failed to understand this definition of predictability and integrity, it reinforced distrust among the advisers. The mortgage bankers taught the advisers to distrust: "Be very careful about who in the firm you let touch your customers. They may destroy the relationships you worked so hard to build."

Communication

Making collaboration work requires superior communication skills in clarifying the goals, interests, capabilities, and commitment of the parties involved and the project at hand. Collaboration entails such a complex series of trade-offs between self-interest and common interest that effective communication becomes a key method of building, sustaining, and repairing trust.

The team leaders who struggle the most with building trust across groups are those who cannot maintain a productive dialogue in collaborative efforts. They typically start out with their group's perspective in mind and then continue to hold on to that perspective too closely. They fail to listen carefully and neglect to adequately inquire about the other team's beliefs and interests. They are so afraid of losing what is important to their own group that, in the end, they lose the trust of the collaborating group and undermine their own success.

With geographical and hierarchical obstacles to information flow contributing to the challenge, communicating effectively in cross-group collaboration can seem like a formidable task. The best approach requires beginning with a win-win or collaborative negotiation process in which the parties think through, communicate, and commit to how they are going to act to promote their own interests, the interests of their partners, and the interests of the enterprise. A collaboration that begins on this basis of clear communication and objective assessment of competing interests is one that is most likely to maintain trust among group members and succeed in its mission. The skills involved in making difficult conversations productive, reviewed in Chapter Five, are essential to effective collaboration across groups.

Communicating and building trust across groups within an organization and among groups collaborating between organizations can be challenging, but they are made even more interesting when we consider the impact that national culture has on the decision to trust.

Ideas for Embedding Trust Through Communication

- Learn how to use inquiry and advocacy to deal with cross-group conflicts
- Learn the other group's language (finance, marketing, as so on)
- Define communication methods and styles that meet the needs of all groups

TRUST ACROSS NATIONAL CULTURES

At the beginning of this chapter, we examined a failure of trust between a German company and an American one, but primarily focused on organizational barriers to trust rather than on cultural differences. Here we deal with the ways in which national culture can be a boundary that affects trust across groups.

Imagine that a team of American executives go to Tokyo to sell their firm's product to a large Japanese company. They meet with a group from the Japanese company, exchange business cards, and engage in conversation to get to know one another. The Japanese delegation asks many questions concerning the American company; the Americans answer but then turn the conversation back to talking about how superior their new product is in comparison to what is on the market now. The Americans then move into a sales pitch of sorts, being careful to focus on the product's features and benefits. At the end of the meeting, the Americans ask the Japanese clients if they would like to place an order. The Japanese clients look at one another and change the subject.

Using the DTM from a cross-cultural perspective, we can understand why this American group has not made the sale and may even have created some distrust with its Japanese trustors. First, more so than in the American culture, in Japan there is an expectation that establishing a relationship should precede doing business. Creating personal comfort is often more important, early on, than having the best product. (The Americans were high on capability but low on benevolence and communication.) At the first meeting, the Americans would have been wise to say nothing about the product or a sale of any kind and instead try to make a personal and group connection.

Second, because Japan is a collectivist culture, the trust calculus starts with the group and then moves to the individual. In the United States, which is an individualistic culture, the trust calculus relies more on the person. Most likely in this meeting, the Japanese in introducing themselves would have mentioned their company first and then their family name second. There was a reason that they spent time inquiring about the company that the Americans represented. In Japan, trust tends to be bound up in group ties and networks more than in individual personality or trustworthiness. These Americans should have carefully expressed their background from a group level and tried to establish some common group ties or connections within their network to the Japanese clients' network. (The Americans were low on similarity and communication.)

Third, given that the Japanese belong to a high-context culture in terms of communication, paying proper respect to the positions and titles of clients is important, and the Americans' failure to adequately pause and focus on their counterparts' business cards and status may have signaled disrespect. (Again, the Americans were low on similarity and communication.) Introductions tend to be more important and more formal in Japan, and business cards that communicate detailed status information that most Americans think of as appropriate only for a resume are seen by Japanese as helpful in understanding the status and position of the person whom they are addressing. Not knowing this information might make them anxious about not addressing someone properly and offending the other party.

Finally, asking for the sale in an early meeting and doing so in a group setting put the Japanese clients in an awkward position. (Again, the Americans were low on benevolence and communication.) In Japan, it is more typical that decisions are made well before a group meeting is called. The Japanese representatives were likely embarrassed at being asked for an on-the-spot decision because they probably needed to take the offer back to other senior executives who were not at the meeting. The Japanese culture values *nemawashi,* which means to "lay the root or groundwork" in advance, rather than spontaneity, which might cause embarrassment or conflict.

The point in raising this subject is to emphasize the importance of developing cultural sensitivity and not trading in cultural stereotypes. The previous chapters have made it abundantly clear that if we wish to build trust, it is best to work from a diagnosis of the actual parties, rather from stereotypes which assume that all people within a culture operate in the same manner. Nor should we assume that people of another culture will behave just as we do, as our story of the American executives shows. Behavioral norms and expectations vary around the world, and we must understand them if we are to increase our adaptability and sensitivity in building trust. Otherwise, we run the risk of causing confusion and suspicion despite our well-intended efforts.

THE DTM FACTORS MOST CRITICAL TO TRUST ACROSS NATIONAL CULTURES

The DTM has been used very successfully in Asia, Europe, and North America to train thousands of executives to manage trust. There is also ample academic work that suggests that the dimensions of the model have relevance across cultures.[13] Given what we know about cultures and about trust, we must keep in mind five important considerations in adapting the DTM for effective use in multiple cultures:

1. The disposition to trust varies by culture and can affect how long it takes to build trust.
2. Like risk-averse personalities, cultures that are high in uncertainty avoidance may take longer to build trust.
3. Collectivist cultures emphasize similarities and in-group status more than individualistic cultures.

4. High-context and low-context cultures will prefer different communication styles to most effectively build trust and to avoid eroding it.
5. The manner in which benevolence, fairness, and integrity should be demonstrated may vary by culture.

Disposition to Trust

The World Values survey data from 2005 to 2008 show a wide range in the willingness to trust among the general population in different countries.[14] (Figure 9.4 shows the World Values Survey data.) People from all over the globe were asked, "Generally speaking, would you say that most people can be trusted, or that you can't be too careful in dealing with people?" About 40 to 50 percent of respondents in Japan, Unites States, Germany, Canada, Indonesia, and Thailand agreed that most people can be trusted. China, Switzerland, Finland, Sweden, and Norway were in the 50 to 70 percent range. At the other end of the spectrum, less than 20 percent of respondents in Mexico, Serbia, Columbia, Chile, Brazil, Peru, and Turkey said that most people can be trusted. Not surprisingly, other research shows that the countries that tend to score lower on trust in the World Values Survey also tend to have more corruption and more civil wars than higher-trust countries.[15]

These data refute the intuitive idea that many of us have in thinking about trust: "If I treat people the way I would want to be treated, of course they will trust me." Not true! Through a complex interplay of national history, religious traditions, and family socialization, people around the world learn to think differently about trust. For example, research shows that one of the reasons that Italy tends to have a higher proportion of family businesses is that in the Italian culture, many are taught to believe that trust belongs foremost within the family.[16] It is therefore wise to be prepared for a more skeptical reception from someone whose national culture encourages cautious dealings with others. For example, people from the Nordic countries should understand that trust may take longer to build when dealing with partners from countries in South America or Africa, where people may

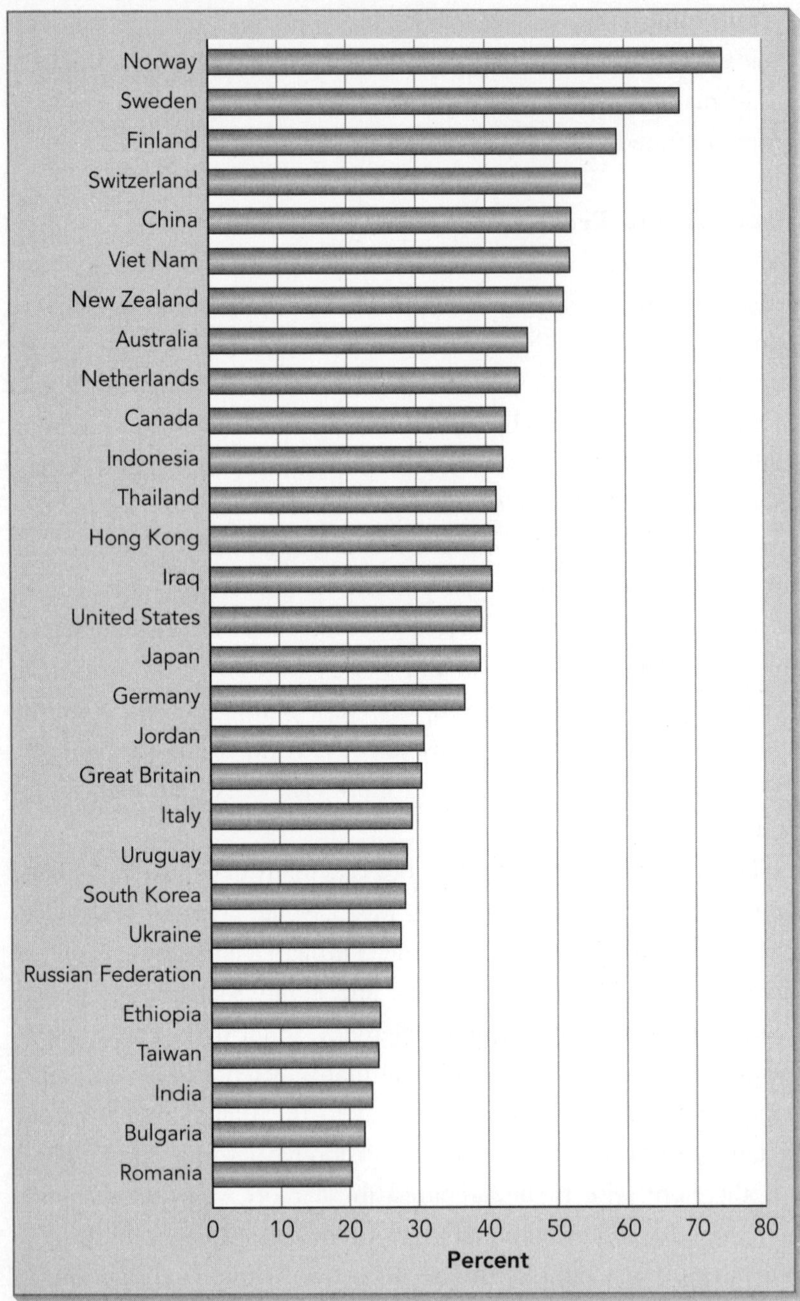

Figure 9.4 Percentage of Those Who Say "Most People Can Be Trusted"

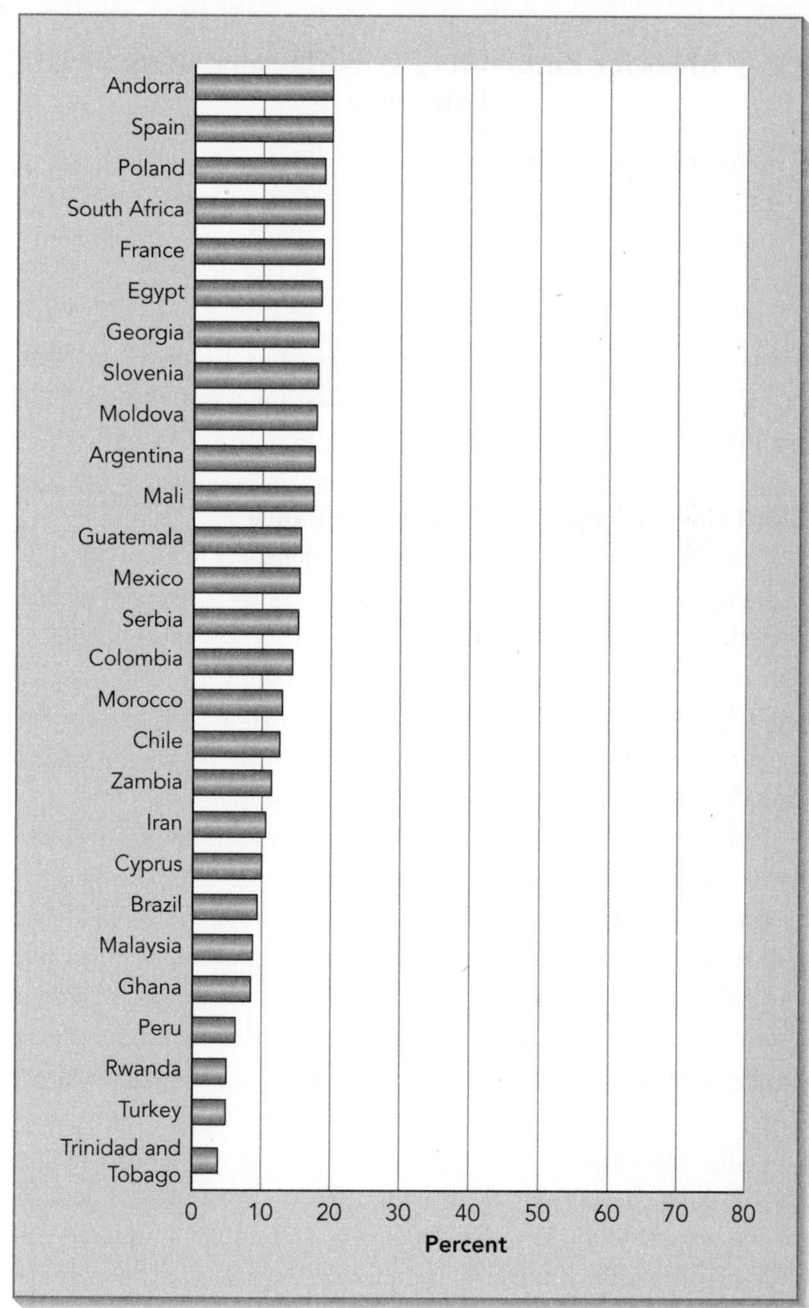

Figure 9.4 *(Continued)*

Ideas for Embedding Trust Through Risk Tolerance

- Provide more assurance to uncertainty-avoidant partners
- Reduce ambiguity through formal and informal meetings, routines, contracts, and so on

have a lower disposition to trust. Increasing our sensitivity to other parties' needs can facilitate the trust-building process and reduce the potential for frustration.

Risk Tolerance and Uncertainty Avoidance

Hofstede's seminal work on national culture defined it as "the collective programming of the mind which distinguishes the members of one group from another."[17] Cultural programming creates filters that affect what we see in others, how we interpret their behavior, and how we respond to them. When we operate using the wrong assumptions and interpretations, it is easy to offend, unintentionally betray, or simply engender discomfort and suspicion among others.

Hofstede's work in studying variation among national cultures showed that the degree of uncertainty avoidance—the inability to tolerate uncertainty and ambiguity—varies by country. People from countries that are high in uncertainty avoidance (for example, Japan and Portugal) are less comfortable with uncertainty and ambiguity and tend to seek rules and structure to eliminate or reduce them. Cultures that are low in uncertainty avoidance (for example, India and the United States) tolerate change, uncertainty, and risk and prefer fewer rules to be imposed. Figure 9.5 plots generalized trust scores against uncertainty avoidance scores for the countries where data exist.[18] The data provide support to the idea that people in cultures that are uncertainty avoidant will, like the risk averse, require more assurances in the decision to trust.

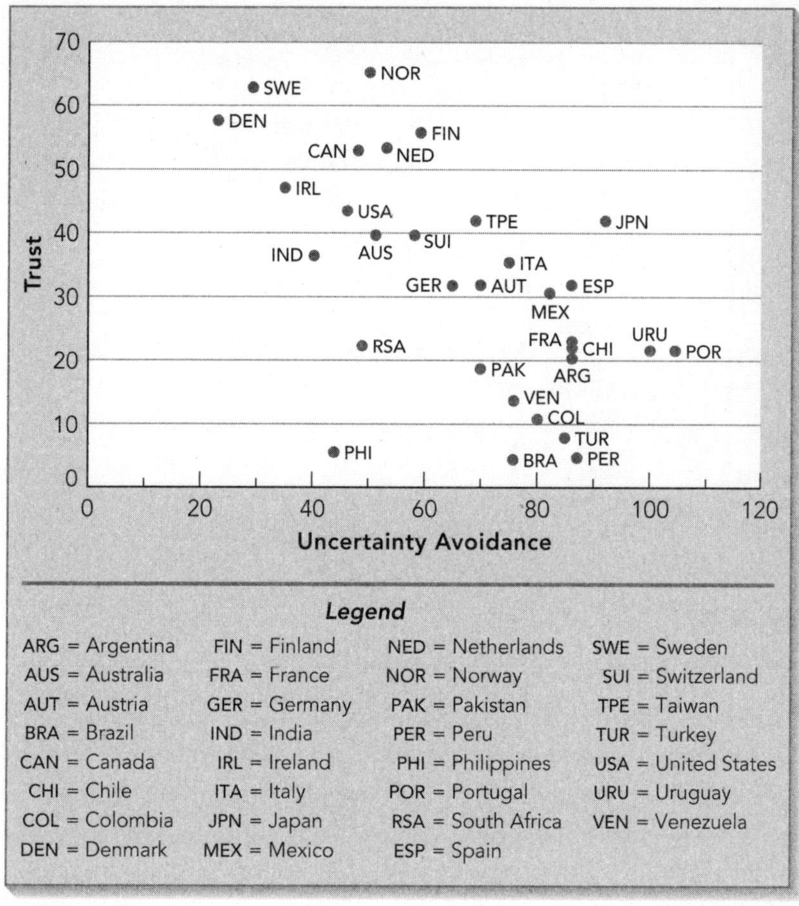

Figure 9.5 Uncertainty Avoidance and Trust Across Countries

Similarities and Collectivism Versus Individualism

Hofstede's cultural dimension of collectivism-individualism considers the degree to which a person's identity as an individual is more or less important than her identity as a member of the group to which she belongs. Individualistic cultures emphasize self-determination and self-responsibility for actions. Collectivist cultures value group membership, offer protection by the group in exchange for loyalty, and de-emphasize individual uniqueness and achievement in favor of the group.

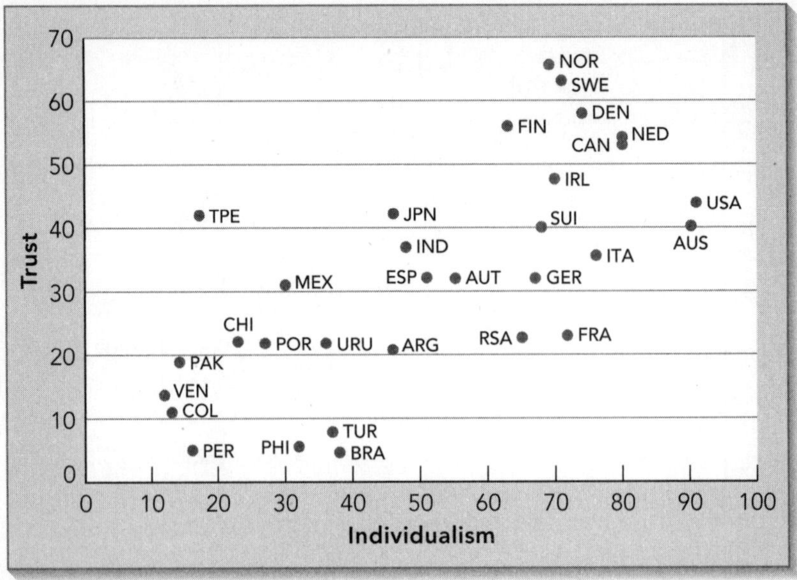

Figure 9.6 Individualism and Trust Across Countries *Note:* Please refer to the country key shown in Figure 9.5.

Research shows that people from collectivist cultures are more wary of contact with foreigners and out-group members than is the case in individualistic cultures. Further, in collectivist cultures, being an "in-group" member confers more status and trust than is the case in individualistic cultures, where group membership is less central to exchange and identity.[19]

Figure 9.6 plots the World Values trust data against the scores on the collectivism-individualism continuum from Hofstede's culture data. The data indicate some positive relationship between individualism and higher trust scores. The theory supporting this is that for collectivist cultures, trust is connected with group membership; therefore, the idea of generalized trust that is independent of in-group status fits more with an individualistic mind-set than it does with a collectivist mind-set.

The effect of similarity on trust operates all over the world, but even more so in collectivist cultures. Outsiders can fit in and become trusted

Ideas for Embedding Trust Through Similarity

- Use a trusted in-group member to facilitate relationship development
- Spend more face-to-face time when dealing with partners from collectivist cultures

in collectivist cultures, but it may take more time, more demonstration of respect of the culture, and even the use of trusted insiders who can facilitate the development of relationships.

Communication and High-Context Versus Low-Context Cultures

From a trust perspective, Hall's theory of high-context and low-context cultures offers the most relevant insight into cultural variations in communication.[20] Table 9.1 summarizes some of the implications of operating in a high- or a low-context culture. In Hall's theory, low-context cultures, which also tend to be individualistic, rely on a communication style that is direct and explicit. High-context cultures, which tend to be collectivist in nature, feature communication styles that are more subtle and ambiguous. In cross-cultural attempts to build trust, people from low-context cultures run the risk of appearing insensitive, impatient, and boorish when they are overly direct with those from high-context cultures. By the same token, individuals from high-context cultures should be careful not to frustrate and alienate potential trustors from low-context cultures, who may misinterpret a lack of directness as a sign of deception, inauthenticity, or untrustworthiness.

Manifesting Trust Factors of Alignment of Interests (Fairness), Benevolence, and Integrity

The trust factors of fairness, benevolence, and integrity are important all over the world, but we must appreciate that how they are defined varies. For example, fairness doesn't have the same meaning

Ideas for Embedding Trust Through Communication

- Communicate in the manner most comfortable for the trustor.
- Test your understanding of messages and your assumptions more carefully when there are high- and low-context partnership relations.

Table 9.1 High- and Low-Context Cultures

High Context	Low Context
Communication is less verbally explicit.	More knowledge is codified, public, external, and accessible.
There is more reliance on tacit understanding.	Knowledge is more often transferable.
Decisions and activities focus around personal relationships.	Decisions and activities focus on tasks and roles.
Implications	
Decisions and information are relayed before meetings.	Decisions and information are relayed during meetings.
The manner and setting of message delivery are important.	The content of the message is important.
People are expected to read between the lines.	People are expected to be explicit.
Example Countries and Regions	
Japan	United States
China	England
Arab	Germany
Latin America	Ireland
	Australia

in every country. In many parts of Asia influenced by Confucianism (China, Taiwan, Japan, Korea, Vietnam, and Singapore), there is a strong cultural value that competition and self-interest are divisive and harmful to social harmony. It is therefore considered fair that group interests should prevail over individual interests. Confucian philosophy emphasizes equity as fairness, but with significant consideration of the needs of others in the group. In Buddhism, the idea of karma suggests that there is no such thing as unexplained or causeless injustice.

What we experience now is due to prior actions, including those in prior lives. Buddhists tend to take an equality perspective on fairness, tempered with concerns for the needs of others. Many countries in the Western world (Australia, Israel, United States, the United Kingdom, Germany), whose cultures are more influenced by the Judeo-Christian view, emphasize individualism and self-reliance and take more of an equity perspective on fairness: people should get what they deserve, which is based on their efforts.[21] These are generalizations, and there can be variance and exceptions. The point is to be aware of how the people with whom you are trying to build trust conceive of fairness, rather than relying on your own cultural assumptions.

The same is true for benevolence. In the United States, the demonstration of benevolence might manifest itself as a manager's taking a junior person to lunch or mentoring him or her, whereas in Turkey it could mean paying for the wedding or childbirth expenses of a subordinate. In China, benevolence tends to be more about being tolerant and taking the other's perspective.[22] There is also some empirical evidence that East Asian and Middle Eastern cultures emphasize benevolence in the form of relational and affective components of trust more than is the case in the United States or Germany.[23] Because benevolence, or caring about others, is the most relational aspect of trust, it is not surprising that it has deep roots in culture and may look very different, and be more or less important, in certain countries.

The definitions of integrity can also vary around the world. Some values are universal; others are culturally relative. For example, it is a universal aspect of ethics to protect human life. In contrast, who should be rewarded, how much deference should be afforded to older people, and the role of women and men in society are all norms that are shaped by the cultural context. We can respect and accept another culture's norms without agreeing with them. Manifesting integrity in a cross-cultural context requires some thoughtful integration of our own values with the norms of the culture in which we are operating. The goal is to be both culturally sensitive and authentic in manifesting integrity.

Conclusion

The DTM has been shown to be effective in practice across multiple cultures around the world. The caveat is that the diagnosis of trust should be based on insight and fact finding that is informed by cultural differences rather than narrowed by stereotypical assumptions. Insight into culture helps us see and understand better how people from different parts of the world make this very important decision to trust—especially when the trustee looks different, sounds different, and maybe even thinks differently than we do.

TEN

Hope for the Future of Trust

Although this book began by lamenting the decline of trust since the 1960s, perhaps this is a good time to point out that returning to that earlier, simpler time is neither possible nor desirable. Scholars have suggested that when trust was higher from the 1940s to the 1960s, it was perhaps a state of naïve trust. Trust was assumed without much basis.[1] Much has changed to rupture our innocence. In the age of twenty-four-hour news, the media has become more negative, aggressive, and salacious. In the United States, we came to know much more about Bill Clinton's life than we ever knew about Roosevelt or Kennedy. The raw opportunism during the financial crisis in 2008 was witnessed on a global scale. Our low trust scores suggest that we have awakened to realize that trust is not always warranted and that key agents of trust are fallible and, in some cases, untrustworthy. In this sense, our current state of low trust is perhaps more accurate, sustainable, and protective.

But all is not lost—there is hope for the future of trust. During the same period of declining trust scores, we have seen trust hold steady and grow with regard to such institutions as the military and the Supreme Court, and, more recently, to large companies such as Microsoft, Google, Ernst and Young, Goldman Sachs, and QuikTrip. There is ample proof that if we make a concerted effort, we can build trustworthiness, and doing so will result in increased perceptions of trust among stakeholders.

According to lessons from some high-trust organizations and the impressive research that has been done by scholars, there are three major areas of focus that seem most critical for the future of trust: improving trustors, improving trustees, and engineering trustworthiness into organizational systems.

IMPROVING TRUSTORS

Trustors' less than rigorous decision-making processes have been outlined in great detail in this book. Whether we're looking at the financial system, politicians, or our boss, we often fail to conduct our due diligence to gauge trustworthiness. We use a limited schema to judge trust and are then shocked at betrayal. This lack of rigor in making good trust decisions creates an incentive for the untrustworthy. We can blame the untrustworthy for the low state of trust, but we also need to look in the mirror. After all, should we expect the untrustworthy to reform themselves? Perhaps the answer is to reform the untrustworthy by withholding our trust. If trustors make better decisions to trust and withhold commitment from untrustworthy agents, Darwinian selection—become fit (trustworthy) or die—will take hold.

Consider the decline of the U.S. auto industry. Up to the 1980s, American automobile manufacturers dominated the market. Years of prosperity and of increasing union wages, benefits, and executive bonuses ensued. Executives, acting opportunistically, approved unsustainable wage packages and raised prices until the 1980s, when Japanese car companies started producing better-quality cars at lower cost. The U.S. car companies improved quality but, again acting opportunistically, also lobbied Congress for protective quotas and exemptions from the clean air statutes. In advertising, the American car companies exhorted members of their tribe to be loyal and "buy American." Quality truly improved only when customers began leaving in large numbers. People started voting with their checkbooks—buying the Japanese cars.

When trustors stop holding trustees accountable, betrayal cannot be far behind. Thomas Jefferson suggested that an ability to hold government accountable and protect liberty was a central reason for public education of the masses: "Every government degenerates when trusted to the rulers of the people alone. The people themselves are its only safe depositories."[2] It is not practical or cost-effective to assume that formal contracts, monitoring, or sanctions themselves will be adequate to ensure trust. Regulating distrust certainly has a role to play, but we also need individual actors, using a clear trust decision process, to hold trustees accountable. The cycle of trust and betrayal is enabled by our tendency to trust as a default, without applying any decision process or vigilance.

This is not to suggest that trustors should become paranoid. The paranoid, like the compulsive micromanager, also make poor trust decisions. Their default is to distrust. This has its own poor outcomes: the loss of valuable relationships, failure to engage others in committed cooperative ventures, and the like. The suggestion here is that responsibility for growing trust falls on both the trustor and the trustee. Everyone in the social system must take responsibility for understanding not just ethical and moral decision making but also the decision to trust. Learning to make better trust decisions disciplines a system and provides a self-correcting mechanism to withdraw resources and support from less trustworthy agents. Regardless of whether or not you agree with the political stance of the Tea Party movement, it was a sign of hope that its members helped remove elected officials from office who they felt had not represented their interests.

IMPROVING TRUSTEES

As we've just discussed, the future of trust requires trustors to create greater disincentives for untrustworthy behavior. At the same time, trustees also need reform. The most powerful place to start is to improve trustworthiness in leaders. Over the long term, an organization or institution cannot be more trustworthy than it leaders.

Chapter Six defined in some detail how leaders can create trust in themselves and in the groups or organizations they direct, but a more fundamental paradigm shift is needed to move the needle on trust. A variety of scholars have used different labels to describe aspects of the paradigm shift that is needed: stakeholder management, stewardship, integrative leadership, adaptive leadership, sustainable management, servant leadership, and values-based leadership. From a trust perspective, the label *integrative stewardship* best captures what is required to restore trust in organizations and institutions.

A good steward is someone who takes care of something of value and preserves it for the next generation.[3] Stewards are good trustees. They are literally "trust worthy." The leader who is an "integrator" encapsulates stakeholders' interests rather than acting opportunistically and competing with stakeholders. He or she tries to move the enterprise forward with a wholeness and integrity that avoids disengagement and splitting stakeholders into competing factions. Thus the integrative steward builds lasting value and engages all stakeholders in the process.

Two fairly fundamental principles are associated with the adoption of an integrative stewardship orientation at the top of any organization. One is that the leader understands that the job requires him or her to cooperate with and serve all stakeholders instead of competing with them. Stewardship is about service, not opportunism. The other is that the authority to solve complex problems and challenges will reside in the system of stakeholders, not in the leader. The leader's job is to energize and facilitate, not dominate and control. Leaders who serve as integrative stewards are those who devote their energies to cultivating and engendering cooperation among stakeholders, aimed at moving the organization forward.

Beyond these two foundational principles are some essential elements that characterize integrative stewardship.

Seven Elements of Integrative Stewardship

1. Service to stakeholders takes priority over self-interest and is central to being a good trustee.
2. Organizational progress proceeds from a complex mix of competition (across networks) and cooperation (within networks).
3. To be sustainable and effective, cooperation requires trust.
4. Winning trust from any person, group, or organization requires a focus on the continuous development of capabilities to serve stakeholders.

5. The development of capability cannot be sustained over the long term by manipulation. It requires leadership that integrates stakeholders as interdependent partners.
6. All trustees and stakeholders must engage in improving the system and accept responsibility for how the system functions. This includes holding trustees accountable for being trustworthy.
7. We must all act as stewards of natural, human, and capital resources that were neither earned nor created by us. We have an obligation to accept accountability for being trustworthy agents and use these resources effectively for current and future generations of stakeholders.

The idea of leaders being integrators and stewards is woven into the fabric of many high-trust companies like SAS, Zappos, and QuikTrip, which have been written about extensively.[4] This is not surprising, because integrative stewardship effectively operationalizes four of the seven key situational factors in the DTM: similarities, alignment of interests, benevolent concern, and communication. Leaders who are focused on integration and being stewards of something larger than themselves will naturally create similarity and a shared identity among stakeholders. The focus of their drive and passion is not self-aggrandizement or self-enrichment but creating something of which all stakeholders can be proud.

Once opportunism and excessive self-interest are constrained with the acceptance of service to others, the alignment of interests also proceeds naturally. The leader explores various stakeholder concerns and does what is right for the whole enterprise. Given that he is not driving his own agenda but leading the agenda of the larger stakeholder group, perceived fairness is forthcoming.

Benevolent concern is demonstrated in every act by a leader who adopts an integrative stewardship approach. The act of trying to integrate all stakeholders' interests is an act of respect for others. Integration is hard, time-consuming, and, at times, frustrating. The leader is motivated to engage in this difficult task out of concern for others.

Those others feel this benevolence, and it engenders trust. Trying to understand and integrate stakeholders' interests requires listening and engagement. An integrative stewardship orientation forces more listening and communication in general. Listening with empathy, respecting others' interests, creating an integrated way forward, and communicating the rationale to stakeholders out of respect—all contribute to improving relationships. Because trust is a relational concept, improving relationships also improves trust.

Integrative stewardship is not necessarily the dominant model of leadership in practice today, but research is increasingly suggesting that such a model is needed. For example, Jim Collins's work showed that great companies tend to have a series of Level 5 leaders (those who are humble and with intense will) with a focus on building something bigger than themselves; they also avoid celebrity CEOs. Collins emphasizes that level 5 leaders do not lack ego strength; they simply direct it toward building something for others.[5] Bill George, a Harvard Business School professor and former CEO of Medtronic, is an advocate of many elements of integrated stewardship. He explicitly says that leaders must make a transition from "I" to "we" in their thinking and decision making as they orient themselves toward a larger purpose from which to lead.[6] Academic research has also recently suggested that stewardship is essential to trust and to effective governance in organizations.[7] Introducing integrative stewardship on a more widespread scale will require a new model of leadership and new approaches to teaching, selecting, and evaluating leaders. For example, boards will need to take as much care in evaluating CEO candidates' values as they do in judging their track records of financial results.

ENGINEERING TRUST INTO ORGANIZATIONAL SYSTEMS

Unfortunately, there is reason to believe that relying on improving trustors and trustees and even teaching leaders to become integrative stewards will not be enough to change the trend of declining trust. The reason is that individual trustors and trustees, in fact all human beings, are creatures with a powerful need to adapt to their environments.[8] We orient ourselves and our behavior to the game that is presented to us; culture trumps personality most of the time.[9]

An experiment at Stanford University demonstrated the importance of the context and environment in which we act. Students participated in a Prisoner's Dilemma study in which they were required to make a decision to cooperate or to defect (compete). Students were told that the game was the "community game." After seven successive rounds of the game, the results showed that 70 percent of the students chose to cooperate and 30 percent chose to defect. The researchers then conducted the exact same experiment with another group of students, with only one change. They told the students that it was the "Wall Street" game. The results were reversed. This time, 70 percent of the students chose to defect![10] This may surprise you, but it makes perfect sense given what we know from research in social psychology. Deutsch many years ago showed that when we are put in a situation where the signals and cues tell us that we are competing, we tend to act opportunistically—we defect and protect our own interests.[11]

This has profound implications for engineering trust. If we teach trustors and trustees about trust but place them in a situation where there are incentives to act opportunistically (pursue self-interest with deception) and where the signals tell them that they are competing with stakeholders, they will tend to act in an untrustworthy manner toward those stakeholders. What makes this situation worse is that this opportunism eventually becomes embedded in the system and induces all players to act this way. This is exactly what happened in the global financial crisis. The crisis did not happen because business people suddenly became more evil. It happened largely because the game at hand, with little regulatory restraint, encouraged agents to take advantage of existing incentives to maximize their income in the short term without regard for others' interests or the long-term health of the economy.

If we want higher levels of trust, we must engineer the rules of the game to promote it and do so effectively, without creating undo bureaucracy or sending a misleading signal of increased trustworthiness (as was the case with most of Sarbanes-Oxley), which inappropriately reduces people's vigilance. This is an intervention at the social, economic, and organizational system level, not the individual level. The central role that a trusting culture plays in the high-trust firms examined in this book is evidence of the importance of systemic approaches to fostering trust. Therefore, the policymaker's job is not merely to model trustworthiness or integrative stewardship. He or she must transform the social environment within which people make choices to trust and cooperate or distrust and compete.

Appendix D, Systemic Trust Interventions, contains specific actions that can be implemented to engineer trust into systems. These include increasing transparency in communication, setting pay policies to ensure fairness, aligning incentives among stakeholders, creating shared common values, and embedding a stewardship orientation in social and economic systems. The idea is to change the context and rules of the game to increase trustworthiness and, eventually, trust. When we compare high-trust nations and companies to those with low trust, it is clear that enablers of trust have been embedded in these more virtuous and effective systems. Ethical and trustworthy behavior occurs not simply because people are good but because they know that trustworthiness will be rewarded and its opposite will be penalized within the system. For example, ethics officers at companies know that ethics training works only when values concerning ethical compliance are embedded in the culture of the firm.[12] In this way, trustworthiness and trust become contagious in the social system and part of how people who enter the system are socialized.

THE FUTURE

A new model is emerging that can produce trust even in risky and uncertain situations, and it is very different than the naïve trust of the 1950s. Whole Foods, which constrains CEO compensation to a ratio of fourteen times the average employee salary, is one example.[13] Similarly,

Zappos' culture includes words like trust and faith, team and family, partnerships, and overcommunicating.[14] True to its values, Zappos solved an alignment of interests issue by partnering with Amazon to buy out its board and venture capital investors, who were more interested in short-term financial return than doing the right thing for the long term. These high-trust companies commonly follow the tenet of competing outside their networks and fostering cooperation and collaboration inside their networks. They tend not to have leaders who act opportunistically to gain advantage over their stakeholders.

As resources and talent become increasingly scarce, low-trust people, teams, companies, and nations will find themselves increasingly at risk. Time and the everyday decisions made by trustors will determine how this path to the future unfolds. The hope is that this book serves as a useful guide for those seeking the high-trust path forward.

APPENDIX A

Research on the Antecedents to Trust

DTM Factor	Antecedents to Trust from Research	Authors
Risk tolerance	Risk tolerance	Boyle & Bonacich (1970)
	Cautiousness	Rotter (1967)
Adjustment	Adjustment	Erikson (1950)
	Disposition, personality to trust	Kee & Knox (1970); Hardin (1992)
Power	Power, deterrence	Kee & Knox (1970); Ring & Van de Ven (1992); Dasgupta (1988); Farrell (2009)
	Autonomy	Hart, Capps, Cangemi, & Caillouet (1986)
Similarities	Shared values, value congruence	Hart, Capps, Cangemi, & Caillouet (1986); Sitkin & Roth (1993)
	Identity, shared	Rousseau, Sitkin, Burt, & Camerer (1998); Gaertner, Dovidio, & Bachman (1996); Brewer (1979)
	In-group bias	Brewer (1979)
	Network trust effects	Ferrin, Dirks, & Shah (2006)
	Group norms	Farris, Senner, & Butterfield (1973)
	Group goals	Rosen & Jerdee (1977)
	Personal attraction	Giffin (1967)
	Reputation, opinions of others	Giffin (1967); Doney, Cannon, & Mullen (1998)
Interests	Interests, motives	Gabarro (1978); Kee & Knox (1970); Hovland, Janis, & Kelley (1953); Hardin (1992)
	Incentives	Kee & Knox (1970)
	Cooperativeness	Deutsch (1960); Zand (1972)
	Group goals	Rosen & Jerdee (1977)
	Fairness	Butler (1991)
	Intention to produce or support	Deutsch (1960); Good (1988); Giffin (1967); Cook & Wall (1980); Barber (1983)

(continued)

DTM Factor	Antecedents to Trust from Research	Authors
Benevolence	Benevolence	Larzelere & Huston (1980); Solomon (1960); Strickland (1958)
	Altruism	Frost, Stimpson, & Maughan (1978)
	Loyalty	Jennings (1971); Butler & Cantrell (1984); Butler (1991); Chow & Holden (1997); Robbins (2001)
	Caring	Mishra (1996); McAllister (1995)
	Goodwill	Ring & Van de Ven (1992)
Capability	Competence, expertness, expertise	Deutsch (1960); Gabarro (1978); Butler (1991); Kee & Knox (1970); Lieberman (1981); Mishra (1996); Giffin (1967); Hovland, Janis, & Kelley (1953); Zand (1972); Robbins (2001)
	Ability	Sitkin & Roth (1993); Jones, James, & Bruni (1975); Cook & Wall (1980); Deutsch (1960); Good (1988)
	Judgment	Gabarro (1978); Rosen & Jerdee (1977)
	Control	Zand (1972)
Predictability and Integrity	Past interactions, previous outcomes, experiments	Boyle & Bonacich (1970); Gabarro (1978); Kee & Knox (1970); Farris, Senner, & Butterfield (1973)
	Credibility of promises	Dasgupta (1988)
	Reliability, consistency	Gabarro (1978); Johnson-George & Swap (1982); Mishra (1996); Butler & Cantrell (1984); Butler (1991); Robbins (2001)
	Integrity, moral integrity	Gabarro (1978); Butler (1991); Lieberman (1981); Ring & Van de Ven (1992); Robbins (2001)
Communication	Communication	Roberts & O'Reilly (1974); Kee & Knox (1970); Rogers (1961); Zand (1972)
	Discreetness, keeping confidence	Gabarro (1978); Butler (1991)
	Openness, receptivity	Farris, Senner, & Butterfield (1973); Gabarro (1978); Mishra (1996); Butler (1991); Robbins (2001)
	Reliability as information source	Giffin (1967)
	Trustees' claims about how they will behave	Good (1988)

REFERENCES

Barber, B. (1983). *The logic and limits to trust.* New Brunswick, N.J.: Rutgers Press.

Boyle, R., & Bonacich, P. (1970). The development of trust and mistrust in mixed-motive games. *Sociometry, 33,* 123–139.

Brewer, M. (1979). In-group bias in the minimal intergroup situation: A cognitive motivational analysis. *Psychological Bulletin, 86,* 307–324.

Butler, I. K. (1991). Toward understanding and measuring conditions of trust: Evolution of a conditions of trust inventory. *Journal of Management, 17,* 643–663.

Butler, I. K., & Cantrell, R. S. (1984). A behavioral decision theory approach to modeling dyadic trust in superiors and subordinates. *Psychological Reports, 55,* 19–28.

Chow, S., & Holden, R. (1997, Fall). Toward an understanding of loyalty: The moderating role of trust. *Journal of Managerial Issues, 9,* 275–298.

Cook, I., & Wall, T. (1980). New work attitude measures of trust, organizational commitment, and personal need nonfulfillment. *Journal of Occupational Psychology, 53,* 39–52.

Dasgupta, P. (1988). Trust as a commodity. In D. G. Gambetta (Ed.), *Trust* (pp. 49–72). New York: Blackwell.

Deutsch, M. (1960). The effect of motivational orientation upon trust and suspicion. *Human Relations, 13,* 123–140.

Doney, P. M., Cannon, J. P., & Mullen, M. R. (1998). Understanding the influence of national culture on the development of trust. *Academy of Management Review, 23,* 601–620.

Erikson, E. H. (1950). *Childhood and society.* New York: Norton.

Farrell, H. (2009). Trust, distrust, and power. In R. Hardin (Ed.), *Distrust.* Thousand Oaks, CA: Sage. www.henryfarrell.net/distrust.pdf.

Farris, G., Senner, E., & Butterfield, D. (1973). Trust, culture, and organizational behavior. *Industrial Relations, 12,* 144–157.

Ferrin, D. L., Dirks, K. T., & Shah, P. (2006, July). Direct and indirect effects of third-party relationships on interpersonal trust. *Journal of Applied Psychology, 9,* 870–883.

Frost, T., Stimpson, D. V., & Maughan, M.R.C. (1978). Some correlates of trust. *Journal of Psychology, 99,* 103–108.

Gabarro, J. (1978). The development of trust, influence, and expectations. In A. G. Athos & J. J. Gabarro (Eds.), *Interpersonal behavior: Communication and understanding in relationships* (pp. 290–303). Upper Saddle River, NJ: Prentice Hall.

Gaertner, S. L., Dovidio, J. F., & Bachman, B. A. (1996). Revisiting the contact hypothesis: The induction of a common ingroup identity. *International Journal of Intercultural Relations, 20,* 271–290.

Giffin, K. (1967). The contribution of studies of source credibility to a theory of interpersonal trust in the communication department. *Psychological Bulletin, 68,* 104–120.

Good, D. (1988). Individuals, interpersonal relations, and trust. In D. G. Gambetta (Ed.), *Trust* (pp. 131–185). New York: Blackwell.

Hardin, R. (1992). The street-level epistemology of trust. *Analyse and Kritik, 14,* 152–176.

Hart, K. M., Capps, H. R., Cangemi, J. P., & Caillouet, L. M. (1986). Exploring organizational trust and its multiple dimensions: A case study of General Motors. *Organization Development Journal, 4*(2) 31–39.

Hovland, C. I., Janis, I. L., & Kelley, H. H. (1953). *Communication and persuasion.* New Haven, CT: Yale University Press.

Jennings, E. E. (1971). *Routes to the executive suite.* New York: McGraw-Hill.

Johnson-George, C., & Swap, W. (1982). Measurement of specific interpersonal trust: Construction and validation of a scale to assess trust in a specific other. *Journal of Personality and Social Psychology, 43,* 1306–1317.

Jones, A. P., James, L. R., & Bruni, J. R. (1975). Perceived leadership behavior and employee confidence in the leader as moderated by job involvement. *Journal of Applied Psychology, 60,* 46–143.

Kee, H. W., & Knox, R. E. (1970). Conceptual and methodological considerations in the study of trust. *Journal of Conflict Resolution, 14,* 357–366.

Larzelere, R., & Huston, T. (1980). The dyadic trust scale: Toward understanding interpersonal trust in close relationships. *Journal of Marriage and the Family, 42,* 595–604.

Lieberman, J. K. (1981). *The litigious society.* New York: Basic Books.

McAllister, D. J. (1995). Affect- and cognition-based trust as foundations for interpersonal cooperation in organizations. *Academy of Management Review, 38,* 24–59.

Mishra, A. K. (1996). Organizational responses to crisis: The centrality of trust. In R. M. Kramer & T. Tyler (Eds.), *Trust in organizations* (pp. 261–287). Thousand Oaks, CA: Sage.

Ring, S. M., & Van de Ven, A. (1992). Structuring cooperative relationships between organizations. *Strategic Management Journal, 13,* 483–498.

Robbins, S. P. (2001). *Organizational behavior* (9th ed.). Upper Saddle River, NJ: Prentice Hall.

Roberts, K. H., & O'Reilly, C. A. (1974). Measuring organizational communication. *Journal of Applied Psychology, 59,* 321–326.

Rogers, C. R. (1961). *On becoming a person.* Boston: Houghton Mifflin.

Rosen, B., & Jerdee, T. H. (1977). Influence of subordinate characteristics on trust and use of participative decision strategies in a management simulation. *Journal of Applied Psychology, 62,* 628–631.

Rotter, J. B. (1967). A new scale for measuring interpersonal trust. *Journal of Personality, 35,* 651–665.

Rousseau, D. M., Sitkin, S. B., Burt, R. S., & Camerer, C. "Not So Different After All: A Cross Discipline View of Trust." *Academy of Management Review,* 1998, *23,* 393–404.

Sitkin, S. B., & Roth, N. L. (1993). Explaining the limited effectiveness of legalistic "remedies" for trust/distrust. *Organization Science, 4,* 367–392.

Solomon, L. (1960). The influence of some types of power relationships and game strategies upon the development of interpersonal trust. *Journal of Abnormal and Social Psychology, 61,* 223–230.

Strickland, L. H. (1958). Surveillance and trust. *Journal of Personality, 26,* 200–215.

APPENDIX B

Trust Diagnosis Worksheet

Model Factor	Trust Score 1 (low) to 5 (high)	Impact Estimate 1 (high) to 5 (low)	Ease of Implementation 1 (easy) to 5 (hard)	Priority Score (Add Across)
Adjustment of Trustor				
Risk Tolerance of Trustor				
Power of Trustor				
Situational Security				
Similarities				
Interests				
Benevolent Concern				
Capability				
Predictability and Integrity				
Communication				

Note: When added across, the lowest scores usually represent the highest-priority areas to enhance trust. These are areas where the trust rating is low, the potential impact is high, and implementation is easier.

APPENDIX C

Trust Interventions

Trust Factor	Some Interventions to Build Trust
Low Adjustment	• Be patient; for some people, building trust takes longer. • Enhance the trustor's confidence by recognizing his or her achievements. • Develop a supportive relationship where you are seen as being "on the trustor's side." • Correct issues or mistakes through positive and nonjudgmental dialogue. • Conduct individual or group sessions where you demonstrate social support. • Place low-adjustment trustors in roles that require less trust for productive and efficient exchange (roles with low variability, low risk, less complexity, fewer stakeholders). • Focus on building trust not just with this individual trustor but also with his or her most trusted colleagues. • Anticipate and then demonstrate the cues of trustworthiness that will reassure the reluctant trustor.
Low Tolerance for Risk	**Strategies to Address Orientation to Trustee** • Spend more time educating, explaining options and risk. (Note: spend less time with risk seekers.) • Acknowledge and respect risk aversion. • Evaluate the process separately from the results. Recognize excellent work even if results are not achieved. • Encourage reluctant trustors to judge each relationship *on its own merits and performance,* not on irrelevant experience of others from the past. • Ask for the trustor to consider taking a low-level risk so that the trustee can demonstrate himself or herself. Build on small exchanges to develop more involved exchanges over time. **Strategies to Facilitate Appropriate Risk in Relationships** • Reduce downside risk with some safety net. • Consider a "bond" or a "hostage asset" to protect the trustor. • Develop stop-loss mechanisms that create a more limited downside scenario. • Develop good informal or formal contracting methods to identify and manage risks.

(continued)

Trust Factor	Some Interventions to Build Trust
	• Find ways to share risk. • Find areas where not trusting may invite more risk or fewer opportunities than trusting. • Be active in helping manage risk. Point to examples where your involvement has avoided or reduce risks. • Provide tangible and emotional support to deal with the anxiety that risk will generate. • Frame education and support efforts as an investment that may pay off in a long-term beneficial relationship. • Match high-assurance trustees with low-risk-tolerance trustors.
Low Power	**To Prevent Coercion** • Provide more choices. • Create norms for teams and organizations that guard against coercion. • Offer mechanisms for voice (ombudsman, open door policy, surveys, dialogue meetings, and the like). • Provide concrete recourse in the event of violations. • To enhance transparency and fairness • Communicate that leadership decisions aren't made arbitrarily but are based on fair process and serve all stakeholder interests. • Use responsibility charting to clearly define roles and influence in decision making. • Change decision-making processes to be more fair and transparent. **To Redistribute Power** • Locate situations where low power is inhibiting trust and engagement and find creative ways to balance authority. • Educate people on personal, positional, and network sources of power.
Low Situational Security	• When risk is high, adjust expectations of trust downward. • Find ways to take risk out of the situation: use constraints, appropriate monitoring, policies, or systems to ensure trustworthy performance. • Expect to invest time in building assurance. • Share risk with other stakeholders or at the group or organizational level. • Devote more resources to identifying and managing risk. • Enable dialogue about risk to increase social support. • During a change process, consult and seek input from employees and keep them informed. • Seek comprehensive information and advice from different parties, including experts, on options and risks.
Few Similarities	• Use the words "us" more and "I" less. • Locate identity elements (organizational, professional, national, ethnic, recreational). Seek out commonalities among these different spheres of people's lives. • Build in regular opportunities for social interaction (lunches, morning tea, off-sites, and the like). • Make more salient what you have in common (values, membership, and so on).

Trust Factor	Some Interventions to Build Trust
	• Create within- and cross-group superordinate values and goals to serve as bridges. • To build similarity, locate people within your network who are positive and whom the trustor likes.
Low Alignment of Interests	• Conduct a candid exploration of stakeholders' interests. • Use formal or informal contracting to ensure alignment. • Choose or change partners to achieve natural alignment. • Focus on understanding the other's interests first. • Communicate how stakeholders' interests were served by decisions. • Align people with the strategy and vision—superordinate goals. • Change incentive and reward systems to increase alignment. • Shape a culture that reinforces doing "the right thing" for the broader group. • Increase flexibility in decision making to encapsulate more stakeholder interests; apply *Getting to Yes*–style principles of negotiation (focus on interests, not positions; separate the person from the process; and so on). • Take a long-term, relationship-oriented perspective rather than a short-term transactional perspective in dealing with stakeholders. • Be explicit in communicating the value you place on identifying and pursuing joint interests.
Lack of Benevolent Concern	• Take the time to inquire about and understand others' concerns. Communicate the ways you can address their concerns, but also describe constraints you may have. • Take actions that demonstrate a concern for those with whom you want to build trust. • On occasion, serve others' interests even if you bear some loss. Find a tactful way to let them know that they won more than you and that they did so through your choice. • Be active in locating stakeholder interests that you can promote that do not cost you too much. • Identify the behaviors that define benevolence toward stakeholders. • Make and implement decisions in ways that demonstrate care and compassion.
Low Capability	• Demonstrate your capability and competence with regard to the matter in which you want trust. • Increase your understanding of what it takes to deliver on expectations. • Share experiences in which you delivered results. • Negotiate a change of scope so that it matches capability. • Consider candidly identifying those areas where capability may not yet be complete. (It may be better to be up front about any weaknesses than to let the other party find them.) • Create reliable systems to eliminate, catch, or mitigate failures. • Create a world-class recovery system to repair failures when they occur. • Identify the resources needed for success and apply them.

(continued)

Trust Factor	Some Interventions to Build Trust
	• Negotiate approaches to compensating for areas where partners are not yet capable. • Demonstrate an ability to delegate, so that you can be effective through other people.
Low Predictability or Integrity	**Interpersonal Level** • Do what you said you would do, and if you can't, explain why. • Be careful about committing to things you do not fully understand. • Underpromise and overdeliver. • Be clear about the values that drive your behavior so that there is a consistent rather than random pattern. • Sincerely apologize for your mistakes and explain how they will be rectified and prevented in the future. **Group Level** • Use role modeling, training, selection, and induction processes to reinforce your organization's code of conduct. • Provide mentoring support for employees facing difficult decisions and ethical dilemmas. • Impose sanctions and disciplinary procedures for integrity breaches and violations of the code of conduct. • Ensure that incentive and reward systems are not encouraging unethical behavior. • Ensure procedural fairness in organizational processes and systems.
Poor Communication	• Increase the openness and frequency of your communication. • Adopt a long-term relationship orientation rather than a short-term transactional perspective when planning communications. • Engage in non-task-related communication and activities (for example, a golf outing or lunch) that can help build a relationship beyond the constraints of your respective roles. • Increase use of inquiry and decrease use of advocacy. • Pitch your communication to your audience—their level of knowledge, their interests, and so on. • Make it easy for people to communicate with you and to raise issues (for example, use a variety of communication channels, have an open door policy, and so on).

APPENDIX D

Systemic Trust Interventions

Trust Factor	Systemic Interventions
Increase Power	• Penalize any use of coercive power (retribution, threat) that does not enhance trust. (Note that fines and prosecution by authorities to enforce laws enhances trust.) • Create low-risk mechanisms for voice (networking Web sites, ombudsman, open door policy, employee surveys, dialogue meetings, and the like). • Provide concrete mechanisms for recourse in the event of violations (for example, litigation, appeal to ombudsman, appeal to regulatory bodies, arbitration, appeal to self-regulatory industry association groups). • Create vehicles for stakeholders to influence policy and decisions (for example, town hall meetings, hearings, participative decision-making processes).
Increase Similarities	• At each level of the collective (industry, organization, group), engage stakeholders in a process to define the purposes and values of the collective. • Embed and make salient the purposes and values of the collective (through frequent communication, stewards modeling and actively promoting values). • Penalize members who violate core values. • Promote members who live by core values. • Create open mechanisms to reaffirm or change core values over time as necessary.
Increase Alignment of Interests	• Work to use a clear set of values to align stakeholders around a common set of goals • Use large-group dialogue and other techniques (search conferences, councils, associations, and the like) to conduct a candid exploration of stakeholders' interests. • Use frequent and transparent communication to explain how stakeholders' interests were served in decisions. • Ensure procedural fairness in processes and systems. • Remove conflicting incentive and reward systems. (For example, bonus structures should align with long-term stakeholder value.)

(continued)

Trust Factor	Systemic Interventions
	• Focus incentives on long-term rather than short-term stakeholder interests. • Embed a long-term relationship perspective rather than a short-term transactional perspective in dealing with stakeholders.
Increase Benevolent Concern	• Penalize excessive focus on self-interest when it conflicts with collective interests. • Reward a stewardship orientation. • Make demonstration of a stewardship orientation a condition for selection among key officers.
Increase Capability	• At every level in the system (industry, board, senior officers, and below), define clear accountability for evaluating and ensuring competence in critical positions and processes. • Create reliable systems to eliminate, catch, and mitigate failures. • Create a world-class recovery system to repair failures when they occur. • Match organizational scope with capability to avoid unmanageable diversity and complexity.
Increase Predictability and Integrity	• Use role modeling, training, selection, and induction processes to reinforce a code of conduct. • Impose sanctions and disciplinary procedures for integrity breaches and violations of the code of conduct. • Ensure that incentive and reward systems are not encouraging unethical behavior.
Increase Communication	• Increase the use of open forums where leaders and followers can communicate. • Increase transparency and communication of information, particularly concerning accountability for trust, codes of conduct, and fairness. • Hold members of the system accountable for keeping informed and keeping those for whom they are stewards informed.

NOTES

Introduction

1. Joseph A. Schumpeter, *Capitalism, Socialism, and Democracy.* (3d ed.) New York: Harper and Brothers, 1942.
2. Robert F. Hurley, "The Decision to Trust." *Harvard Business Review,* Sept. 2006, pp. 55–62.

Chapter 1

1. This research is reviewed in the following books: Eric Uslaner, *The Moral Foundations of Trust.* New York: Cambridge University Press, 2002; Jared Diamond, *Guns, Germs, and Steel: The Fates of Human Societies.* New York: Norton, 1997; Francis Fukuyama, *Trust: The Social Virtues and the Creation of Prosperity.* New York: Free Press, 1995; Robert D. Putnam, *Bowling Alone: The Collapse and Revival of American Community.* New York: Simon & Schuster, 2000.
2. Detlef Fetchenauer and David Dunnin, "Why So Cynical? Asymmetric Feedback Underlies Misguided Skepticism Regarding the Trustworthiness of Others." *Psychological Science,* 2010, *21*(2), 189–193.
3. For example, see Daniel Gilbert, *Stumbling on Happiness.* New York: Vintage Books, 2005, and the research suggesting that relationships are one of the key sources of happiness.
4. See a summary of Morton Deutsch's experiments on cooperation and competition in his chapter "Trust and Suspicion: Theoretical Notes." In Deutsch, *The Resolution of Conflict.* New Haven, Conn.: Yale University Press, 1977.

5. Much of this research is summarized in Deutsch, *Resolution of Conflict*; Kirk T. Dirks and Donald L. Ferrin, "Trust in Leadership." *Journal of Applied Psychology*, 2002, *87*(4), 611–628; Reinhard Bachmann and Akbar Zaheer (eds.), *Handbook of Trust Research.* Cheltenham, UK: Elgar, 2006. Concerning trust and happiness, see Julian B. Rotter, "Interpersonal Trust, Trustworthiness and Gullibility." *American Psychologist,* 1980, *35*(1), 1–7.
6. Most notably Deutsch, *Resolution of Conflict*; also Roderick M. Kramer, "Trust as Situated Cognition." In Bachmann and Zaheer (eds.), *Handbook of Trust Research.*
7. Rotter, "Interpersonal Trust, Trustworthiness and Gullibility."
8. See Uslaner, *Moral Foundations of Trust,* for an excellent review of trends in measures of trust over time in the United States. For a summary of global trends, see Gabriela Catterberg and Alejandro Moreno, "The Individual Basis of Political Trust: Trends in New and Established Democracies," *Journal of Public Opinion Research,* 2006, *18*(2), 31–48; and Russell J. Dalton, "The Social Transformation of Trust in Government," *International Review of Sociology,* 2005, *15*(1), 133–154.
9. The database contains over fifty thousand interviews and can be found at http://publicdata.norc.org:41000/gssbeta/GSSVariables_subject.html and by choosing "trust" as the subject. The data shown here start in 1987 because that is when they began being collected on a regular basis.
10. All of the Harris Poll data used in this chapter can be found in the article "Virtually No Change in Annual Harris Poll Confidence Index from Last Year," Mar. 9, 2010. www.businesswire.com/news/home/20100309005415/en/Virtually-Change-Annual-Harris-Poll-Confidence-Index.
11. Pew Research Center for the People & the Press, "Press Accuracy Rating Hits Two Decade Low," Sept. 13, 2009. http://people-press.org/2009/09/13/press-accuracy-rating-hits-two-decade-low/.
12. See the 2009 Edelman Trust Barometer, www.edelman.com/trust/2009/. The Edelman Trust Barometer study of trust and credibility involved a thirty-minute telephone survey of 4,475 people (ages twenty-five to sixty-four) in twenty countries on five continents between Nov. 5 and Dec. 14, 2008. The sample consisted of college-educated people with household income in the top quartile of their country and who report significant media consumption and engagement in business news and public policy.
13. Ibid.

14. Paola Sapienza and Luigi Zingales, "The Results: Wave I." Financial Trust Index, University of Chicago Booth School of Business and Kellogg School of Management, 2009. www.financialtrustindex.org/resultswave1.htm.
15. See Frederic Mishkin and Franklin Edwards, "The Decline of Traditional Banking: Implications for Financial Stability and Regulatory Policy." *Federal Reserve Bank of New York Economic Policy Review,* July 1995. www.ny.frb.org/research/epr/95v01n2/9507edwa.pdf.
16. Russell Hardin, *Trust.* Cambridge: Polit Press, 2006.
17. See Derek Bok, "Measuring the Performance of Government." In Joseph S. Nye, Philip D. Zeliko, and David C. King (eds.), *Why People Don't Trust Government.* Cambridge, Mass.: Harvard University Press, 1997.
18. "Business Briefing." *Financial Times Weekend Supplement,* Aug. 15, 2009, p. 31.
19. See Gary Orren, "Fall from Grace: The Public's Loss of Faith in Government," and Jane Mansbridge, "Social and Cultural Causes of Dissatisfaction with U.S. Government." In Joseph S. Nye, Philip D. Zelikow, and David C. King (eds.), *Why People Don't Trust Government.* Cambridge, Mass.: Harvard University Press, 1997.
20. Hardin, in *Trust,* pp. 5–10, goes into this argument in more detail.
21. See complete statistical analysis in Uslaner, *Moral Foundations of Trust.*
22. Ibid., p. 109.
23. Center for Creative Leadership, "World Leadership Survey." Jan. 2009. www.ccl.org/leadership/pdf/research/WLSSnapshotReport0109.pdf.
24. See Uslaner, *Moral Foundations of Trust,* and Putnam, *Bowling Alone.*
25. Putnam, *Bowling Alone.*
26. See the 2010 Edelman Trust Barometer, www.edelman.com/trust/2010/.
27. See Paul R. Lawrence and Nitin Nohria, *Driven: How Human Nature Shapes Our Choices.* San Francisco: Jossey-Bass, 2002; see also Paul R. Lawrence, *Being Human: A Darwinian Theory of Human Behavior.* www.prlawrence.com/.
28. See Louis V. Gerstner, *Who Says Elephants Can't Dance? Inside IBM's Historic Turnaround.* New York: HarperCollins, 2002; and William M. Bulkeley, "IBM to Export Highly Paid Jobs to India, China." *Wall Street Journal,* Dec. 15, 2003, pp. B1–B3. www.ibmemployee.com/PDFs/WSJ.com%20-%20IBM%20to%20Export%20Highly%20Paid%20Jobs%20To%20India,%20China.pdf.
29. Morton Deutsch, "Trust and Suspicion." *Journal of Conflict Resolution,* 1958, *2*(4), 265–279.

30. Joseph A. Schumpeter, *Capitalism, Socialism, and Democracy*. (3d ed.) New York: Harper and Brothers, 1942; see also William J. Baumol, Robert E. Litan, and Carl J. Schramm, *Good Capitalism, Bad Capitalism, and the Economics of Growth and Prosperity*. New Haven, Conn.: Yale University Press, 2007.
31. Oliver E. Williamson, "Calculativeness, Trust and Economic Organization." In Roderick M. Kramer (ed.), *Organizational Trust*. New York: Oxford University Press, 2006; Sumantra Ghosal and Peter Moran, "Bad for Practice: A Critique of the Transaction Cost Theory." *Academy of Management Review*, 1996, *21*(1), 13–47.
32. Shawn Berman, Andrew Wicks, Suresh Kotha, and Tom Jones, "Does Stakeholder Orientation Matter? An Empirical Examination of the Relationship Between Stakeholder Management Models and Firm Financial Performance." *Academy of Management Journal*, 1999, *42*(5), 488–506.
33. Ghosal and Moran, "Bad for Practice."
34. See an excellent summary of these ideas in Bradely Agle and others, "Dialogue: Toward Superior Stakeholder Theory." *Business Ethics Quarterly*, 2008, *18*(2), 153–190.
35. Baumol, Litan, and Schramm, *Good Capitalism, Bad Capitalism*.
36. Robert J. Blendon and others, "Changing Attitudes in America." In Nye, Zelikow, and King (eds.), *Why People Don't Trust Government*.
37. Valdimer Orlando Key, *Public Opinion and American Democracy*. New York: Knopf, 1961.
38. Thomas Patterson, *Out of Order*. New York: Knopf, 1993.
39. Bill Bradley, "Foreword." In Joseph Cooper (ed.), *Congress and the Decline of Public Trust*. Boulder, Colo.: Westview Press, 1999, p. xi.
40. Nicole Gillespie, Robert F. Hurley, Graham Dietz, and Reinhard Bachmann, "Restoring Institutional Trust After the Global Financial Crisis: A Systemic Approach." In Roderick M. Kramer and Todd Pittinsky (eds.), *Restoring Trust*. New York: Oxford University Press, forthcoming.
41. K. Bijlsma and P. Koopman, "Trust Within Organizations." *Personnel Review*, 2003, *32*(5), 556–568; Tony Simons, "The High Cost of Lost Trust." *Harvard Business Review*, Sept. 2002, 18–19.
42. Paul Zak and Stephen Knack, "Trust and Growth." *Economic Journal*, Apr. 2001, *111*(470), 295–321. http://pdf.usaid.gov/pdf_docs/PNACD585.pdf.
43. For a summary of findings on the performance effects of trust, see Bill McEvily and Akbar Zaheer, "Does Trust Still Matter? Research on the

Role of Trust in Inter-Organizational Exchange." In Bachmann and Zaheer (eds.), *Handbook of Trust Research.* See also Dirks and Ferrin, "Trust in Leadership."

Chapter 2

1. Denise M. Rousseau, Sim B. Sitkin, Ronald S. Burt, and Colin Camerer, "Not So Different After All: A Cross Discipline View of Trust." *Academy of Management Review*, 1998, *23*(3), 393–404.
2. Morton Deutsch, *The Resolution of Conflict.* New Haven, Conn.: Yale University Press, 1977.
3. Deutsch, *Resolution of Conflict;* also Roderick M. Kramer, "Trust as Situated Cognition." In Reinhard Bachmann and Akbar Zaheer (eds.), *Handbook of Trust Research.* Cheltenham, UK: Elgar, 2006.
4. Roy J. Lewicki, Daniel J. McAllister, and Robert J. Bies, "Trust and Distrust: New Relationships and Realities." *Academy of Management Review,* 1998, *23*(3), 438–458.
5. Ibid.
6. For system trust, see Niklas Luhmann, "Familiarity, Confidence, Trust: Problems and Alternatives." In Diego Gambetta (ed.), *Trust: Making and Breaking Cooperative Relations.* Oxford: Blackwell, 1988. For different weights across cultures, see Donald L. Ferrin and Nicole Gillespie, "Trust Differences Across National-Societal Cultures: Much to Do, or Much Ado About Nothing?" In Mark N. Saunders, Denise Skinner, Graham Dietz, Nicole Gillespie, and Roy J. Lewicki (eds.), *Organizational Trust: A Cultural Perspective.* New York: Cambridge University Press, 2010.
7. Daniel J. McAllister, "Affect and Cognition Based Trust as Foundations for Interpersonal Cooperation in Organizations." *Academy of Management Journal*, 1995, *38*(1), 24–59.
8. "James-Lange Theory of Emotion," Changing Minds. http://changingminds.org/explanations/theories/james_lange_emotion.htm.
9. Paul Krugman. "All the President's Friends." *New York Times,* Sept. 12, 2005. www.nytimes.com/2005/09/12/opinion/12krugman.html.
10. W. Chan Kim and Renee Maughborne, "Fair Process: Managing in the Knowledge Economy." *Harvard Business Review,* Jan. 2003, pp. 127–136; see also Joel Brockner, "Why It's So Hard to Be Fair." *Harvard Business Review,* Mar. 2006, pp. 122–129.

11. Sanjay Banerjee, Norman E. Bowie, and Carla Pavone, "An Ethical Analysis of the Trust Relationship." In Bachmann and Zaheer (eds.), *Handbook of Trust Research,* p. 308.
12. Protagoras, in "Man Is the Measure" (in John Mansley Robinson, ed., *An Introduction to the Early Greek Philosophy.* New York: Houghton-Mifflin, 1968), suggested that self-interest must be constrained to protect freedom; John Rawls, in *Theory of Justice* (Cambridge, Mass.: Harvard University Press, 1967), indicated that fairness and distributive justice are part of ethical behavior. Emmanuel Kant, in *Groundwork for the Metaphysics of Morals* (New York: Harper and Row, 1964), argued that ethics includes respecting others' rights.
13. Plato, in *The Republic* (New York: Random House, 1955), and Aristotle, in *Nichomachean Ethics* (in Richard McKeon, ed., *Introduction to Aristotle.* New York: Random House, 1947), suggested that courteous treatment, honesty, and truthfulness were part of leading a virtuous life. Kant (*Groundwork for the Metaphysics of Morals*) suggested that reciprocity and treating others as you would want to be treated were part of ethics.
14. Plato (*The Republic*) and Aristotle (*Nichomachean Ethics*) indicated that honoring one's word and truthfulness are essential to ethics.

Chapter 3

1. Jess Feist and Gregory Feist, *Theories of Personality.* New York: McGraw-Hill, 2002.
2. Erik H. Erikson, *Childhood and Society.* New York: Norton, 1950.
3. Edward Glaeser, David Laibson, Jose Scheinkman, and Christine Soutter. "Measuring Trust." *Quarterly Journal of Economics,* 2000, *115*(3), 811–846. http://dash.harvard.edu/handle/1/4481497. These researchers found that minority students in the United States were less likely to trust. Nava Ashraf, Iris Bohnet, and Nikita Piankov, "Is Trust a Bad Investment?" Working paper, Kennedy School of Government, Harvard University, 2003. These researchers recorded similar results in a cross-cultural study.

Chapter 4

1. Tom Hays, Larry Neumeister, and Shlomo Shamir, "Extent of Madoff Fraud Now Estimated at Far Below $50b." *Associated Press,* Mar. 6, 2009. www.haaretz.com/news/extent-of-madoff-fraud-now-estimated-at-far-below-50b-1.271672.

2. Michael Ocrant, "I Rang the Alarm Bells Seven Years Ago but People Kept Rushing to Invest." *Sunday Times,* Dec. 21, 2008. http://business.timesonline.co.uk/tol/business/industry_sectors/banking_and_finance/article5375374.ece.
3. Diana B. Henriques, "Madoff Scheme Kept Rippling Outward, Crossing Borders." *New York Times,* Dec. 20, 2008, p. A1. www.nytimes.com/2008/12/20/business/20madoff.html.
4. Claudio Da Rold, "Three Golden Rules of Cost and Risk Reduction in Outsourcing." *Gartner,* Jan. 15, 2009. www.syntelinc.com/uploadedFiles/Syntel/Digital_Lounge/White_Papers/Syntel_Gartner_AMO.pdf.
5. Milton Rokeach, *The Open and Closed Mind: Investigations into the Nature of Belief Systems and Personality Systems.* New York: Basic Books, 1960; Fang F. Chen and Douglas T. Kenrick, "Repulsion or Attraction? Group Membership and Assumed Attitude Similarity." *Journal of Personality and Social Psychology,* 2002, *83,* 111–125.
6. "USAF Reports on Thunderbirds Crash." *Aviation Week & Space Technology,* May 17, 1982, p. 195.
7. Roy J. Lewicki and Barbara Benedict Bunker, "Developing and Maintaining Trust in Work Relationships." In Roderick M. Kramer and Tom R. Tyler (eds.), *Trust in Organizations: Frontiers of Theory and Research.* Thousand Oaks, Calif.: Sage, 1996.
8. Daniel Bryne, "Interpersonal Attraction and Attitude Similarity." *Journal of Abnormal and Social Psychology,* 1961, *62*(3), 713–715; Thomas W. Dougherty, Daniel B. Turban, and John C. Callender, "Confirming First Impressions in the Employment Interview: A Field Study of Interviewer Behavior." *Journal of Applied Psychology,* 1994, *79*(5), 659–665.
9. Ronald S. Burt and Marc Knez, "Trust and Third-Party Gossip." In Kramer and Tyler (eds.), *Trust in Organizations.*
10. Henri Tajfel and John C. Turner, "The Social Identity Theory of Intergroup Behavior." In Stephen Worchel and L. William Austin (eds.), *Psychology of Intergroup Relations.* Chicago: Nelson-Hall, 1986.
11. Tom R. Tyler and Roderick M. Kramer, "Whither Trust?" In Kramer and Tyler (eds.), *Trust in Organizations.*
12. Oliver E. Williamson, "Calculativeness, Trust and Economic Organization." In Roderick M. Kramer (ed.), *Organizational Trust.* New York: Oxford University Press, 2006.

13. Morton Deutsch, *The Resolution of Conflict.* New Haven, Conn.: Yale University Press, 1977.
14. W. Chan Kim and Renee Maughborne, "Fair Process: Managing in the Knowledge Economy." *Harvard Business Review,* Jan. 2003, pp. 127–136; see also Joel Brockner, "Why It's So Hard to Be Fair." *Harvard Business Review,* Mar. 2006, pp. 122–129.
15. I am grateful to Graham Dietz at Durham University in the United Kingdom for suggesting this exercise for our trust seminars.
16. See an excellent summary of these experiments in Williamson, "Calculativeness, Trust and Economic Organization."
17. Roger C. Mayer, James H. Davis, and F. David Schoorman, "An Integrative Model of Organizational Trust." *Academy of Management Review,* 1995, *20*(3), 709–734.
18. Data can be found on the Web sites for Gallup (www.gallup.com/) and Harris Interactive (www.harrisinteractive.com/). Search for "trust" or "confidence" to locate data.
19. Larry Bossidy and Ram Charan, *Execution: The Discipline of Getting Things Done.* New York: Crown Business, 2002.
20. This incident and the subsequent trust repair were witnessed by the author.

Chapter 5

1. Figure is adapted from Peter H. Kim, Kurt T. Dirks, and Cecily D. Cooper, "The Repair of Trust: A Dynamic Bilateral Perspective and Multilevel Conceptualization." *Academy of Management Review*, 2009, *34*(3), 401–422.
2. Roderick M. Kramer and Roy J. Lewicki, "Repairing and Enhancing Trust: Approaches to Reducing Organizational Trust Deficits." *Academy of Management Annals*, 2010, *4*(1), 245–277.
3. Roy J. Lewicki and Barbara Benedict Bunker, "Developing and Maintaining Trust in Work Relationships." In Roderick M. Kramer and Tom R. Tyler (eds.), *Trust in Organizations: Frontiers of Theory and Research.* Thousand Oaks, Calif.: Sage, 1996.
4. Nicole Gillespie and Graham Dietz, "Trust Repair After an Organization-Level Failure." *Academy of Management Review,* 2009, *34*(1), 127–145.
5. Debra L. Shapiro, "The Effects of Explanations on Negative Reactions to Deceit." *Administrative Science Quarterly*, 1991, *36*(4), 614–630.

6. Edward C. Tomlinson, Brian A. Dineen, and Roy J. Lewicki, "The Road to Reconciliation: Antecedents of Victim Willingness to Reconcile Following a Broken Promise." *Journal of Management,* 2004, *30*(2), 165–187.
7. Donald L. Ferrin, W. Chan Kim, Cecily D. Cooper, and Kirk T. Dirks, "Silence Speaks Volumes: The Effectiveness of Reticence in Comparison to Apology and Denial for Responding to Integrity- and Competence-Based Trust Violations." *Journal of Applied Psychology*, 2007, *92*(4), 893–908.
8. Ibid.
9. Barry R. Schleker, Beth A. Pontari, and Andrew N. Christopher, "Excuses and Character: Personal and Social Implications of Excuses." *Personality and Social Psychology Bulletin,* 2001, *5*(1), 15–32.
10. William P. Bottom, Kevin Gibson, Steven E. Daniels, and J. Keith Murnighan, "When Talk Is Not Cheap: Substantive Penance and Expressions of Intent in the Reestablishment of Cooperation." *Organizational Science*, 2002, *13*(5), 497–513.
11. Nicole Gillespie, Robert F. Hurley, Graham Dietz, and Reinhard Bachmann, "Trust Repair in the Context of the Global Financial Crisis." In Roderick M. Kramer and Todd Pittinsky (eds.), *Restoring Trust.* New York: Oxford University Press, forthcoming.
12. Kramer and Lewicki, "Repairing and Enhancing Trust."

Chapter 6

1. See Kirk T. Dirks, "Three Fundamental Questions Regarding Trust in Leaders." In Reinhard Bachmann and Akbar Zaheer (eds.), *Handbook of Trust Research.* Cheltenham, UK: Elgar, 2006; Kirk T. Dirks and Donald L. Ferrin, "Trust in Leadership." *Journal of Applied Psychology*, 2002, *87*(4), 611–628.
2. A fuller description of Dunlap's flawed leadership appears in Barbara Kellerman, *Bad Leadership: What It Is, How it Happens, Why It Matters.* Boston: Harvard Business Press, 2004, chap. 7.
3. According to my conversations with multiple private equity funds, the typical investor is looking for a three- to five-year time frame and returns in excess of 20 percent. The Private Equity Growth Capital Council estimates that the average holding period is five years; see "Private Equity: Frequently Asked Questions," www.pegcc.org/just-the-facts/private-equity-frequently-asked-questions/.

4. Brian J. Hall, Rakesh Khurana, and Carleen Madigan, "Al Dunlap at Sunbeam," Harvard Business School Case 9-899-218, Apr. 12, 1999.
5. Quotes from Mathew Schifrin, "The Dunlap Effect," *Forbes*, Mar. 25, 1997, p. 42. See also John A. Byrne, *Chainsaw: The Notorious Career of Al Dunlap in the Era of Profit-at-Any-Price*. New York: HarperBusiness, 1999.
6. Chester Cadieux, *From Lucky to Smart*. Tulsa, Okla.: Müllerhaus Publishing Group, 2008.
7. The 2010 Edelman Trust Barometer (www.edelman.com/trust/2010/) is the tenth annual trust and credibility survey. The survey was produced by the research firm StrategyOne and consisted of twenty-five-minute telephone interviews using the fielding services of World One from Sept. 29 through Dec. 6, 2009. The 2010 Edelman Trust Barometer survey sampled 4,875 informed publics in two age groups (25–34 and 35–64). All informed publics met the following criteria: college-educated; household income in the top quartile for their age in their country; read or watch business/news media at least several times a week; follow public policy issues in the news at least several times a week.
8. Ronald A. Heifetz, Marty Linsky, and Alexander Grashow, *The Practice of Adaptive Leadership: Tools and Tactics for Changing Your Organization and the World*. Boston: Harvard Business School Press, 2009.
9. A Great Place to Work, "Creating Trust: It's Worth the Effort." White paper. 2008. http://resources.greatplacetowork.com/article/pdf/creatingtrustit%27sworththeeffort.pdf.
10. Jack Welch, Great-Quotes.com. Gledhill Enterprises, 2011. www.great-quotes.com/quote/61638.
11. Albert Bandura, *Self-Efficacy: The Exercise of Control*. New York: Worth Publishers, 1997. For an example of the effect of situation on confidence independent of individual ability, see Suzanne G. Brainard, Suzanne Laurich-McIntyre, and Linda Carlin, "Retaining Female Undergraduate Students in Engineering and Science." *Journal of Women and Minorities in Science and Engineering*, 1995, *2*(4), 255–267.
12. The Hogan instrument that measures potential career derailers refers to this as excessive cautiousness due to an elevated fear of failure or embarrassment. See Hogan Assessment Systems validation manual for the Hogan Challenges instrument. www.hoganassessments.com/white-papers.

13. Henry M. Paulson Jr., *On the Brink: Inside the Race to Stop the Collapse of the Global Financial System.* New York: Business Plus. 2010.
14. Patrizia Frazier, Jason Steward, and Heather Mortensen. "Perceived Control and Adjustment to Trauma: A Comparison Across Events." *Journal of Social and Clinical Psychology*, 2004, *23*(3), 303–324.
15. W. Warner Burke, "Leadership as Empowering Others." In Suresh Srivastva and Associates (ed.), *Executive Power: How Executives Influence People and Organizations.* San Francisco: Jossey-Bass, 1986.
16. IBM. "Capitalizing on Complexity." IBM Institute for Business Value, 2010. http://public.dhe.ibm.com/common/ssi/ecm/en/gbe03297usen/GBE03297USEN.PDF.
17. General Electric 2000 annual report. Available at www.ge.com/annual00/.
18. Manual of the U.S. Army. Available at www.enlisted.info/about/values.shtml.
19. Richard C. Rothermel, "Mann Gulch Fire: A Race That Couldn't Be Won." United States Department of Agriculture Forest Service: General Technical Report INT-GTR-299, 1993. Available at www.fs.fed.us/rm/pubs_int/int_gtr299/.
20. Karl E. Weick, "Drop Your Tools: An Allegory for Organizational Studies." *Administrative Science Quarterly*, June 1996, *41*(2), 301; Mark Matthews, "The Development of Safety Training After Mann Gulch," Spring 2009. www.wildfirelessons.net/Additional.aspx?Page=186.
21. Gary A. Yukl, *Leadership in Organizations.* (3rd ed.) Upper Saddle River, N.J.: Prentice Hall, 1994; Gary A. Yukl and Rick Lepsinger, *Flexible Leadership: Creating Value by Balancing Multiple Challenges and Choices.* San Francisco: Jossey-Bass, 2004.
22. Jack Welch with John A. Byrne, Jack, *Straight from the Gut.* New York: Warner Books, p. 422.
23. From a talk by McDonald at MIT Sloan School, Mar. 3, 2009.
24. Bill George with Peter Sims, *True North: Discover Your Authentic Leadership.* San Francisco: Jossey-Bass, 2007.
25. Quoted in Ben W. Heineman, "Avoiding Integrity Land Mines." *Harvard Business Review*, Apr. 2007, pp. 100–108, 142.
26. See the GE Web site for its code of conduct; for further details about the GE integrity infrastructure, see Heineman, "Avoiding Integrity Land Mines."

27. Dennis S. Reina and Michelle L. Reina, *Trust and Betrayal in the Workplace: Building Effective Relationships in Your Organization.* (2nd ed.) San Francisco: Berrett-Koehler, 2006.
28. Ibid., p. 50.
29. Nicole Gillespie and Leon Mann, "Transformational Leadership and Shared Values: The Building Blocks of Trust." *Journal of Managerial Psychology*, 2004, *19*(6), 588–607.

Chapter 7

1. These data were collected by my colleagues and I from 2009 to 2011. Employees were asked to describe the top three trust issues that they confront in their work. Responses were content-analyzed to arrive at frequency counts.
2. Edelman Trust Barometer study of trust and credibility (www.edelman.com/trust/2009) involved a thirty-minute telephone survey of 4,475 people (ages twenty-five to sixty-four) in twenty countries on five continents between Nov. 5 and Dec. 14, 2008. The sample consisted of college-educated people with household income in the top quartile of their country and who report significant media consumption and engagement in business news and public policy.
3. Akbar Zaheer, Bill McEvily, and Vincenzo Perrone, "Does Trust Matter? Exploring the Effects of Interorganizatonal Trust on Performance." *Organization Science*, 1998, *9*(2), 141–159.
4. Wesley Shrum, Ivan Chompalov, and Joel Genuth, "Trust, Conflict and Performance in Scientific Collaborations," *Social Studies of Science*, 2001, *31*(5), 681–730.
5. Jeffrey H. Dyer and Wujin Chu, "The Role of Trustworthiness in Reducing Transaction Costs and Improving Performance." *Organization Science*, 2003, *14*(1), 57–68.
6. Bill McEvily and Akbar Zaheer, "Does Trust Still Matter? Research on the Role of Trust in Interorganizational Exchange." In Reinhard Bachmann and Akbar Zaheer (eds.), *Handbook of Trust Research.* Cheltenham, UK: Elgar, 2006.
7. Paul A. Pavlou, "Institution-Based Trust in Interorganizational Exchange Relationships." *Journal of Strategic Information Systems*, 2002, *11*(3–4), 215–243.

8. Alex Edmans, "Does the Stock Market Fully Value Intangibles? Employee Satisfaction and Equity Prices." Working paper, Wharton School, University of Pennsylvania, 2010.
9. Kirk T. Dirks and Donald L. Ferrin, "The Role of Trust in Organizational Settings." *Organization Science*, 2001, *12*(4), 450–467.
10. Michael Burchell and Jennifer Robin, *The Great Workplace: How to Build It, How to Keep It, and Why It Matters.* San Francisco: Jossey-Bass, 2011.
11. See the Proctor & Gamble Web site, which includes the impressive list of external awards: www.pg.com/en_US/company/external_recognition.shtml.
12. David A. Nadler and Michael L. Tushman, "A Model for Diagnosing Organizational Behavior." In M. L. Tushman and W. L. Moore (eds.), *Readings in the Management of Innovation.* New York: Harper Business, 1988; W. Warner Burke, and George H. Litwin, "A Causal Model of Organizational Performance and Change." *Journal of Management,* 1992, *18*(3), 523–545.
13. William J. Holstein, "Toyota Recall Highlights Deep Organizational Failures." BNET CBS News, Feb. 9, 2010. www.bnet.com/article/toyota-recall-highlights-deep-organizational-failures/391889.
14. Akio Toyoda, president of Toyota Motor Corporation, press conference with U.S. secretary of transportation, May 10, 2010. http://articles.latimes.com/2010/may/10/business/la-fiw-toyota-lahood11-20100511.
15. Robert F. Hurley, *The Innovative Culture and Its Effects on Performance.* Doctoral dissertation, Columbia University, 1992.
16. Google, "Our Philosophy: Ten Things We Know to Be True." www.google.com/about/corporate/company/tenthings.html.
17. David Drummond, "A New Approach to China," Jan. 12, 2010. http://googleblog.blogspot.com/2010/01/new-approach-to-china.html.
18. Amy Lyman, "Building Trust by Welcoming Employees." Great Place to Work Institute, 2007. http://resources.greatplacetowork.com/article/pdf/building_trust_-_welcoming_employees.pdf; Burchell and Robin, *Great Workplace.*
19. Ibid.
20. Tony Hsieh, *Delivering Happiness.* New York: Business Plus, 2010.
21. Richard S. Tedlow and Wendy K. Smith, "James Burke: A Career in American Business (B)." Harvard Business School Case 305S14, Apr. 20, 1989 (updated in 2005).

22. Kevin Maney, "SAS Workers Won When Greed Lost." *USA Today,* Apr. 21, 2004. www.usatoday.com/money/industries/technology/2004-04-21-sas-culture_x.htm.
23. Susan Svoboda and Stuart Hart, "Case A: McDonald's Environmental Strategy." National Pollution Prevention Center for Higher Education. Mar. 1995. Available at www.umich.edu/~nppcpub/resources/compendia/CORPpdfs/CORPcaseA.pdf.
24. Greg Farrell and Francesco Guerrera, "Thain Admits $1.2m Office Refit 'Mistake.'" *Financial Times,* Jan. 27, 2009, p. 17.
25. W. Chan Kim and Renee Maughborne, "Fair Process: Managing in the Knowledge Economy." *Harvard Business Review,* Jan. 2003, pp. 127–136.
26. Burchell and Robin, *Great Workplace.*
27. The examples come from press reports, company Web sites, and in some cases my firsthand experience with the companies.
28. The details of this story are from press reports and my actual experience with the firm and key employees.
29. Larry Bossidy and Ram Charan, *Execution: The Discipline of Getting Things Done.* New York: Crown Business, 2002.
30. Maria Palma, "Business Week's Top 25 Customer Service 'Champs.'" *Customers Are Always,* Feb. 25, 2007. www.customersarealways.com/2007/02/business_weeks_top_25_customer.html; and "100 Best Companies to Work For." *CNNMoney,* 2011. http://money.cnn.com/magazines/fortune/bestcompanies/2011/snapshots/67.html.
31. Warren Thayer, "Why Publix Is So Darn Good." *RFF Retailer,* Aug. 28, 2008, pp. 14–18, 20, 24–25.
32. Ben W. Heineman, "Avoiding Integrity Land Mines." *Harvard Business Review,* Apr. 2007, pp. 100-108, 142.
33. Ibid.
34. More information on these examples can be found on the Web site of the Great Place to Work Institute (www.greatplacetowork.com).
35. Nicole Gillespie, Robert F. Hurley, Graham Dietz, and Reinhard Bachmann, "Trust Repair in the Context of the Global Financial Crisis." In Roderick M. Kramer and Todd Pittinsky (eds.), *Restoring Trust.* New York: Oxford University Press, forthcoming.
36. Amy Lyman, "Building Trust in the Workplace," Nov. 2003. http://resources.greatplacetowork.com/article/pdf/building-trust.pdf.

Chapter 8

1. Jon R. Katzenbach and Douglas K. Smith, *The Wisdom of Teams*. New York: HarperBusiness, 1994.
2. Vanessa Urch Druskat and Steven B. Wolf, "Building the Emotional Intelligence of Groups." *Harvard Business Review,* Mar. 2001. www.talentfactor.nl/publicaties/Building_The_Emotional_Intelligence_of_Groups_HBR_spring_2008.pdf.
3. Henri Tajfel and John C. Turner, "The Social Identity Theory of Intergroup Behavior." In Stephen Worchel and L. William Austin (eds.), *Psychology of Intergroup Relations*. Chicago: Nelson-Hall, 1986.
4. Carl Larkin, "From Device to Vice: Social Control and Intergroup Conflict at Rajneeshpuram." *Sociological Analysis,* 1991, *52*(4), 363–378.
5. HayGroup, "Managing Performance: Achieving Outstanding Performance Through a 'Culture of Dialogue.'" HayGroup working paper, 2002. www.b21pubs.com/pdf/managingperformance.pdf.
6. Bruce Tuckman, "Developmental Sequence in Small Groups." *Psychological Bulletin,* 1965, *63*(6), 384–399.

Chapter 9

1. Details of the Daimler-Chrysler story are from Sydney Finkelstein, "The DaimlerChrysler Merger." Tuck School of Business, Dartmouth College, 2002; Bill Vlasic and Bradely Stertz, *Taken for a Ride: How Daimler-Benz Drove Off with Chrysler*. New York: HarperCollins, 2001.
2. Richard Schonberger, *Building a Chain of Customers*. New York: Free Press, 1990.
3. Frank Ostroff, *The Horizontal Organization: What the Organization of the Future Actually Looks Like and How It Delivers Value to Customers*. New York: Oxford University Press, 1990.
4. IBM Global Business Services. "The New Value Integrator: Insights from the Global Financial Officer Study." (Executive summary) Mar. 2010. http://public.dhe.ibm.com/common/ssi/ecm/en/gbe03282usen/GBE03282USEN.PDF; Johnny Barnes, "How IBM Saved Billions Through IT Consolidation." IBM Center for the Business of Government, Jan. 31, 2011. www.businessofgovernment.org/blog/strategies-font-color-redcut-costsfont-and-improve-performance/monday-jan-31-how-ibm-saved-bill.

5. Ranjay Gulati, *Reorganize for Resilience.* Boston: Harvard Business School Press, 2009.
6. Peter Sanders, "Boeing Delays 787 Fuselage Shipments." *Wall Street Journal* (Online), Apr. 28, 2010.
7. See Morten T. Hansen, *Collaboration: How Leaders Avoid the Traps, Create Unity, and Reap Big Results.* Boston: Harvard Business School Press, 2009.
8. See Morton Deutsch, *The Resolution of Conflict.* New Haven, Conn.: Yale University Press, 1977.
9. Gulati, *Reorganize for Resilience.*
10. Ibid.
11. Barry Shore, Global Project Strategy, 2009, www.globalprojectstrategy.com; also Alan MacCormack, Theodore Forbath, Peter Brooks, and Patrick Kalher, "Innovation Through Global Collaboration: A New Source of Competitive Advantage." Harvard Business School Working Paper 07-180, Aug. 14, 2007. www.hbs.edu/research/pdf/07-079.pdf.
12. Michael Burchell and Jennifer Robin, *The Great Workplace: How to Build It, How to Keep It, and Why It Matters.* San Francisco: Jossey-Bass, 2011.
13. Donald L. Ferrin and Nicole Gillespie, "Trust Differences Across National-Societal Cultures: Much to Do, or Much Ado About Nothing?" In Mark N. Saunders, Denise Skinner, Graham Dietz, Nicole Gillespie, and Roy J. Lewicki (eds.), *Organizational Trust: A Cultural Perspective.* New York: Cambridge University Press, 2010.
14. This World Values data were collected in a wave from 2005 to 2008 from approximately sixty thousand people in sixty countries. Surveys employed a combination of face-to-face interviews and questionnaires; the average sample size per country was over one thousand. The score represents the percentage of people who said "most people can be trusted." The World Values Survey data and instructions are available at www.wvsevsdb.com/wvs/WVSAnalize.jsp?Idioma=I.
15. See Eric Uslaner, *The Moral Foundations of Trust.* New York: Cambridge University Press, 2002.
16. Francis Fukuyama, *Trust: The Social Virtues and the Creation of Prosperity.* New York: Free Press, 1995.
17. Geert Hofstede, *Culture's Consequences: International Differences in Work Related Values.* Thousand Oaks, Calif.: Sage, 1984, p. 21.

18. The Hofstede culture data was collected at IBM from 1967 to 1973. A few notes about interpreting these data. First, many factors affect a country's overall disposition to trust, so we should not expect there to be a strong correlation of only one cultural dimension with trust. Second, these data are from different time periods, which is not very problematic because national culture and disposition to trust change slowly over time, but things may have shifted. We should treat these two-dimensional plots as a way to explore differences rather than as determinative. The trust scores represent World Value survey data averaged from 1991 and 1995–1998 data collection waves, as found in the article: Arjun Bhardwaj, Joerg Dietz, and Paul W. Beamish, "Host Country Cultural Influences on Foreign Direct Investment." *Management International Review,* 2007, *47*(1), 29–50.
19. Lilach Sagiv and Shalom H. Schwartz, "Value Priorities and Readiness for Out-Group Social Contact." *Journal of Personality and Social Psychology,* 1995, *69*(3), 437–448; Lenard Huff and Lane Kelley, "Levels of Organizational Trust in Individualist Versus Collectivist Societies: A Seven-Nation Study." *Organization Science,* 2003, *14*(1), 81–90; Jean L. Johnson, John B. Cullen, Tomoaki Sakano, and Hideyuki Takenouchi, "Setting the Stage for Trust and Strategic Integration in Japanese-U.S. Cooperative." *Journal of International Business Studies,* 1996, *27*(5), 981–1004.
20. Edward T. Hall and Mildred Reed Hall, *Understanding Cultural Differences.* Yarmouth, Maine: Intercultural Press, 1990.
21. Nina Cole, "Cross-Cultural Conceptions of Organizational Justice: The Impact of Eastern Religions/Philosophies." Proceedings of the International Business and Management Research Annual Conference, Honolulu, 2009. Abstract available at *Business Review, Cambridge,* 2009, *12*(2). www.jaabc.com/brcv12n2preview.html.
22. See Hwee Hoon Tan and Syeda Arzu Wasti, *Why Do I Trust My Coworkers? Comparison of Factors of Trustworthiness Among Peers Across Turkey and China.* Paper presented at the 27th International Congress of Applied Psychology, Melbourne, Australia, 2010.
23. Jeffrey Sanchez-Burks and Fiona Lee, "Culture and Workways." In Shinobu Kitayama and Dov Cohen (eds.), *Handbook of Cultural Psychology,* Vol. 1. New York: Guilford Press, 2007; Harry C. Triandis, *Individualism and Collectivism.* Boulder, Colo.: Westview Press, 1995.

Chapter 10

1. Carol A. Heimer, "Solving the Problem of Trust." In Karen. S. Cook (ed.), *Trust in Society*. New York: Russell Sage Foundation, 2001; Roderick M. Kramer, "When Paranoia Makes Sense." *Harvard Business Review*, July 2002, pp. 62–69, 124.
2. Saul K. Padover, *Thomas Jefferson on Democracy*. New York: Appleton-Century, 1939.
3. Peter Block, *Stewardship: Choosing Service Over Self-Interest*. San Francisco: Berrett-Koehler, 1996.
4. For SAS Institute, see David Russo, *17 Rules Successful Companies Use to Attract and Keep Top Talent: Why Engaged Employees Are Your Greatest Sustainable Advantage*. Upper Saddle River, N.J.: Financial Times Press, 2010; for Zappos, see Tony Hsieh, *Delivering Happiness*. New York: Business Plus, 2010; for QuikTrip, see Chester Cadieux, *From Lucky to Smart*. Tulsa, Okla.: Müllerhaus Publishing Group, 2008.
5. James C. Collins, *Good to Great*. New York: HarperCollins, 2001.
6. Bill George with Peter Sims, *True North: Discover Your Authentic Leadership*. San Francisco: Jossey-Bass, 2007.
7. See Chamu Sundaramurthy and Marianne Lewis, "Control and Collaboration: Paradoxes of Governance." *Academy of Management Review*, 2003, *28*(3), 397–415; Cam Caldwell, Linda A. Hayes, Ranjan Karri, and Patricia Bernal, "Ethical Stewardship: Implications for Leadership and Trust." *Journal of Business Ethics*, 2008, *78*(1–2), 53–164; Bradley Agle and others, "Dialogue: Toward Superior Stakeholder Theory." *Business Ethics Quarterly*, 2008, *18*(2), 153–190.
8. Morton Deutsch, *The Resolution of Conflict*. New Haven, Conn.: Yale University Press, 1977.
9. Walter Mischel, *Personality and Assessment*. Hoboken, N.J.: Wiley, 1968.
10. Varda Liberman, Steven M. Samuels, and Lee Ross, "The Name of the Game: Predictive Power of Reputations Versus Situational Labels in Determining Prisoner's Dilemma Game Moves." *Personality and Social Psychology Bulletin*, 2004, *30*(9), 1175–1185.
11. Deutsch, *Resolution of Conflict*.
12. Zabihollah Rezaee, *Corporate Governance Post Sarbanes-Oxley: Regulations, Requirements, and Integrated Processes*. Hoboken, N.J.: Wiley, 2007.

13. Gary Shorter and Marc Labonte, "The Economics of Corporate Executive Pay." Report RL33935. Congressional Research Service. Mar. 22, 2007. Available at http://digitalcommons.ilr.cornell.edu/cgi/viewcontent.cgi?article=1035&context=crs.
14. Hsieh, *Delivering Happiness.*

ACKNOWLEDGMENTS

This book would not have been possible without a great deal of help. First, many scholars have produced a tremendous body of research that enabled me to create the DTM. First and foremost among these scholars is Morton Deutsch, who pioneered the field of trust research in social psychology and with whom I was fortunate to study during my PhD program at Columbia University. Also Reinhard Bachmann, Robert Bies, Joel Brockner, Phil Bromiley, Ronald Burt, Karen Cook, Graham Dietz, Kirk Dirks, Donald Ferrin, Francis Fukuyama, Diego Gambetta, Nicole Gillespie, Ranjay Gulati, Russell Hardin, Peter Kim, Roderick Kramer, Roy Lewicki, Niklas Luhman, Deepak Malhotra, Roger Mayer, Daniel McAllister, Bill McEvily, Bart Nooteboom, Robert Putnam, Denise Rousseau, Julian Rotter, David Schoorman, Blair Shepard, Sim Sitkin, Marla Tuchinsky, Tom Tyler, Eric Uslaner, Akbar Zaheer, and Lynne Zucker, along with Mort Deutsch, are the people on whose work this book rests. I hope I have contributed to making their fine research more actionable in the world of practice. One other person at Columbia University deserves special mention: Warner Burke at Teachers College has taught me more about how organizations and teams work that anyone else. I am in his debt, and his impact can be found on many of these pages. I am also indebted to Amy Lyman of the Great Place to Work Institute, whose fine work on trust in practice provided so many compelling examples, and to

Edelman, a public relations firm that has done some excellent survey research on trust.

There are a great many executives and companies I have worked with over the years that have helped me learn about leadership, teams, organizations, and trust. I thank Columbia Business School, Duke Corporate Education, Fordham University, Ernst and Young, PriceWaterhouseCoopers, QuikTrip Convenience Stores, Sheetz Convenience Stores, QuikChek, and State Farm Insurance for helping me learn about how trust can be built in large organizations when we understand what we are doing and are committed to doing the right thing.

As an author who has written many academic articles but no previous books, I must express my appreciation to some people without whom this work would never have appeared. My students and research assistants Robert Ahern, Patrick Bertschy, Krithika Chandrasekaran, John DeSilvestri, Dawin Efe-Ekici, Ryan Faulkingham, Artem Khlevner, Amber Law, Caterina Miduri, Carolina Poli, Ilyssa Schlager, Juergen Urban, and Eric Westphal, whose research and editing helped enormously. I am grateful to Schon Beechler, Bob Bollinger, Graham Dietz, Donald Ferrin, Nicole Gillespie, Ken Hirokawa, Sharon Livesey, and Michael Pirson, who did the yeoman's work of reading and commenting on earlier drafts or chapters of this book. At Fordham, early on Dean Robert Himmelberg saw the importance of this work and helped me find the time to get it done; and, at key points, Dean Donna Rapaccioli's leadership and support were instrumental and greatly appreciated. Sarah Cliffe at *Harvard Business Review* deserves recognition for seeing the need for a practical approach to the subject of trust. I am also grateful to my agent Esmond Harmsworth, who read my *Harvard Business Review* article, decided the world needed this book, and helped make it happen.

In addition to Esmond, I received significant help in crafting this book from Noel Weyrich, a talented writer, and the team at Jossey Bass, including Mary Garrett, Michele Jones, and Karen Murphy.

My final thanks go to my family. My children, Frank, Steve, and Katie, were understanding when my mind was elsewhere and offered support that was needed along the way. The most important person in this entire effort was my wife, to whom this book is dedicated. She did it all—reading, editing, encouraging, and tolerating the absence and stress that producing a book entails. She is my trusted partner in all my important life adventures, of which writing this book was one.

ABOUT THE AUTHOR

Robert Hurley, PhD, is a professor at Fordham University and president of Hurley Associates. At Fordham, Hurley has been recognized by the student body for his excellence in teaching with the Gladys and Henry Crown Award for faculty excellence. Hurley and his colleagues have designed and led seminars on trust throughout Asia, Europe, and North America. He also consults with organizations on leadership development, top team development, coaching, managing transformational change, and developing and implementing strategies to maximize stakeholder value. Hurley has done consulting in the banking, insurance, retail, real estate, and manufacturing industries. He has been a core faculty member in Columbia Business School's High Impact Leadership Program for executives since 1987. Earlier in his career, Hurley was a senior consultant with W. Warner Burke Associates, a firm specializing in organization consultation. He was also a product manager at Kraft Foods, where he led and managed new product development and established-brands teams. He began his career as a CPA working for Ernst and Whinney and Arthur Andersen, where he consulted with large and medium-size companies in the financial area.

Hurley has a BS from Fordham University and an MBA from Wharton School. He received his doctorate from Columbia University. He has published more than twenty articles and book chapters, including articles in the *Harvard Business Review* and the *California Management Review*. For more information, Hurley can be reached at Drbobhurley@yahoo.com.

INDEX

H

I

J

K

L

M